THE I TATTI
RENAISSANCE LIBRARY

James Hankins, General Editor

PLATINA

LIVES OF THE POPES

VOLUME I

ITRL 30

BARTOLOMEO PLATINA

✦ ✦ ✦

LIVES OF THE POPES

VOLUME I ✦ ANTIQUITY

EDITED AND TRANSLATED BY

ANTHONY F. D'ELIA

THE I TATTI RENAISSANCE LIBRARY

HARVARD UNIVERSITY PRESS

CAMBRIDGE, MASSACHUSETTS

LONDON, ENGLAND

2008

Series design by Dean Bornstein

Library of Congress Cataloging-in-Publication Data

Platina, 1421–1481.
[Historia de vitis pontificum Romanorum English]
Lives of the popes : antiquity /
Bartolomeo Platina ; edited and translated
by Anthony F. D'Elia.
p.   cm. — (The I Tatti Renaissance library ; 30)
Includes bibliographical references and index.
ISBN 978-0-674-02819-7 (cloth : alk. paper)
1. Popes — Biography — Early works to 1800.
I. D'Elia, Anthony F., 1967–   II. Title.
BX953.P7513 2008
282.092′2 — dc22   2007041314

Contents

৵৻৵

Introduction   ix

LIVES OF THE POPES

Preface   2

Life of Christ   8

· CONTENTS ·

· CONTENTS ·

Introduction

🦅🦚🦅

Bartolomeo Platina's *Lives of Christ and the Popes* demonstrates both the success and the failure of humanist attempts to blur the lines between pagan and Christian antiquity. In the early lives contained in this volume (through AD 461), Roman history and pagan culture are given precedence. The lives of the popes, surprisingly, take second place to lengthy and sometimes lurid accounts of good and bad pagan emperors. The biographical compendium quickly reveals itself as a work of papal propaganda, however, as with the advancing years the popes gradually become the new emperors and preservers of classical civilization. The first biographical sketch, a humanist retelling of Christ's life, comes after the emperor Augustus is praised for his patronage of writers and building projects. "The felicity of his rule was great," Platina continues, launching smoothly into his biography of the Christian founder, "but it was certainly made greater still by the most salutiferous birth of Christ our King." Roman popes gradually merge with Roman emperors; even Christ is given the inapt epithet of "emperor of the Christians." Popes, emperors, and Jesus Christ are linked by falling under the same topics of praise. By starting his history of the popes with a life of Christ and calling Christ "our pontiff," Platina asserts the unique legitimacy of the Petrine succession. Christianity and the Roman Church are mutually legitimated by their common origins in the Golden Age of Augustus; the Roman papacy inherits the Roman empire.

Platina's lives, however, not only reveal what a Renaissance humanist thought about Christian antiquity. The past forces Platina to think about the present and he often compares the virtuous saints of Christian antiquity with the corrupt clergy of his own day. A preeminent example of humanist historiography, the *Lives*

innovate upon traditional papal histories like the *Liber pontificalis* with respect both to the wide range of pagan and Christian sources they employ and to the sometimes critical and skeptical way that Platina uses those sources. History for Renaissance humanists, of course, had a didactic purpose. Platina himself says in his preface, "Now the true knowledge of things past that history embraces is that from which we glean the excellent deeds not of one age, but of all ages. And taking past events as our guide to life, even as private citizens we may think ourselves worthy of command of any kind." We study history in order to become better people by imitating the virtues while avoiding the vices of the past. Did Platina see the *Lives* as a way to reform the Church? Perhaps he hoped to provoke in his readers the same response he himself had when contemplating the early history of the Church: a sense of moral outrage and impending disaster consequent upon comparing ancient sanctity with the corrupt contemporary Church.

Life and Works

Little is known about the early life of Bartolomeo Sacchi, better known as Platina.[1] He was born in 1421 in Piadena (latinized as *Platina*) near Cremona and as a youth dedicated himself to the military life. He served for four years in the armies of Francesco Sforza and then Niccolò Piccinino. Perhaps disillusioned with this life, he then settled in Mantua in 1449 and studied under Ognibene da Lonigo, who had been a student of the famous humanist teacher Vittorino da Feltre. In 1453 Platina began tutoring the children of the Marquis Ludovico Gonzaga, the ruler of Mantua. Then in 1457 he moved to Florence to study Greek with the Byzantine émigré John Argyropoulos. While in Florence he befriended the major humanists of the day, including Poggio Bracciolini, Francesco Filelfo, Marsilio Ficino, Cristoforo Landino, and Leon Battista Alberti. Platina acted as an agent for Ludovico

Gonzaga while in Florence and obtained copies of Vergilian manuscripts and Hebrew and Greek Bibles for the marquis.

After Francesco Gonzaga became a cardinal in 1461, Platina followed him to Rome, where he grew acquainted with Cardinal Bessarion and became a principal member of Pomponio Leto's Roman Academy. Soon after this, the humanist pope Pius II (1458–1464) recognized Platina's talents and appointed him to the College of Abbreviators. The abbreviators were secretaries responsible for all papal correspondence, encyclicals and decrees, and an elegant, even eloquent Latin style was a prerequisite for the position. A humanistic education was by the fifteenth century the best preparation for such posts; indeed, apart from teaching and secretarial work, humanists had few chances to earn a living from their classical erudition and eloquence.[2] So when Pius II dramatically increased the number of abbreviators to sixty in 1464, many humanists suddenly found financial stability, and Pius earned their gratitude and praise. But only a few months later the humanist pope was dead.

The next pope, Paul II (1464–1471), was intent on reforming papal finance.[3] He not only disbanded the College of Abbreviators, but demanded that the recently hired humanists return all the papal funds they had already received. Platina lost his temper. During a papal audience he at first demanded the revocation of the decree, then questioned its validity and insisted it be examined by the Sacred Roman Rota, the legal tribunal of the Holy See. Paul was unresponsive. After failing to obtain a second audience, Platina sent the pope an open letter in which he called on kings and princes to convoke a council in order to force the pope to justify his robbing the humanists of their legitimate livelihood. Platina was arrested, tortured, and imprisoned for four long months in Castel Sant'Angelo. His patron, Cardinal Gonzaga, tried to excuse his conduct by declaring him mad. Platina was eventually released in early 1465. Embittered by clerical life, he

wanted to flee Rome but Gonzaga convinced him to stay. He longed for the days of Pius II and even wrote a laudatory life of the deceased pope.

Over the next few years Platina composed a history of Mantua and a famous cookbook, often reprinted.[4] In February, 1468, he tried to win back papal favor with a panegyric of the pope, in which he praised Paul as the bringer of peace to Italy.[5] But then the skies fell again. Suddenly, in the middle of Carnival, twenty humanists of the Roman Academy, including Platina, were accused of plotting to murder the pope. They were arrested, questioned, tortured, and imprisoned in Castel Sant'Angelo. There is much debate about whether there was an actual humanist conspiracy.[6] Whether or not he was guilty, however, Platina suffered permanent damage to his shoulder from the rack and endured over a year of harsh incarceration in Castel Sant'Angelo.[7] While in prison, Platina wrote numerous letters pleading desperately for help from friends and patrons and for mercy from the pope. He also composed and dedicated to Paul a dialogue in which he criticized pagan philosophy.[8] After his release, Platina revised various of his works for publication and kept a low profile. Among these works was a short treatise, *On the Prince*, which he presented to his old patron Ludovico Gonzaga.[9]

When Paul II died in 1471, Platina's hopes were revived of landing a lucrative curial post and he immediately tried to ingratiate himself with the next pope, Sixtus IV (1471–1484). This pope was more receptive and assigned to him the honor of delivering a funeral oration for Cardinal Bessarion, who had died on November 18, 1472.[10] Encouraged by this, Platina began work on his *magnum opus*, a history of the popes. He finished it in only three years and presented the work to Pope Sixtus IV in 1474. For his efforts, Platina received the greatest reward a humanist could have hoped for. In 1475 Sixtus appointed him prefect of the Vatican Library, a post he enjoyed for only a few years until his death from plague

in 1481.[11] The *Lives* was immediately successful, went through twenty-five printings before the mid-seventeenth century, and was translated into Italian, French, German, Dutch, and, eventually, English. It was in due course corrected and expanded by Onofrio Panvinio in 1557 to become the standard biographical compendium of the popes for early modern Europe.[12]

Sources and Historical Method

It is still sometimes claimed that Platina's lives are nothing more than a stylistic reworking of the medieval *Liber Pontificalis* (*The Book of the Pontiffs*, henceforth *Pontiffs*), a reference work compiled over many centuries by multiple authors.[13] (Platina believed, mistakenly, that the parts of it prior to the fourth century had been composed by Pope Damasus I.)[14] But though Platina constantly uses the *Pontiffs* and often silently quotes whole lines, to describe the book as a mere *rifacimento* hardly does it justice. To start with, the *Pontiffs* begins with Saint Peter but Platina chose to begin his history with a life of Christ. This is already a forceful message about the divine origins and legitimacy of the popes. The *Pontiffs*, moreover, continue down, rather sketchily, to the pontificate of Martin V (1417–31).[15] Platina's much fuller lives of the fifteenth-century popes are, therefore, a new and an important source for the Renaissance popes, replete with unique historical details. In general most of the lives included in the *Pontiffs*, especially the early ones, are notably short by comparison with Platina's lives. From the *Pontiffs* Platina gleans, to be sure, much factual information on each pope's family background, the length of his pontificate, his most important decrees, the number of his ordinations, church constructions and the gifts made to the church during his reign, and so forth. But Platina also discusses at length many topics not treated in the *Pontiffs*. For example, he includes long sections on Roman political history, on famous Christian writers, and on

the persecutions and the heresies of the early Church. He constructs his history out of a wide variety of sources. In presenting ecclesiastical affairs and religious history, he relies on many ancient sources, Greek and Latin, among them the New Testament, Josephus, Eusebius, Jerome, Orosius, Augustine, and Rufinus. He also refers to the fifth-century church historians Socrates and Sozomenes, probably via a compendium of Cassiodorus. For secular history, he draws on Suetonius, Eutropius, Tacitus, Ammianus Marcellinus, and the *Scriptores Historiae Augustae*. He also uses Isidore of Seville's seventh-century *Etymologies* and Paulus Diaconus' eighth-century continuation of Eutropius' history. His more recent sources include the medieval ecclesiastical and secular history of Ptolemy of Lucca (1236–1327), Aeneas Sylvius Piccolomini's epitome of Flavio Biondo's *Decades*, and Matteo Palmieri's chronicle. Much more innovative still was his use of the epigraphical evidence he found all around him in Rome: "In Sixtus' time, they say, bishop Peter, an Illyrian by birth, built the church of Saint Sabina . . . But I think this was done in the time of Celestine the First, as the following inscription in epic verse, which can still be read, indicates: 'When Celestine held the apostolic summit . . .'" (46.6).

In other places, Platina uses evidence from his own field researches to support or correct his sources. When discussing the cemetery of St. Calixtus, he says: "Out of devotion, I have gone to see this place with some friends. The ashes and bones of martyrs are still seen, as are the chapels" (17.3). So, while Platina certainly draws extensively on the *Pontiffs*, he adds and synthesizes a fair amount of information on secular and ecclesiastical history from a wide variety of other sources as well. He also subjects the *Pontiffs* to historical criticism and includes his own observations based on his own personal experience.

Platina is most critical of his sources on the issue of the alleged Arianism of the Emperor Constantine. This was no doubt an out-

growth of the revival of interest in the first Christian emperor in fifteenth-century art and literature.[16] In his life of Mark I, he attacks detractors of Constantine with two arguments. "These historians," he first says, "were deceived by a similarity of names, and ascribed to the father the wicked deed of the son" (35.1). They fell into a classic case of misidentification, which Platina reiterates in his life of Felix II: "As soon as Felix began his pontificate, he proclaimed Constantius, the son of Constantine the Great, to be a heretic. . . . In this we may detect the error that led some to ascribe this heresy to Constantine the Great—a charge which, as you see from history, neither should nor could fall upon so great an emperor and lover of the Christian faith" (38.3).

In the life of Mark I, Platina next argues from probability and character: "It is not probable that this wisest of emperors would approve of something that he had always condemned, especially at a time of life when one is given wisdom" (35.1). The emperor's religious devotion, he says, and the existence of a baptistery built by him in Rome demonstrate that he was not an Arian, but that he had been "thoroughly instructed in the faith by Sylvester." Finally, Platina appeals to the majority: "Let them confuse the matter as they wish, and let us believe what almost everyone thinks, that Constantine, who so often conquered enemies in the sign of the Cross . . . would also . . . have wanted to fortify himself against the enemy of humanity with the imprint of baptism . . . I am certainly not unaware of what Socrates and Sozomen in the *Tripartita Historia* and many others believe, but I follow the truth, which is fitting to the religious devotion and piety of the best of emperors" (35.2).[17] Constantine in fact directly attacked Arius and the Arians. But Platina seems not to have been aware of this. For Platina, Constantine was the first Christian emperor; a supporter of the Church, a patron and a legitimizer of the papacy and the embodiment of the union of Christian and classical cultures. He could not have been a heretic.[18]

Platina weighs his sources and applies historical criticism on another thorny issue in the same life: "In no way do I believe the commonly-told story that he had contracted leprosy and was cured by baptism. . . . I follow Socrates in this matter, who maintains that when Constantine reached the age of sixty-five he fell ill and for health reasons left the city of Constantinople for the baths; there is no mention of leprosy. Besides, no mention is made of this by any writer; not even by our own [Christian] writers, to say nothing of the pagans. Orosius would not have been silent about this, nor Eutropius, nor those who wrote down as diligently as possible the deeds of Constantine" (35.2).

Constantine's leprosy was a key part of the legend connected with the so-called Donation of Constantine. This document supposedly demonstrated that, in thanks for curing his leprosy, the Emperor Constantine granted to Pope Sylvester and the Church temporal (i.e. political) power over all the lands of the empire. Although there were skeptics in the Middle Ages, commentators on Gratian gave the document some legitimacy by including parts of the Donation in his twelfth-century compilation of canon law. Conciliarism, questions about spiritual poverty, and the expanding territorial ambitions of the papacy in the fifteenth century led to increased scrutiny of the foundations of the Church's temporal power. In 1440, Lorenzo Valla wrote his famous demolition of the Donation, directed against Pope Eugene IV, who was enmeshed in a territorial struggle at the time with Valla's patron, Alfonso of Aragon, king of Naples.[19] In an amazing display of humanist philological, historical, and textual criticism, Valla demonstrated that the supposed fourth-century document was really a later forgery. Supporters of papal power replied to Valla's polemic not so much with logical arguments as with renewed affirmations of the Donation's authenticity.[20] In his discussion of Constantine, Platina does not refer to the Donation or to the controversy at all. Instead, he lists the numerous specific donations

that Constantine made to Pope Sylvester and the Church. Nevertheless, by forcefully arguing against the story of Constantine's leprosy, Platina indirectly questions the Donation. The close cooperation between popes and emperors often depicted in Platina's *Lives*, his image of the heroic and pious Christian emperor, Constantine, as the defender and patron of the faith, and his description of the impressive amounts of imperial largesse towards the Church perhaps reveal unconsciously what Platina believed should be the true relationship between Church and State.[21]

Such a view would have been risky enough. But a charge of Arianism, this time against a pope, even leads Platina to disagree with the authority of a leading Church Father, Jerome. Saint Jerome was much admired for his erudition and classical learning by the humanists in the Renaissance.[22] Platina nevertheless criticizes Jerome when his assertions fail to harmonize with Platina's own agenda. In his life of Felix, he writes: "But for my part I wonder about [Jerome's report] that he appointed Felix, an Arian bishop, to replace Liberius in Rome, for it is surely evident that Felix was Catholic, as I have written, and that he always condemned the Arians. In short, since Felix held fast to his orthodox faith, he was seized by his enemies and killed along with many orthodox believers" (38.4). In all of these examples, Platina emerges less as a critical historian and more as an apologist of papal claims to legitimacy through an orthodox tradition.[23]

The Popes and Classical Antiquity

The tendency of Roman humanists to harmonize ancient Roman history and papal propaganda is evident in both the themes and organization of the *Lives*. The popes are presented as the heirs to the good pagan emperors and, eventually, as the successors to Rome's emperors. The biographies of the early popes are indeed overshadowed by the accounts of Roman emperors and pagan

writers with which they are linked; sometimes the life of a pope is nothing more than a convenient peg upon which to hang an epitome of Roman imperial history. This is no doubt partially because of Platina's limited sources for these pontiffs, but it also reflects the Renaissance taste for antiquity and its penchant for assimilating the Christian to the pagan, the papal to imperial. Platina's goal is in part to overcome the traditional separation between ecclesiastical and political history, for on his (perfectly sound) view, each casts light on the other. As he says in his preface: "If you consider the first emperors who opposed the Christians and the last who favored them, they are so closely connected that one could not be fully explained without the other." In his life of Peter, he explicitly justifies including extensive accounts of bad emperors. After discussing the Emperor Tiberius and the lust of Caligula, Platina remarks: "I have taken the opportunity to describe these monsters in detail in order to make it more readily apparent that God would have hardly been able to avoid destroying the whole world if he had not sent His Son and His Apostles, by whose blood humankind, though imitating the cruelty of Lycaon, might be redeemed from destruction." The argument that including accounts of cruel emperors brings the virtues of holy apostles or popes into higher relief is not wholly convincing, however, since Platina cannot resist praising even the cruelest persecutors of Christians such as Nero, Aurelianus and Pertinax for their magnificent building projects, patronage of literature, and feats of engineering.[24] And once Christianity becomes the state religion of Rome in the fourth century, the same worldly topics of praise are employed for the popes themselves.

The argument that Christians needed to make use of pagan culture was hardly a new one in the Renaissance: Augustine, for one, had forcefully argued for the preservation and utility of some parts of pagan philosophy and culture. Just as the Hebrews in the Bible, he writes, were enjoined to steal what was useful from the

Egyptians, so should the Christians use pagan learning.[25] In his life of Linus, Platina praises the Platonist Philo of Alexandria and says that Philo befriended St. Peter in Rome and wrote much that was favorable to the Christians (2.6). The idea that the first pope, an uneducated fisherman, was a friend of the foremost Platonist of the day supports the humanist conviction of the value of pagan philosophy.

Similarly, Christian esteem for and preservation of the pagan monuments is a running theme. Platina defends Gregory the Great, for example, from the charge of destroying ancient monuments. Gregory was primarily responsible for the transformation of Rome from a pagan city into a major destination of pilgrimage in the sixth century. He popularized the cult of relics and built altars and churches over martyrs' tombs. Guidebooks from this period ignore the pagan antiquities and monuments and celebrate the Christian sites.[26] Like Jerome, Gregory reportedly saw triumphal arches and the monuments of antiquity as dangerous distractions from Christian landmarks. Nevertheless, Platina asserts: "No such reproach can be made, since Gregory was a native Roman and he esteemed his homeland, after God, more than his own life. Certainly, many of those monuments were ruined by time and many, as we see today, might have been pulled down to build new houses. Others were probably demolished for the brass set into the arches not only by barbarians but by the Romans themselves."[27] In his life of Sabinian I, Platina again defends Gregory from the charge of "mutilating and throwing down statues of the ancients."[28] In his history, the popes are the inheritors and restorers of the Eternal City's pagan past. They unite and care for both its classical and Christian inheritances.

Such a forceful theme makes Platina's first jibe at the Renaissance pope, Paul II, all the more pointed. Platina, twice imprisoned and tortured by Paul II, famously took an exquisite literary revenge by writing a scathing account of the pope's life.[29] In his life

of Zephyrinus, Platina praises the emperor Septimius Severus for building the Septizonium, then remarks: "It was only a little while ago that stone-cutters at the command of Pope Paul II demolished the last surviving part of the Septizodium." Later, in his life of Paul, Platina will present Paul as an uncultured oaf.

Platina's emphasis on pagan antiquity sometimes comes at the cost of neglecting Christian heroes such as the early martyrs. This cannot be said to be typical of the humanist movement in general. The martyrdom of the early Christians was a popular theme in fifteenth-century literature and art.[30] Flavio Biondo, Piero da Monte, Antonio degli Agli, and other humanists stress the Christian foundation of Rome. The Rome of the papacy, they declare, was founded not by the pagan emperors but on the blood of the Christian martyrs.[31] Yet despite this revival of interest in early Christian martyrs and their propagandistic value to the Roman See, Platina includes many fewer martyrdoms and provides much less detail than does his major source, the early Christian historian Eusebius. Eusebius spreads himself for page after page on the heroism of the martyrs. Polycarp, for example, is "bound like a noble ram and set aflame," a bright flame arises from his pyre "not like burning flesh, but like gold and silver being refined in a furnace."[32] In contrast, Platina's Polycarp is a man "celebrated for his religion and learning" who is burnt in Smyrna by order of the proconsul during the reign of Commodus. He is not the Christian athlete and noble warrior of Eusebius. Platina does little more than mention the martyrdom of Ignatius of Antioch, who was devoured by ten leopards; the scolding pitch poured upon Potamiena's head; and the exploits of the great orator Justin Martyr who "delivered a speech in defense of Christianity in the Senate." During the persecution of Emperor Diocletian, Platina reports, Christians were flayed with potsherds and had vinegar and salt rubbed into their exposed flesh until they died; sharp reeds shoved under their nails, and their eyes burned out with searing irons. "No torment," he

writes, "could be invented which the Christians did not undergo." Pope Marcellus, condemned to work in the emperor's camel and horse stables, suffers martyrdom from stench and filthy drudgery. Despite such images, Platina's treatment of the Christian martyrs is disproportionately small compared to the space he dedicates to the Roman emperors, especially in comparison with his sources.

Saint Peter and the Origins of the Papacy

Platina's selective historical method is most evident in his life of the first and most important pope, Peter. The basis of the papal claim to legitimacy, of course, rests on the Roman Church's link to Jesus Christ via the Petrine tradition. In his biography, Platina conjures an heroic image of Peter, closer in form and content to Eusebius' account than to the one in the popular medieval *Golden Legend*.

Peter's battle with Simon Magus forms the central part of Platina's life of the Apostle.[33] Peter comes to Rome "both because he judged it a fitting seat for the pontifical dignity and because he understood that the Samaritan Simon Magus had gone there."[34] Simon and his consort, the former prostitute Selena, were both being worshipped as gods. In Platina's telling, Simon and Peter have two contests. While Simon uses his power of illusion to make a dead child appear to move, Peter instantly revives the child with the word of Jesus. In the next trial, during Simon's magical flight from the Capitoline Hill to the Aventine, Peter invokes God against Simon who in mid-flight falls to the ground, breaks his leg, and soon after dies of his injury.

In the book of Acts in the New Testament there is only a short battle between the Apostles Philip and Peter and Simon Magus, and in Samaria, not in Rome. Eusebius refers to the Samaria episode, describes the evil lunacy of Simon, and reports his fall at the hands of Peter.[35] Eusebius presents Peter as a powerful crusader.

"Close on [Simon's] heels . . . the all-gracious and kindly Providence of the universe brought to Rome to deal with this terrible threat to the world the strong and great Apostle, chosen for his merits to be spokesman for all the others, Peter himself. Clad in divine armor, like a noble captain of God, he brought the precious merchandise of the spiritual light. . . ."[36] Platina's image of Peter reflects the heroic language of Eusebius' account.

Another popular account of the episode in the Renaissance was in Jacobus de Voragine's thirteenth-century *Golden Legend*. Here extensive dialogues between Peter and Simon are included. Peter first vanquishes Simon in debate in Jerusalem, then follows him to Rome where he defeats him in five different trials. In Rome Simon ingratiates himself with Nero through tricks of illusion. He changes his appearance at will to be young or old. Claiming to be the Son of God, he orders Nero to behead him, boasting that he would rise from the dead on the third day. He then astonishes the emperor with acts of bilocation. Simon achieved all these things with the help of demons and was acclaimed a god by both emperor and people. At this point Peter arrives in Rome and denounces Simon to Nero. "If there is any divinity in him," Peter asserts, "let him tell me what I am thinking or what I am doing; but first I shall whisper in your ear what I am thinking so that he won't dare lie!"[37] Then Peter secretly obtains and conceals in his sleeve a loaf of bread. Unable to guess, Simon quickly challenges Peter to say "what he is thinking." In another trial, Simon places a ferocious dog outside the house of one of Peter's disciples. Peter blesses the dog and turns it against Simon. The dog tears off the magician's clothes and chases him naked out of the city.[38] Not surprisingly, Platina does not include such parlor-game miracles. While Platina uses some medieval sources, he constructs his history of the early church for the most part from ancient sources. The *Golden Legend* was a collection of lives of the saints written for a popular lay audience. Platina does not include much of these

apocryphal details, both because he is critical of his sources and because such trivial miracles would have detracted from the heroic image of Peter, appropriate for the first pope, and from the moral dignity Platina would like to confer on Christendom's highest priest.

Accordingly, Peter's worst moment, his denial of Jesus (Matthew 26:69–75) is not included in Platina's account (nor in that of Eusebius or the *Pontiffs*). In the Biblical account, while Jesus is being questioned before the Jewish high priest, Peter in the courtyard below denies knowing Christ in three separate incidents. After the third denial a cock crows and Peter remembers Jesus' prediction that he would deny him. Peter leaves the courtyard and weeps bitterly. It is not surprising that a writer like Platina does not include such a difficult passage, in which the first pope actually turns against Jesus. The *Golden Legend* tells us that his sense of guilt made him weep continually, so much that "his whole face burned with tears."[39] He even carried a towel under his tunic for this purpose. In the sixth century, Pope Gregory the Great saw God's tremendous mercy in allowing Peter to sin. He allowed this, Gregory writes, "so that he who was to be shepherd of the Church might discern in his own sin how to have compassion for others and to recognize in his own weakness how to act mercifully with the weaknesses of others."[40] The fifteenth-century Franciscan preacher Bernardino of Siena refers to teary-eyed Peter as the penitent's model. In another sermon in 1427, Bernardino interprets Peter's denial as a moral exemplar of compassion: "When you see a sinner fallen into sin, remember, Peter, how you yourself fell into sin." Like the first sin of Adam, Peter had to deny Christ in order to be forgiven, to show the way to redemption. "He who has not fallen," Bernardino states, "knows not how to have compassion for the fallen."[41] Peter's denial is depicted in Duccio's 1308 *Maestà* altarpiece, but seems to have fallen out of favor as a subject for art in the fifteenth century. It becomes popular again only in the post-

Tridentine Church of Catholic reform, when the penitent Peter once again becomes a subject for Caravaggio and his followers. In the fifteenth century, however, the denial was out of place in a humanist account of Peter's life. It would have jeopardized the image of the heroic first pope.

While Platina does not mention the denial in his life of Peter, he refers to it obliquely in his life of Pope Marcellinus (296–304). Having been compelled to sacrifice to pagan idols, Marcellinus repented and asked forgiveness at the council of Sinuessa. "There was not one man," Platina writes, "who would pass judgement on him. They all agreed that he had lapsed in the same way that St. Peter himself did." Like Peter, Pope Marcellinus is forgiven and becomes a better and stronger man for it. "Would that we could imitate him and return to health! . . . He recognized his own mistake of failing in faith, returned to himself and . . . suffered martyrdom for the Christian faith with a steadfast spirit" (30.7). In the penitent Marcellinus and Peter Platina sees the state of the Church. Just as Eusebius explained the persecutions of early Christians by blaming the corruption of the clergy, so Platina asserts that the avarice, lust, ambition, pride, idleness, and ignorance of the fifteenth-century clergy is the reason why God is permitting the Ottoman invasions. "Believe me — and would that I were a false prophet! — the Turk will come, a crueler enemy of Christianity than Diocletian and Maximian. He is already knocking on the gates of Italy! Lazy and half asleep, we await universal destruction, more concerned with our own private pleasure than with public utility" (30.6).[42] Early Church history was directly relevant to the most pressing issue in Platina's day.

The martyrdom of Peter is central to Rome's claim to supremacy. As in other contemporary works, Platina includes the famous *Quo vadis?* episode to emphasize that Christ divinely ordained the martyrdom in Rome of Peter his successor. After firmly establishing the papal succession by describing Peter as formally handing

down his authority to Clement, Platina has Peter crucified upside-down (since he felt unworthy of imitating Christ's death) by order of Nero. In the *Golden Legend* two other reasons are ascribed to Peter for wishing to be crucified upside-down: to signify the fall of man in Adam, and to reflect the inverted logic of the times, "right is left and left is right."[43] Platina's Peter is heroic even in death, nobly choosing his own martyrdom rather than being a victim of circumstance.

Critic of the Renaissance Church

Platina often makes negative comparisons between the virtuous Christians of the early centuries and the corrupt clergy of his own day. One such example has just been mentioned. But there are many other places where Platina criticizes the corrupt clergy of his own day. In his life of Pope Julius I, he presents an image of an illiterate and morally reprehensible clergy: "In our time most, not to say all, are so ignorant of letters that they barely know how to write their own name in Latin, let alone record the deeds of others. I do not wish to discuss morals, since certain men have been brought into this order from the ranks of pimps and parasites" (36.4). In his life of Zosimus, he similarly says: "Nowadays, not only servants and bastards are admitted to the priesthood, but also all the disgraceful men born of disgraceful parents, from whose wicked deeds the Church of God in the end will experience some great misfortune" (43.4). Comments like these demonstrate why sixteenth-century reformers would later find Platina an ally in their fight against church corruption, and why the *Lives* would eventually be put on the Index of Forbidden Books, then republished in censored form in the later sixteenth and seventeenth centuries.[44]

Platina, however, does not limit his attack to the lower clergy. After describing Antherus' decree concerning bishoprics, Platina

comments on the greedy bishops of his day: "Today most bishops do the opposite; considering their own advantage, or rather pleasure, they always look upon a richer bishopric as a source of plunder. They don't ask how large the flock is or how to feed them, but inquire how much the see brings in every year. Little mention is made of the care of souls, but much of increasing revenues, so that they may support more horses and more lazy and stupid servants in their homes" (20.2). In his life of Sylvester, Platina in a similar vein compares unfavorably the legislation of holy Pope Sylvester with the corruption of the contemporary Church, with its absentee bishops, its pluralism and its unedifying hunt for benefices: "It was also decreed in a sacred spirit that a council should be held every year in the province to address any wrongs. I do not see why the popes of our age have abolished this sacred institution, unless because they fear the censure of the pious and orthodox. . . . It was decreed that no one should leave a smaller church for a larger one out of ambition or greed. This decree is certainly not observed today, since, like hungry wolves with thirsty mouths, by prayers, promises, gifts, and bribes they all seek and demand fatter bishoprics, having abandoned their first ones" (34.7).

Platina also criticizes the cardinals of his day. In his 1438 dialogue on the Roman curia, Lapo da Castiglionchio had complained that splendor and magnificence had replaced the ideal of apostolic poverty for cardinals.[45] Sixtus IV later increased the number of cardinals significantly. In his life of Dionysius, Platina describes Paul of Samosata's arrogance and finds occasion to criticize the pompous luxury of teenage cardinals: "But what would they make of our time, when no pride or pomp, not to say luxury, is lacking? What if they were to see the many silk- and scarlet-clad youths parading on high-spirited, prettily caparisoned horses, and a crowd of priests following them with parti-colored, gold-embossed riding cloaks hanging from their horses? I know well that they would despise them; they would say that they have nothing

in common with Christ apart from a kind of similarity of religion"
(26.3). Platina had been attached to the household of Cardinal
Gonzaga and a long-time employee of the Vatican. Such direct
criticism is astonishing, and astonishingly courageous, in a work
commissioned by and presented to a pope. By holding up ancient Christianity for admiration, thus highlighting contemporary
abuses, Platina both underscores the need for reform and suggests
a way to achieve it: through a rebirth of the wisdom, piety and virtue of ancient Christians.

The series editor, Professor James Hankins, has made numerous
invaluable corrections, additions, and revisions to the entire volume. Professor David Marsh carefully edited the translation and
in particular smoothed out syntactical complexities. The volume
would not have been possible without my first and greatest Latin
teacher, Father Reginald Foster. A modern day Platina, Reginald
passionately showed me the beautiful depths of the Latin language
and the eloquence of Christian antiquity. My father and mother
have never wavered in their support. But the greatest thanks go to
my loving and patient family: my wife, Una, and daughter Lucia.
Our second beautiful daughter, Zoe, was born in July 2007.

A.F.D.
Kingston, Ontario
October 2007

NOTES

1. On Platina's life, see the Gaida edition of the *Liber de vita Christi ac omnium pontificum*, IX–XXXIV; Mary Milham's "Introduction" to
Bartolomeo Platina, *De honesta voluptate et valetudine*, tr. Mary E. Milham
(Tempe, Arizona: Medieval and Renaissance Texts and Studies, 1998), 1–
45; Stefan Bauer, "Platina, Bartolomeo." (Full references may be found in
the Bibliography.)

2. D'Amico, *Renaissance Humanism*, 25–35, 238–240; Partner, *The Pope's Men*, 111–49.

3. D'Amico, 92–97; Stinger, *Renaissance in Rome*, 8.

4. *Historia urbis Mantuae*, in Rerum Italicarum Scriptores, II serie, XX: 641–862; *De honesta voluptate et valetudine*, trans. Milham.

5. Platina, *Liber*, ed. Gaida, XVI; Platina, *De honesta voluptate*, tr. Milham, 18.

6. The best account is still Platina, *Liber*, ed. Gaida, XVI–XXVII. See also, Platina, *De honesta voluptate*, tr. Milham, 18–23; D'Amico, *Renaissance Humanism*, 92–97; and Anna Modigliani, "Paolo II," *Enciclopedia degli Papi* (Treccani: Rome, 2000), 685–701; eadem, "Paolo II e il sogno abbandonato di una piazza imperiale," in *Antiquaria a Roma: intorno a Pomponio Leto e Paolo II* (Rome: Roma nel Rinascimento, 2003), 125–161, esp. 152–154.

7. Platina, *Liber*, ed. Gaida, XXVII; Platina, *De honesta voluptate*, tr. Milham, 21–22.

8. *De falso et vero bono*, ed. Maria Grazia Blasio (Rome: Edizioni di storia e letteratura, 1999). For the dating, see Platina, *Liber*, ed. Gaida, XXII.

9. *De principe*, ed. Giacomo Ferraù (Palermo: Il Vespro, 1979).

10. Platina, *Liber*, ed. Gaida, XXXI.

11. Ibid., IV; Platina, *De honesta voluptate*, tr. Milham, 28–33.

12. Platina, *Liber*, ed. Gaida, IV–V, XCII–XCVIII. For the editions see the Bibliography. On the reception of the *Lives* more generally in the sixteenth and seventeenth centuries, see Stefan Bauer, "'Platina non vitas, sed vitia scripsit'," and idem, *The Censorship and Fortuna of Platina's Lives.*

13. For a more detailed discussion of Platina's sources, see Platina, *Liber*, ed. Gaida, XXXV–LXXII.

14. See *Lives*, 39.7, note. It was also widely believed in the Renaissance that St. Jerome was the author of *Pontiffs* down to his own time.

15. Platina, *Liber*, ed. Gaida, III.

16. On this, see Stinger, *Renaissance in Rome*, 247–254; Robert Black, "The Donation of Constantine: A New Source for the Concept of the Renaissance," in *Languages and Images of Renaissance Italy*, ed. Alison Brown (Oxford: Oxford University Press, 1995), 51–85.

17. On the controversy over Constantine's baptism in the Renaissance, see Stinger, *Renaissance in Rome*, 253.

18. For evidence of Constantine's disapproval of Arius, see Timothy D. Barnes, *Constantine and Eusebius* (Cambridge, Mass.: Harvard University Press, 1981), 233; A. H. M. Jones, *Constantine and the Conversion of Europe* (Toronto: Toronto University Press, 1978), 157–158.

19. See Lorenzo Valla, *On the Donation of Constantine*, ed. and tr. Glen W. Bowersock (Cambridge, Mass.: Harvard University Press, 2007). On the historical context and reception of Valla's critique, see Stinger, *Renaissance in Rome*, 248–254. Christopher S. Celenza *The Lost Italian Renaissance: Humanists, Historians, and Latin's Legacy* (Baltimore: Johns Hopkins University Press, 2004), 89–91, argues that Valla's attack on the Donation constitutes a serious call for Christian reform.

20. On the reception of the *Donation*, see Anna Modigliani, "Pio II e Roma," in *Il sogno di Pio II e il viaggio da Roma a Mantova*, ed. A. Calzona, F. P. Fiore, A. Tenenti, C. Vasoli (Florence: Olschki, 2000), 103–5; Giovanni Antonazzi, *Lorenzo Valla e la polemica sulla Donazione di Costantino* (Rome: Storia e letteratura, 1985), 121–28; Stinger, *Renaissance in Rome*, 248–54; Black, "The Donation of Constantine," 70–77.

21. See 35.3, note 5, for further comments.

22. Eugene F. Rice, Jr., *Saint Jerome in the Renaissance* (Baltimore: Johns Hopkins University Press, 1985), 84–115.

23. On attitudes of humanists to forgery and criticism in general see Anthony Grafton, *Forgers and Critics: Creativity and Duplicity in Western Scholarship* (Princeton: Princeton University Press, 1990).

24. On this, see Stinger, *Renaissance in Rome*, 247.

25. Augustine, *Confessions*, 7.9.15.

26. On this, see Carole Ellen Straw, *Gregory the Great: Perfection in Imperfection* (Berkeley: University of California Press, 1988), 66–67.

27. Platina, *Liber*, ed. Gaida, 98.

28. Ibid., 99

29. On this, see ibid., XI–XVI.

30. On the "Renaissance of martyrs," see Alison Knowles Frazier, *Possible Lives: Authors and Saints in Renaissance Italy* (New York: Columbia University Press, 2005), 45–99.

31. Stinger, *Renaissance in Rome*, 170–1.

32. Eusebius, *Ecclesiastical History*, 4.15.

33. For an exhaustive survey of the apocryphal tradition and sources concerning Simon Magus, see James I. Shotwell and Louise Ropes Loomis, *The See of Peter* (New York: Octagon Books, 1965), 120–207.

34. See also Stinger, *Renaissance in Rome*, 189.

35. Eusebius, *Ecclesiastical History*, 2.13–15.

36. Ibid. 2.14.

37. Jacobus de Voragine, *The Golden Legend: Readings on the Saints*, trans. William Granger Ryan (Princeton: Princeton University Press, 1993), vol. 1, 343.

38. Ibid., 344.

39. Ibid., 341.

40. Quoted and discussed in Straw, 256 (note 26).

41. Bernardino da Siena, *Prediche volgari sul campo di Siena 1427*, ed. Carlo Delcorno (Milan: Rusconi, 1989), vol. 1. 434; vol. 2, 1370.

42. Ascribing Ottoman victories to Christian moral degeneracy was a commonplace in the fifteenth century. On this, see James Hankins, "Renaissance Crusaders: Humanist Crusade Literature in the Age of Mehmed II," *Dumbarton Oaks Papers* 49 (1995): 114, 132, 134, reprinted in idem, *Humanism and Platonism in the Italian Renaissance*, 2 vols. (Rome: Edizioni di Storia e Letteratura, 2003–04), vol. 1, 292–424; Robert

Schwoebel, *The Shadow of the Crescent: the Renaissance Image of the Turk (1453–1517)* (New York: St. Martin's, 1967), 14–23.

43. *Golden Legend*, vol. 1, 346.

44. See Luther's *Augsburg Confession*, Article XXIII.2. Platina's lives were translated into German in 1546 by the Reformer Caspar Hedio. On the reception of the *Lives*, see the works of Bauer cited in note 12, above.

45. On Lapo and clerical wealth, see Christopher S. Celenza, *Renaissance Humanism and the Papal Curia: Lapo da Castiglionchio the Younger's De curiae commodis* (Ann Arbor: University of Michigan Press, 1999), 71–80 and passim.

LIVES OF THE POPES

Prohemium Platinae in Vitas Pontificum
Ad Sixtum Quartum Pontificem Maximum

1 Multa quidem in vita utilia esse, beatissime pontifex, et humano generi commoda nemo est qui ambigat. Scripsere philosophi multa, scripsere mathematici excogitata et inventa ad ingenia hominum excolenda. Magnum fuit, ne mentiar, rimari secreta naturae et caelos scandere atque inde ad nos doctrinam et artem earum rerum traducere, quae auctor et parens omnium Deus procul ab oculis mortalium collocaverat ut, cum tantam pulchritudinem, tantum ac tam[1] perpetuum ordinem admirantes intueremur, maiestatem divini numinis merito collauderemus. Negari certe non potest quin ex hac philosophandi ratione magna utilitas ad homines pervenerit, ingenio praesertim utentes; quippe pulchritudine divinitatis commoti, humana contemnentes, vitam caelestem in terris ducere nituntur. Verum, ut ait poeta, non omnia possumus omnes. Invenienda igitur via fuit quae omnibus aditum ad felicitatem praestaret, ne solis philosophis consultum videretur. Ea certe rerum antea[2] gestarum cognitio est, quas ipsa historia continet, ex qua non quid una, sed quid omnes aetates egregie fecerint colligentes, magistram vitae nostrae vetustatem ipsam habituri, privati etiam, quovis imperio digni existimamur. Praeterea vero ex hac cognitione ad prudentiam, ad fortitudinem, ad modestiam, ad omnes denique virtutes animi hominum ita concitantur, ut laude ipsa nil antiquius, turpitudini autem nil detestabilius existiment. Quod si veteres illi, apud quos virtus in pretio fuit, celebrari maiorum suorum statuas in foro collocatas, pro templis ac aliis[3] in locis publicis volebant ad utilitatem hominum respicientes, quanti a nobis facienda est historia, quae non muta, ut statuae, non vana, ut picturae, veras praeclarorum virorum imagines nobis exprimit, quibuscum loqui, quos consulere et imitari ut vivos fas est?

Preface

Most blessed pontiff, no one doubts that life offers many things 1
that are useful and beneficial to humankind. In their writings, philosophers and mathematicians have devised and discovered much that has improved men's minds. It was, honestly, a great task to probe the secrets of nature and ascend the heavens, and from thence to convey to mortals the knowledge and science of subjects that God, the creator and parent of us all, had placed far from mortal eyes. Hence, when we look with wonder at such great beauty and so great and so universal an order, we justly praise the majesty of God's power. Certainly no one can deny that the practice of philosophy has conferred great benefits on men, especially those who use their intellect, for, moved by the beauty of divinity and disdaining what is human, they strive to lead a heavenly life on earth. But, as the poet says, we cannot all do all things.[1] A way had to be found, therefore, to let all people achieve happiness, so that it might not seem that philosophers alone had been cared for. Now the true knowledge of things past that history embraces is that from which we glean the excellent deeds, not of one age, but of all ages. And taking past events as our guide to life, even as private citizens we may think ourselves worthy of command of any kind. From this knowledge, moreover, people's minds are so roused to practice prudence, fortitude, modesty, and indeed all virtues, that they think nothing more excellent than praise and nothing more abominable than disgrace. Now, if those ancients who esteemed virtue chose to honor the statues of their ancestors by placing them in the forum, in front of temples, and in other public places for the betterment of humanity, how greatly should we value history, which expresses neither dumb images like statues nor empty images like pictures, but the true images of outstanding men, with whom we may fitly speak, take counsel, and imitate as if they were still living?

3

2   Addo praeterea quod historiae lectio, quae vitam hominum continet, ad eloquentiam, ad urbanitatem,[4] ad usum rerum quavis facultate gerendarum confert plurimum, atque adeo quidem ut eos etiam qui rebus gestis nequaquam interfuere, dum aliquid composite atque eleganter narrant, supra ceteros sapere et intelligere arbitremur.[5] Tu itaque theologorum ac philosophorum princeps, maxime Pontifex, hac hominum utilitate motus simulque dignitati ecclesiasticae consulens, non frustra mandasti ut res gestas pontificum scriberem, ne illorum benefacta perirent negligentia scriptorum, qui suo sudore et sanguine hanc rempublicam Christianam tam amplam nobis tamque praeclaram reliquere, utque deinceps haberent posteri nostri quo ad bene beateque vivendum incitarentur, cum legendo perdiscerent quid imitari quidve fugere oporteret.

3   Non sum tamen nescius futuros quosdam qui dicant me hoc onus frustra suscepisse, cum id antea a plerisque factum sit. Leguntur certe multi (Damasum semper excipio) qui nullum florem orationis, nullam compositionem et elegantiam sequuntur, non de industria, ut ipsi iactitant, ornatum fugientes quod eleganti stilo res sacrae scribi non debeant, sed inscitia et ignoratione bonarum literarum. Iis autem obiicere Augustini, Hieronymi, Ambrosii, Gregorii, Leonis, Cypriani, Lactantii eruditionem et doctrinam sit satis, qui hac in re Ciceronis auctoritatem sequentes, arbitrati sunt nil esse tam incultum et horridum quod non splendesceret oratione. Non negaverim tamen huic generi scribendi difficultatem quandam inesse, cum nudis verbis interdum ac minus latinis quaedam exprimenda sunt quae in nostra theologia continentur. Haec autem ad latinitatem qui referat, magnas perturbationes ingeniis nostrorum temporum hac consuetudine imbutis afferat necesse est, mutatis praesertim terminis unde omnis disputandi ac rationandi series colligitur. Sed habeat hanc quoque auctoritatem aetas

In addition to this, the reading of history, which embraces the   2
life of humanity, contributes greatly to eloquence, refinement and
the conduct of affairs, whatever one's ability, so much so that we
regard as wiser and more intelligent those who give a coherent and
elegant account of events, even if they have never witnessed them.
Hence, you, the prince of theologians and philosophers, highest
pontiff, moved by this benefit to humanity and considering the
dignity of the Church, have bidden me write a history of the
popes. And not in vain. For you feared that through the negligence
of writers we might forget the good deeds of those men who by
their sweat and blood left us this Christian republic, so vast and so
splendid. And you wished that posterity might be inspired to live
well and happily, since from their reading they will learn what to
imitate and what to avoid.

I am not unaware that some people will say that I have under-   3
taken this task in vain, since many have accomplished this task before me. And indeed, we do read many authors who (excepting always Damasus) attempt no ornate speech, artistic composition, or
elegance.[2] But they avoid ornament, not on purpose, as they
themselves boast, saying that holy matters ought not to be written
in an elegant style, but because of their ignorance of good literature. Let the erudition and learning of Augustine, Jerome,
Ambrose, Gregory, Leo, Cyprian, and Lactantius suffice to refute
them. Following Cicero's authority, these writers believed that
there was no subject so uncouth or rough that it could not be
made bright with eloquence. I would not deny, nevertheless, that
there is a certain difficulty in this kind of writing, since certain
parts of our theology require to be expressed with unembellished
and impure Latinity. Anyone who judges such things according to
the standards of good Latin must perforce blame the great troubles affecting the minds of our day, which are permeated with such
usages, especially as the terminology has changed on which every
sequence of argument and reasoning depends. But let our age too,

nostra, vel christiana theologia potius. Fingat nova vocabula, latina faciat, ne veteribus tantummodo id licuisse videatur.

4   Verum iam tandem huic prohemio finem imponam, ubi lecturos prius admonuero non esse mirandum, si, cum pontificum vitas et mores scripturum me pollicitus sum, imperatorum quoque, principum ac ducum res gestas inseruerim. Adeo enim haec simul connexa sunt, si primos imperatores dum Christianis adversantur, si ultimos dum favent inspicis, ut alterum integre sine altero exprimi nequiverit. Legant ergo aequo animo, et si quid emolumenti ex hac scriptione nostra perceperint, tibi soli, pontifex optime, gratias agant, cuius sanctissimo imperio libenter obtemperavi.

or rather Christian theology, be granted this authority. Let it create a new vocabulary and fashion new Latin words, so that this privilege does not seem permitted to the ancients alone.

But let me now end this preface by warning readers not to be   4 amazed, if, having promised to write the lives and characters of the popes, I have also included the deeds of emperors, princes, and generals. If you consider the first emperors who opposed the Christians and the last who favored them, they are so closely connected that one cannot fully be explained without the other. Let my readers read patiently, therefore; and if they gain some benefit from my work, let them thank you alone, most virtuous pontiff, whose most holy command I have willingly obeyed.

LIBER DE VITA CHRISTI AC PONTIFICUM OMNIUM[1]

1   Nobilitatis maximam partem duci ex his maioribus qui clari ius-
tique fuere quique ob singularem aliquam virtutem imperaverunt,
nemo est qui ambigat, nisi qui Platonis auctoritatem non adeo
probat, cuius quadripartitam de nobilitate divisionem, quantum
ad genus pertinet, Christus rex noster consecutus est. Quem enim
ex gentilibus habemus qui gloria et nomine cum David et Salo-
mone quique sapientia et doctrina cum Christo ipso conferri merito debeat ac possit? Neminem certe.

2   Nascitur Christus ex tribu Iuda, nobilissima quidem ob vetustatem et imperium inter Hebraeos, unde propheta Iacob inquit:
'Non auferetur sceptrum de tribu Iuda, quoad venerit qui mitten-
dus est: is erit profecto expectatio gentium.' Quot autem reges vel
duces vel pontifices in ea tribu fuerint, non attinet dicere, cum libri
tum Novi tum Veteris Testamenti huius nobilissimae genealogiae
mentionem faciant.

3   Verum cum post longissima tempora inter Aristobolum et Hir-
canum, Alexandri regis et pontificis filios, orta seditio de principatu esset, tandem Herodi alienigenae regnum Iudaeorum a Romanis traditur; ex patre enim Idumaeo et matre Arabe natus, et
Iudaeorum legisperitos interfecit et genealogias incendit ad inte-
gendam generis sui notam.[2] Cessavit ergo, ac merito quidem, eorum unctio, hoc est imperium, quia ex Danielis sententia sanctus
sanctorum venerat quem Maria Virgo angelo annunciante ex Spiritu Sancto concepit et peperit in Bethleem Iudae, Cyrino tum
Syriae praeside, anno ab Urbe condita septingentesimo quinquage-
simo secundo; imperii vero Augusti Caesaris, qui tum orbi imperi-
tabat, anno quadragesimo secundo.

LIVES OF CHRIST AND
THE POPES[1]

No one doubts that the greatest part of a person's nobility derives 1
from those ancestors who were famous and just and whose rule
depended on their unique virtue. Unless, of course, there is someone who does not fully approve of Plato's authority, whose four-
part division of nobility Christ, our king, attained, insofar as his
ancestry is concerned.[2] For who among the Gentiles can or de-
serves to be compared with David and Solomon for glory and renown, or with Christ himself for wisdom and learning? Surely no
one.[3]

Christ was born of the tribe of Judah, the most noble tribe on 2
account of its age and its supreme authority among the Hebrews,
whence the prophet Jacob says: "The sceptre shall not depart from
the tribe of Judah until tribute comes to him, and the obedience of
peoples is his."[4] There is no point in recounting how many kings
or leaders or high priests there were in that tribe,[5] since both the
New and the Old Testament report this most noble genealogy.

Now it was only after a very long time, when a civil war over 3
the kingdom broke out between Aristobulus and Hyrcanus, the
sons of the king and high priest Alexander, that the Romans gave
the kingdom of the Jews to the foreigner Herod. Since his father
was Idumaean and his mother Arabian, Herod killed the Jews' legal experts and burned the genealogies to cover up any sign of his
birth. Thus, and rightly so, their anointing (that is, their supreme
authority) came to an end. For as Daniel writes, the Holy of
Holies had come, whom the Virgin Mary conceived of the Holy
Spirit at the Annunciation and bore in Bethlehem of Judaea, when
Cyrinus was prefect of Syria in the year 752 since Rome's founding
and the forty-second year of the rule of Augustus Caesar, who at
that time ruled the world.[6]

9

4   Imperium enim a Caio Caesare tum propinquitatis[3] tum haere-
ditatis iure accipiens, vel potius pulsis ac interfectis parricidis ty-
rannisque rempublicam usurpare conantibus, monarchiam orbis
terrarum in meliorem formam redigens, suis temporibus miram
felicitatem praestitit. Nam pacatis rebus tum externis tum domesticis, tanto in honore non solum apud suos, verum etiam apud ex-
teros reges fuit, ut eius nomine civitates conderent quas Sebastias
vel[4] Caesareas appellarunt. Venere etiam multi reges ad Urbem vi-
sendi hominis causa, quos ita comiter et perbenigne suscepit, ut ex
amicis sibi amicissimos redderet. Cum civibus autem suis huma-
nissime vixit, in delinquentes clemens, erga amicos liberalissimus
est habitus; in comparandis amicis rarus, in retinendis constantis-
simus. Liberalium artium adeo studiosus fuit, ut nullus paene laberetur dies in quo non legeret aliquid aut scriberet aut declama-
ret. Ingenio et doctrina Sallustii, Livii, Virgilii, Horatii, Asinii
Pollionis, Messalae Corvini oratoris insignis delectatus est, quorum scriptis etiam eius res gestae immortalitati commendatae
sunt. Urbem Romam ita exornavit, ut gloriatus sit se urbem lateri-
ciam invenisse, marmoream relinquere.[5]

5   Hanc felicitatem quae, ne mentiar, magna fuit, maiorem certe
reddidit saluberrimo ortu suo Christus rex noster. Intercessere autem a creatione mundi usque ad hunc felicissimum natalem diem
anni quinque milia, centum et nonaginta novem. Nascitur puer[6]
sine dolore matris, quippe qui divinus erat, non humanus partus,
unde mater integra statim surrexit et infantem de more pannis in-
voluit. E taberna autem meritoria in Transtiberina regione ex terra
oleum erupit, ut ait Eusebius, fluxitque toto die sine intervallo,
Christi gratiam gentibus ostendens. Narrat Orosius Augustum
Caesarem eadem die mandasse ne quis se dominum deinceps vocaret, divinantem, credo, verum principem orbis terrarum ac
mundi totius natum esse. Idem quoque mandavit ut in orbe Romano omnium hominum capita censu notarentur, ac si maiori

Augustus had inherited the empire from Julius Caesar by right   4
of kinship and hereditary succession—or rather, he defeated and
killed the traitors and usurpers who were trying to usurp the Republic—and reformed the monarchy of the world into a better
form, bestowing wondrous happiness on his age.[7] After pacifying
foreign and domestic affairs, he was held in such great honor, not
only by his people but also by foreign kings, that they built cities
in his name, which they called Sebaste and Caesarea.[8] Many kings
came to Rome to see him, and he received them with such kindness and courtesy that he turned them into his best friends. He
lived most humanely with his own citizens; he was held to be
clement toward criminals and very generous to his friends. He
made friends sparingly, but kept them with the greatest constancy.
He was so fond of the liberal arts that hardly a day passed without
his reading, writing or declaiming something. He delighted in the
wit and learning of Sallust, Livy, Virgil, Horace, Asinius Pollio,
and the outstanding orator Messala Corvinus; and they immortal-
ized all his deeds in their writings. He so beautified Rome that he
boasted that he had found a city of brick and was leaving a marble
one.[9]

The felicity of his rule was great, honestly, but it was certainly   5
made greater still by the most salutiferous birth of Christ our
King. Now between the creation of the world and this most joy-
ous birthday there had elapsed 5190 years. A child is born without
causing his mother pain, for his birth was divine, not human; his
mother immediately arose, still a virgin, and wrapped the child in
swaddling clothes in the usual way. Eusebius writes that oil
erupted from the ground at an inn in Trastevere and gushed forth
the entire day without pause, revealing the grace of Christ to the
nations. Orosius reports that on that same day Augustus Caesar
commanded that no one should henceforth call him "lord," foreseeing, I believe, that the true prince of the whole world had been
born.[10] He also ordered that all the people in the Roman world be

principi rationem gubernati imperii aliquando redditurus esset. Huic autem censui Cyrinum,[7] virum consularem, ex senatus consulto praefecit.

6 Pax praeterea et quies tanta fuit, cum domi tum foris, quanta nunquam antea. Hunc enim iustitiae et pacis regem prophetae appellarunt. Defertur autem octava die ad templum circumcisionis causa; neque enim venerat abrogare legem sed adimplere. Erat autem circumcisio testamenti signum inter Deum et homines, ut ait Augustinus. Die vero tertio decimo adoratur a Magis et muneribus donatur qui ex oriente Hierosolymam eius rei causa venerant. Magos enim quidam orientales populi reges suos et sapientes appellant. Ne vero legem Moyseos praetermittere videretur, mater purificationem sumptura, licet intacta et incorrupta lustratione minime indigeret, puerum ad templum defert. Hunc autem Simeon, vir iustus[8] et singularis religionis, in ulnis retinens, divino numine afflatus, regem suum et salvatorem profitetur, unde Iesus Christus appellatus est. Nam Iesus nomen salvatoris est, Christus vero regis qui, mystico illo chrismate unctus[9] quo reges omnes, 'Messias' hebraice dicitur. Ut enim Romani imperatores purpura, sic Hebraeorum reges unguento ceteris insigniores habebantur. Idem facit Anna spiritu prophetico incitata. Quid de Christo senserint Sibyllae, non est cur scribamus, cum omnes fere eius saluberrimum adventum praedixerint.

7 Celebrata hac lustratione recognitoque iure primogenitorum[10] secundum legem divinam, in Nazareth patriam rediere, civitatem Galilaeae, ubi per quietem Ioseph, existimatus Christi pater, ab angelo admonetur ut fugiens in Aegyptum, puerum secum et matrem deferat; futurum enim paulo post, nisi id fecerit, ut Herodes puerum occideret. Verum id agere tunc quod destinaverat, homo crudelissimus non potuit; a filiis enim ob saevitiam accusatus, Romam ad causam dicendam proficiscitur; qui simulata concordia in

registered in a census, as if he would some day render an account of the empire he governed to a greater prince; and by senatorial decree he placed the consul Cyrinus in charge of the census.[11]

There had never been such great peace and tranquillity at home 6 or abroad. For the prophets called Christ the prince of justice and of peace.[12] On the eighth day he was brought to the temple to be circumcised; for he had not come to annul the law but to fulfill it. The circumcision was a sign of the covenant between God and man, as Augustine says.[13] On the thirteenth day the Magi, who had come to Jerusalem from the East to see him, adored him and presented him with gifts. Certain Eastern peoples call their kings Magi and wise men. Lest she seem to neglect the law of Moses, his mother undertook purification (although, intact and uncorrupt, she in no way needed cleansing), and brought her child to the temple. Simeon, a just man of singular holiness, held him in his arms, and being divinely inspired, declared him his king and Saviour, whence he was called Jesus Christ. (For Jesus is the word for Saviour, and Christ the word for a king 'anointed' with the mystic chrism of all kings; in Hebrew the word is Messiah. Just as the Roman emperors were considered as set above others by their purple, so were the Hebrew kings by their chrism.[14]) Anna too was inspired by a prophetic spirit and did the same as Simeon. There is no reason to record what the Sybils prophesied about Christ, although they nearly all predicted his most salutiferous coming.

Once the purification was over and the right of the firstborn 7 was recognized according to divine law, they returned to Nazareth, their homeland, and the city of Galilee, where Joseph, considered Christ's father, was warned in his sleep by an angel to flee to Egypt with the boy and his mother, as otherwise Herod would kill the boy. But Herod, cruelest of men, was unable to do what he had planned; for as his sons had accused him of savagery, he went to Rome to defend himself. After a pretended reconciliation he returned to the province and in Caesarea hanged his young sons

provinciam rediens, Aristobulum et Alexandrum filios, adolescentes quidem egregios et doctos, quippe qui apud Caesarem Augustum fuerant educati, in Caesarea laqueo peremit. Ad necem deinde puerorum conversus, homo regnandi cupidus, quod natum esse alterum regem Iudaeorum a prophetis intellexerat, omnes qui tum in Bethleem erant et finibus suis a bimatu et infra occidi iubet, secundum tempus quod a Magis exquisierat; nec filio proprio eius aetatis parcit. Unde ferunt Augustum Caesarem, crudelitatem hominis detestatum, hoc dixisse: 'Maluissem Herodis porcus esse quam filius.' Iudaei enim ex lege non modo degustare, sed tangere etiam suillam carnem prohibentur; quare fit ut neque eos alant, neque comedant; hanc ob rem in porcos clementes dicuntur.

8   Ioseph autem septennio in Aegypto commoratus, ubi Herodem tyrannum tabo et sacro igne mortuum intellexit, Hierosolymam cum puero proficiscitur, nec diu ibi immoratus, quod Archelaum Herodis filium regnare intellexerat, in partes Galilaeae, alterius imperio obtemperantes, secessit et Nazareth civitatem incoluit, unde puer Nazareni nomen sumpsit. Dum autem in Aegypto esset, cecidere, ut Hieronymus ait, deorum omnium simulacra, cessarunt oracula, et mors quorundam daemonum subsecuta est ex vaticinio prophetae: 'Ecce,' inquit, 'levem nubem conscendet, et movebuntur simulacra Aegypti ab eius conspectu, et cor Aegypti in eius medio tabescet.'

9   Annum vero duodecimum agens, Hierosolymam cum parentibus de more ad diem festum celebrandum proficiscitur. Hi vero postea peracto sacro abeuntes, cum puerum subsequi non viderent, solicitudine pleni ad templum redeunt eumque doctores sciscitantem offendunt, quod maxime adolescentem deceret. Supra aetatem enim sapiebat, quia, ut Evangelista ait, Dei gratia et virtus

Aristobulus and Alexander, who were distinguished and learned, having been brought up in Caesar Augustus' household. Then this power-hungry man turned to the slaughter of boys, since he had learned from prophets that a second king of the Jews had been born. He ordered that all boys in Bethlehem and the lands bordering it be slain who were two years old and younger, for this was the age he had heard from the Magi; and he did not spare even his own son of that age. Because of this they say that Augustus Caesar hated the man's cruelty and said: "I would rather be Herod's pig than his son." For according to their law the Jews are prohibited not only to taste pork but even to touch it. Thus they neither feed nor eat them, and on account of this they are said to be kind to pigs.[15]

8   Joseph stayed in Egypt for seven years. When he heard that Herod the tyrant had died of consumption and erysipelas, he set out for Jerusalem with the child. But he did not stay long, as he had learned that Herod's son Archelaus was ruling there, and set out for the region of Galilee, which was under someone else's rule. There he settled in the city of Nazareth, from which the child took the name of "the Nazarene." While He was in Egypt, as Jerome says, the statues of all the gods fell, the oracles ceased, and the death of certain demons ensued, according to the Prophet's prediction: "See, the Lord is riding on a swift cloud, and the idols of Egypt will tremble at his presence, and the heart of the Egyptians will melt within them.[16] Behold He shall climb a light cloud and all the idols of Egypt will be moved by His sight and the heart of Egypt shall languish in His midst."[17]

9   When He was twelve, He set out for Jerusalem with His parents to celebrate, as was customary, the feast of Passover. When the service ended, his parents left the temple; but not seeing the boy follow them, they anxiously returned and found Him questioning the elders, which was especially fitting for an adolescent. For He was wise beyond his years, since, as the Evangelist says,

in illo erat. Parentes deinde bene monentes secutus, in patriam revertitur. Quid vero egerit in hac aetate usque ad trigesimum annum quo a Ioanne Zachariae filio aqua baptizatus est, dicere praetermittam, cum non solum Evangelia et Epistolae rebus a se optime ac sanctissime gestis plenae sint, verum etiam eorum libri qui ab eius vita, moribus et institutis abhorruere. Flavius ille Iosephus, qui lingua graeca *Antiquitatem iudaicam* viginti libris conscripsit, cum ad Tiberii principis imperium venisset, 'Fuit,' inquit, eisdem temporibus Iesus vir quidam sapiens, si tamen virum eum nominare fas est. Erat enim mirabilium operum effector ac hominum doctor, eorum maxime qui quae vera sunt libenter audiunt; hanc ob rem multos tum ex Iudaeis tum ex gentibus sibi adiunxit; Christus hic erat.'

10   Hunc autem, cum Pilatus a principibus nostrae gentis instigatus, in crucem agendum censuisset, non tamen ii deseruere qui eum ab initio dilexerant. Eisdem praeterea die tertio post mortem vivus apparuit, quemadmodum, divinitus inspirati, prophetae et haec et alia de eo innumerabilia miracula futura esse praedixere. Perseverat et usque in hodiernum diem celebre christianorum nomen ab ipso sumptum; perseverat et genus. Idem quoque Iosephus Ioannem Baptistam, verum prophetam et ob eam rem ab omnibus in pretio habitum, iussu Herodis, magni Herodis filii, paulo ante mortem Christi caesum fuisse affirmat in castello Machaerunta, non quod sibi et regno timeret, ut idem ait, sed quod Herodiadem, Agrippae sororem ac Philippi fratris viri optimi[11] uxorem, incestis nuptiis sibi coniunxerat. Hic est ille Ioannes, quo nemo maior inter natos mulierum fuit, Salvatoris nostri sententia.

11   Interficitur[12] etiam Christus, verus Dei filius, veritatis iustitiae pietatis religionis assertor, anno decimo octavo Tiberii Caesaris, aetatis vero suae anno tertio et trigesimo,[13] et eo magis, quod ei vita propagata est ab VIII Kalendas ianuarii usque ad VIII Kalen-

the grace and virtue of God was in Him. Following His parents' good advice, He then returned to his homeland.[18] I shall omit to mention what He did from this time until the age of thirty, when He was baptized by John, the son of Zachariah, since not only are the Gospels and the Epistles filled with His great and holy deeds, but so are the books of those who abhorred His life, habits, and teachings. The famed Flavius Josephus, who composed twenty books of *Jewish Antiquities* in Greek, in his account of the reign of the emperor Tiberius says: "There was a certain wise man named Jesus at that time, if it is right to call Him a man. For He was a worker of miracles and a teacher of men, especially of those who willingly listened to the truth; on account of this, he attracted many followers, both Jews and Gentiles. He was the Christ."[19]

Now, after Pilate was goaded by the leaders of our people and 10 condemned Him to be crucified, He was not abandoned by those who had loved Him from the beginning. On the third day after His death, moreover, He appeared alive to them, just as the divinely inspired prophets predicted, foreseeing these and countless other miracles concerning Him. Even today the famous name of the Christians, derived from Him, continues; and his people continue. Josephus also says that the true and universally esteemed prophet John the Baptist was slain in the stronghold of Macherunta shortly before the death of Christ. Herod, the son of the great Herod, ordered this, not because he feared him as a threat to his kingdom, as Josephus says, but because he had contracted an incestuous marriage with Herodias, Agrippa's sister and his virtuous brother Philip's wife. In our Saviour's opinion, among those born of women there was no one greater than John.[20]

Christ, the true son of God and champion of truth, justice, 11 piety, and religion, was killed in the eighteenth year of Tiberius Caesar's reign and the thirty-third year of His life. His life extended from the eighth day before the Kalends of January (December 25) until the eighth day before the Kalends of April

das aprilis, quo die conceptus in Virginis utero est de Spiritu
Sancto. Accusatus a Iudaeis quod sabbatis non vacaret, saluti hominum quovis tempore consulens, et quod baptismum circumci-
sioni anteferret et quod abstinentiam suillae carnis auferret, quibus
in rebus iudaicae religionis sacramenta consisterent.

12   Caedis autem tam nefariae etiam caeli ipsi signa dedere. Nam
et solis tanta defectio facta est hora sexta diei, ut et dies in obscu-
ram noctem versus sit, et Bithynia etiam, licet multum ab Hierosolymis distet,[14] terraemotu concussa, et multa Nicenae urbis aedificia corruere, et velum templi, quod separabat duo tabernacula,
scissum; audita et vox ex adyto templi Hierosolymitani: 'Transmi-
gremus, cives, ex his sedibus.' Admonitus Tiberius a Pilato de
Christi morte ac dogmate, ad senatum retulit censuitque Christum in deos referendum ac templo honorandum. Fieri id non
modo senatus vetuit, quod non ad se prius sed ad Tiberium scrip-
sisset Pilatus, verum etiam pellendos urbe tota Christianos censuit. Proposita sunt accusatoribus praemia, quos Tiberius a tanto
scelere minis et morte prohibuit. Auctores autem tam nefarii par-
ricidii poenas dedere. Nam et Iudas laqueo vitam finivit, et Pilatus
maximis calamitatibus vexatus, sibi manum iniecit, licet sint qui
scribant eum sceleris[15] paenituisse ac veniam a Deo meritum. Iudaei autem, amissa libertate, iusti sanguinis meritas poenas adhuc
luunt.

13   Haec sunt fere quae de vita Christi regia ac pontificis nostri
quam brevissime scribenda censui, quo et mihi facilior aditus ad
opus mente conceptum daretur, et legentibus gratior fieret lectio,

(March 25), on which day He was conceived by the Holy Spirit in the womb of the Virgin.[21] The Jews accused Him of not respecting the Sabbath (as He was always attending to the salvation of men), of preferring baptism to circumcision, and of dispensing with the abstention from pork. These were all sacraments basic to the Jewish religion.[22]

His murder was so horrible that the heavens themselves 12 showed signs of it. For at the sixth hour of the day, there was an eclipse of the sun so great that day turned into dark night. Although it is far from Jerusalem, Bithynia was struck by an earthquake; and many buildings in Nicaea toppled. The curtain of the temple that separated the two tabernacles was torn in two, and a voice was heard from the entrance of the temple of Jerusalem saying: "Let us leave this dwelling-place." Tiberius, whom Pilate had informed about Christ's death and teaching, reported it to the Senate and recommended that Christ be counted among the gods and honored with a temple. The Senate not only opposed doing this, since Pilate had written first to Tiberius rather than to them, but decreed the expulsion of the Christians from the entire city. Rewards were offered to informers, whom Tiberius had deterred from so great a crime with threats and executions.[23] But the authors of this horrible betrayal paid the price. For Judas ended his life by hanging; and Pilate, after suffering the greatest misfortunes, killed himself—although there are some who write that he repented of his wicked deed and earned God's forgiveness. The Jews lost their liberty and are still paying the price they deserve for the shedding of just blood.[24]

The foregoing is more or less what I have decided to write, in 13 the briefest possible way, about the royal life of Christ and of our pontiff, so that I might more easily approach my intended work, and so that readers might enjoy my text the more, because like a

quae tamquam irriguus fons ab imperatore Christianorum in pontifices Romanos per ordinem usque ad tempora Sixti Quarti deri-
varetur.

: I :

Petrus

1 Post Christi mortem et resurrectionem, completis iam diebus Pen-
tecostes, Spiritum Sanctum accepere discipuli; quo imbuti, variis
linguis res gestas summi Dei locuti sunt, etsi plerique eorum sine
ulla eruditione sint habiti, maxime vero Petrus et Ioannes. Eorum
autem vita ad utilitatem communem respiciebat: nil proprii habebant, quicquid ante pedes eorum ob religionem ponebatur, id to-
tum vel partiebantur inter se ad commoda naturae vel pauperibus
erogabant. Ii vero provincias partiti sunt: Thomas Parthos sortitus
est, Matthaeus Aethiopiam, Bartholomaeus Indiam citeriorem,
Andreas Scythiam, Ioannes Asiam; unde et apud Ephesum commoratus, post longos labores et diutinas solicitudines e medio sublatus est.[1] Petro autem principi apostolorum Pontus, Galatia, Bithynia, Cappadocia obtigit. Is enim natione Galilaeus ex Bethsaide
civitate, Ioannis filius, Andreae apostoli frater, primus sedit annis
septem in episcopali sede apud Antiochiam Tiberii tempore.

2   Qui, Augusti privignus et haeres, annis tribus et viginti varie
imperavit. Neque enim inter malos omnino neque inter bonos
principes numerari potest. In homine[2] fuit multa litteratura et gra-
vis eloquentia; bella per se nunquam, sed per legatos gessit; tumultus exortos prudenter suppressit. Multos reges a se blanditiis evo-
catos nunquam remisit, maxime vero Archelaum Cappadocem,

refreshing spring it flows from the emperor of the Christians and continues in order through the Roman pontiffs up until the time of Sixtus IV.

: I :

Peter
[d. ca. 64]

After the death and resurrection of Christ and the completion of   1
the days of Pentecost, the disciples received the Holy Spirit. Being
filled with the Spirit, they preached the deeds of the highest God
in different languages, though most of them, especially Peter and
John, were considered illiterate. Their life was dedicated to the
common good. They had nothing of their own; whatever was
placed at their feet out of piety they either divided among themselves for their natural needs or distributed to the poor. They divided up the provinces: Thomas took Parthia, Matthew Ethiopia,
Bartholomew western India, Andrew Scythia, and John Asia Minor, where, dwelling in Ephesus, he died after much toil and care.
To Peter, prince of the Apostles, fell Pontus, Galatia, Bithynia and
Cappadocia.[1] By birth Peter was a Galilean from the city of
Bethsaida, the son of John and brother of the apostle Andrew, and
he first occupied the episcopal see of Antioch for seven years in
the time of Tiberius.[2]

Augustus' son-in-law and heir, Tiberius, ruled for twenty-three   2
years with varying success and can be counted neither among the
bad emperors nor the good. He was a man of great learning and
dignified eloquence. He never waged war on his own but through
his lieutenants, and prudently suppressed uprisings when they occurred. He summoned many kings with flattery and never let

cuius regnum in provinciam vertit. Multos senatores proscripsit; quosdam etiam interfecit; magnis quoque suppliciis ab eodem necatur C. Asinius Gallus orator, Asinii Pollionis filius. Moritur et Vocienus Montanus, Narbonensis orator, in Balearibus; eo enim relegatus a Tiberio fuerat. Fratrem quoque Drusum veneno eius iussu necatum tradunt historici. Hac tamen moderatione usus est, ut publicanis quibusdam et praesidibus provinciarum augenda esse vectigalia dicentibus, responderit boni pastoris esse tondere pecus, non deglutire.

3   Mortuo Tiberio Gaius Claudius, cognomento Callicula, a castrensi loco[3] ducto, imperium occupat. Filius enim Drusi, Augusti Caesaris privigni, et ipsius Tiberii nepos habebatur, homo omnium scelestissimus. Nil enim vel domi vel foris strenue gestit. Avaritia omnia expilavit. Tantae libidinis fuit, ut etiam sororibus stuprum intulerit; tantae crudelitatis, ut saepius exclamasse dicatur, 'Utinam populus Romanus unam cervicem haberet.' Exules quoque omnes interfici iussit, nam cum unum ab exilio revocasset quaereretque quid potissimum exules optarent, cum ille imprudenter respondisset mortem principis, omnes passim sustulit. De conditione temporum suorum saepe etiam quaestus est, quod nullis calamitatibus publicis insignirentur, velut Tiberii tempora, quibus obtrita ferunt ad viginti milia hominum casu theatri apud Tarracinam. Ita autem Virgilii et Livii gloriae invidit, ut paulum abfuerit quin eorum scripta et imagines ex omnibus bibliothecis amoveret, quorum alterum ut nullius ingenii minimaeque doctrinae, alterum ut verbosum in historia negligentemque carpebat. Dicebat Senecam harenam esse sine calce. Praeterea[4] Agrippam Herodis regis filium, a Tiberio in carcerum coniectum quod Herodem accusaverat,[5] liberat et regem Iudaeae facit; ipsum autem He-

them leave, especially Archelaus of Cappadocia, whose kingdom he turned into a province of the empire. He proscribed many senators and even killed some of them. He put the orator C. Asinius Gallus, son of Asinius Pollio, to death with awful tortures. The orator Vocienus Montanus of Narbo died in the Balearic Islands, where Tiberius had banished him. Historians report that his brother Drusus was poisoned on Tiberius' orders. Yet he exercised such moderation that, when certain publicans and governors of provinces said that taxes should be raised, he replied that it is the job of a good shepherd to shear his sheep, not to flay them.[3]

When Tiberius died, Gaius Claudius, who had acquired the nickname Caligula from the site of a military camp,[4] succeeded him. For he was the son of Drusus, Augustus' son–in–law, and was considered Tiberius' grandson, and the wickedest of all men. He performed no strenuous deeds either at home or abroad. His avarice stripped everything bare. His lust was so great that he even raped his sisters; his cruelty so great that he is said to have repeatedly exclaimed: "Would that the Roman people had one neck!" He ordered all exiles to be killed. For having recalled one exile and having asked him what the exiles most desired, the man imprudently answered "the emperor's death," whereupon Caligula executed them all indiscriminately. He would often complain about the condition of his times, that they were not rendered remarkable by any public calamities, as those of Tiberius had been, when, they say, about twenty thousand men were crushed to death after a theatre collapsed at Terracina. He so envied the glory of Virgil and Livy that he came close to removing their writings and images entirely from the libraries. He criticized the former as a man of no talent and little learning and the latter as a verbose and careless historian. He used to say that Seneca was sand without lime. Moreover, Caligula freed Agrippa, the son of King Herod, whom Tiberius had imprisoned for making accusations against his father, and made him king of Judaea. He confined Herod himself to per-

3

23

rodem perpetuo exilio Lugdunum relegat.⁶ Seipsum vero in deos
transfert; imagines in templo Hierosolymitano collocat. Postremo
autem⁷ a suis tandem necatur imperii anno tertio, mense decimo.
Duo libelli in scriptis eius reperti sunt: quorum alteri pugio, alteri
gladius pro signo erat impressus. Ambo lectissimorum virorum
utriusque ordinis senatorii⁸ et equestris nomina et notas contine-
bant morti destinatorum. Inventa est et ingens arca variorum ve-
nenorum, quibus mox Claudio Caesare iubente demersis, infecta
maria traduntur, non sine magna piscium interitu, quos evectos in
proxima littora passim aestus eiecit.

4   Libuit hominum monstra perscribere, quo facilius appareret
Deum vix⁹ potuisse tum retineri ab excidio orbis terrarum mun-
dique totius, nisi et filium misisset et apostolos, quorum sanguine
humanum genus,¹⁰ Lycaonem imitatum, ab interitu redimeretur.
Horum itaque temporibus fuit Petrus ille, quem his verbis Christus allocutus est: 'Beatus es Simon Bariona, quia caro et sanguis
non revelavit tibi, sed pater meus qui in caelis est' et 'Tu¹¹ es Petrus, et super hanc petram aedificabo ecclesiam meam ac tibi dabo
claves regni caelestis potestatemque ligandi et solvendi.' Is vero,
omnium diligentissimus, ubi Asiaticas ecclesias satis confirmasset,
confutatis eorum opinionibus qui circumcisionem approbabant,
secundo Claudii anno in Italiam venit.

5   Claudius enim, Gaii Calliculae patruus, quem nepos in ludi-
brium reservaverat, imperium accipiens quintus ab Augusto, Britanniam, quam neque ante Iulium Caesarem neque post eum quis-
quam attingere ausus est, in deditionem accepit. Orchadas insulas
Romano adiecit imperio; Iudaeos tumultuantes Roma expulit;
compressit et seditiones in Iudaea a quibusdam pseudoprophetis
concitatas. Obtrita etiam sunt triginta milia Iudaeorum in portis

petual exile in Lyons. He set himself among the gods and put images of himself in the temple of Jerusalem. He was finally murdered by his own men in the third year and tenth month of his reign. Among his writings were found two lists, one sealed with the sign of a dagger, the other of a sword. They contained the names, along with marks of condemnation, of the noblest men of both the senatorial and the equestrian order whom he planned to kill. There was also found a large chest that held various poisons, which Claudius Caesar later ordered to be thrown into the sea. The seas, it is said, were tainted and many fish died which the tide cast up in vast numbers on the neighbouring shores.[5]

I have taken the opportunity to describe these monsters in detail in order to make it more readily apparent that God would have hardly been able to avoid destroying the whole world if he had not sent His Son and His Apostles, by whose blood humankind, though imitating the cruelty of Lycaon,[6] might be redeemed from destruction. In their times lived that Peter, whom Christ addressed with the following words: "Blessed are you, Simon bar-Jonah, for flesh and blood has not revealed this to you, but my Father in heaven. You are Peter, and upon this rock I shall build My church, and I shall give you the keys of the kingdom of heaven and the power of binding and loosing." The most zealous of all the apostles, Peter firmly established the churches of Asia Minor and refuted the opinions of the proponents of circumcision. Then in the second year of Claudius' reign he came to Italy.[7]

Claudius, Caligula's uncle, had been spared by his nephew so as to make a laughing-stock of him. Now emperor (the fifth after Augustus), he forced Britain into submission, a feat which no one either before or after Julius Caesar had ever dared to undertake. He also added the Orkney Islands to the Roman empire. He expelled seditious Jews from Rome and suppressed insurrections sparked by certain false prophets in Judaea. While Cumanus was procurator of Judaea, whom he had appointed, thirty thousand

Hierosolymitani templi azymorum diebus, Cumano eius iussu procurante Iudaeam. Laboratum eodem quoque tempore annonae caritate ubique est, Agabo propheta tantam calamitatem praedicente. Ab externo hoste securus, perfecit aquaeductum, cuius ruinas apud Lateranum cernimus, a Caio incohatum. Emittere quoque Fucinum lacum est aggressus, non minus compendii spe quam gloriae, cum quidam[12] privato sumptu emissurum se polliceretur, si sibi siccati agri concederentur. Per tria autem passuum milia, partim effosso monte, partim exciso, cuniculum aegre absolvit post undecim annos, triginta milibus hominum ibi sine intermissione elaborantibus. Portum quoque Ostiensem, quem adhuc cum admiratione intuemur, extruxit, ductu dextra laevaque brachio ad coercendos maris fluctus. Messalina uxore convicta probri et interfecta, Agrippinam, Germanici fratris sui filiam, contra ius fasque ducit uxorem, a qua postea, imperii quarto decimo anno, boletis veneno illitis[13] necatur.

6   Petrus itaque Romam caput orbis terrarum tunc venit, et quod hanc sedem pontificali dignitati convenientem cernebat et huc profectum intellexerat Simonem Magum, Samaritanum quendam, qui praestigiis suis eo erroris iam deduxerat populum Romanum, ut Deus crederetur. Romae enim iam titulum adeptus erat inter duos pontes positum ac latinis literis sic scriptum: 'Simoni Deo sancto.' Hic, dum in Samaria esset, tamdiu se credere in Christum simulavit quoad baptismum a Philippo, uno ex septem diaconis,[14] acciperet, quo quidem postea in malam partem utens, multarum haeresum fundamenta iecit, cum Selene impudica muliere quam sceleris sociam habuit. Provocare Petrum miraculis morte pueri homo nefarius ausus est; quem eius carmina primo movere visa sunt. Verum, cum postea nihilominus puer iaceret, in nomine

Jews were crushed to death under the porticos of the temple in Jerusalem during the days of Passover. At the same time there was great suffering everywhere due to the high price of grain, which the prophet Agabus had predicted. Untroubled by foreign enemies, Claudius finished the aqueduct that had been begun by Caligula, whose ruins can still be seen near the Lateran. He tried to drain the Fucine Lake, hoping both to achieve glory and to save money, since a certain individual promised to do it at his own expense if the drained land were given to him. Partly by digging out and partly by cutting through three miles of mountain, he with difficulty completed an underground passage after eleven years and with thirty thousand men working non-stop. Claudius also constructed the harbor of Ostia by extending two moles on either side to control the waves. We still marvel at this today. Having executed his wife Messalina for adultery, against both human and divine law he married Agrippina, the daughter of his brother Germanicus. In the fourteenth year of his reign, Agrippina murdered Claudius with poisoned mushrooms.[8]

At that time Peter came to Rome, the capital of the world, both 6 because he judged it a fitting seat for the pontifical dignity and because he had understood that the Samaritan Simon Magus had gone there.[9] Simon's impostures had brought the Roman people to such a pitch of error that they believed him to be a god. Indeed, he had already been honored by an inscription between two bridges in Rome that read in Latin: "To Simon the Holy God."[10] When he was in Samaria, Simon pretended to believe in Christ until he was able to obtain baptism from Philip, one of the seven deacons. He then used his baptism for ill purposes and, along with Selene, a shameless woman and his partner in evil, he laid the foundations for many heresies. This wicked man dared challenge Peter by working miracles over a dead child. At first Simon's charm appeared to move the child, but when it lay still dead, Peter commanded it in the name of Jesus, and the child arose. At this

Iesu, Petro iubente, surrexit. Hanc ob rem indignatus, Simon vidente populo se volaturum ex Capitolino monte in Aventinum pollicetur, si Petrus subsequi vellet; ea ratione dinosci posse[15] uter ipsorum sanctior haberetur et Deo carior. Cum iam volaret, rogatu Petri ad caelum manum tendentis ac rogantis Deum ne deludi magicis artibus tantum populum sineret, Simon decidit ac crus infregit, cuius dolore non ita multo post Aritiae mortuus est, nam eo post tantam ignominiam delatus a suis fuerat. Hinc Simoniaci haeretici originem habent, qui donum Spiritus Sancti emere ac vendere consuevissent quique affirmabant creaturam non a Deo esse, sed ex superna quadam virtute provenire.

7 Conversus deinde ad propagandum verbum Dei Petrus sermone et exemplo, rogatur a Romanis ut Ioanni, cognomento Marco, eius in baptismate filio, conscribendi Evangelii negotium tradat. Probata namque erat eius vita, probati mores. Is enim, ut Hieronymus ait, 'in Israel sacerdotium agens secundum carnem Levita,' id est, additus vel appositus, 'ad Christi fidem conversus, in Italia evangelium scripsit, ostendens quid generi suo deberet et Christo.' Extant eius evangelia, testimonio Petri comprobata. Deinde vero in Aegyptum missus, ut ait Philo Iudaeus scriptor egregius, ubi docendo et scribendo Alexandrinam ecclesiam optime constituisset, doctrina ac moribus insignis, octavo Neronis anno Alexandriae moritur et sepelitur, in locumque demortui Anianus sufficitur.

8 Anno vero antea[16] moritur et Iacobus, cognomento Iustus, Domini frater. Nam ex Ioseph et alia uxore natus erat vel, ut alii volunt, ex sorore Mariae, Christi matris. Hic enim, ut Hegesippus ait (apostolorum temporibus vicinus), in utero matris sanctus fuit,

Simon became enraged and promised that, if Peter would like to follow him, he would fly from the Capitoline to the Aventine hill as the people watched. By this method, he said, they could discern which of them might be considered the holier and dearer to God. While Simon was flying, Peter raised his hands to heaven and begged God not to allow such a great multitude of people to be duped by magical arts; and down Simon fell and broke his leg.[11] Simon soon afterwards died from the pain of his injury in Aricia, where his followers had brought him after this great disgrace. The heretics called Simoniacs originate from him.[12] They habitually bought and sold the gift of the Holy Ghost and asserted that creation was not from God but proceeded from a kind of celestial power.[13]

After this Peter turned his attention to propagating the Word   7
of God by speech and example. The Roman Christians asked him to assign the task of writing the Gospel to John, surnamed Mark, who was his son in baptism and a man of honorable life and character. For, as Jerome states, "John exercised the priesthood in Israel and was a Levite by race" — the name Levi means added or joined — "and after his conversion to the Christian faith John wrote the Gospel in Italy, in which he revealed what he owed to his race and to Christ."[14] His Gospel was approved by Peter's testimony and is still extant. After this John was sent into Egypt, as the famous writer Philo the Jew relates, where by his teaching and writing he firmly established the Alexandrian Church. Outstanding in learning and habits, John died in the eighth year of the Emperor Nero, was buried in Alexandria, and was succeeded by Anianus.[15]

In the previous year James also died, who was surnamed the   8
Just and the Brother of Our Lord, as he was the son of Joseph by another wife, or, as some maintain, he was born from the sister of Mary, the mother of Christ. Hegesippus, who lived near the time of the Apostles, says that James was holy in his mother's womb,

vinum et siceram non bibit, nil carnis degustavit unquam; inton-
sus, nec balneo nec unguento usus est; vestibus lineis tantummodo
indutus. Sancta sanctorum ingressus, ita assidue flexis genibus pro
salute populi orabat, ut eius genua camelorum more occalluerint.
Verum abeunte ex Iudaea Festo, ipsius provinciae gubernatore,
priusquam ei Albinus succederet, pontifex Avanus Avani filius,
compellens publice Iacobum Christum Dei filium negare, recusan-
tem lapidibus obrui iussit. Qui, cum praeceps de pinna templi
deiectus esset, semivivus adhuc et manus ad caelum tendens pro
persecutoribus oraret, fuste, quo fullones utuntur, tandem necatur.
Refert autem[17] Iosephus hunc tantae sanctitatis fuisse ut propter
eius necem publice creditum sit Hierosolymam esse subversam.
Hic est ille Iacobus, cui Dominus post resurrectionem apparuit
cuique panem benedicens ac frangens dixit: 'Mi frater, comede panem tuum, quia filius hominis e morte resurrexit.' Annis vero triginta Hierosolymitanae ecclesiae praefuit, id est usque ad septi-
mum Neronis annum. Cuius[18] sepulchrum iuxta templum unde
deiectus fuerat, cum titulo, Hadriani temporibus adhuc extabat.

9   Mortuum quoque Barnabam Cyprium, qui Ioseph Levites co-
gnominatus est, ante Petri martyrium constat. Hic enim cum
Paulo gentium apostolus electus, unam tantam epistolam ad ecclesiam pertinentem conscripsit, licet ea quoque inter apocryphas
scripturas habeatur. Dissentiens item a Paulo ob Marcum discipulum in Cyprum proficiscitur, Marco comite, ubi Christi fidem
praedicans, martyrio coronatur.

10   Paulus autem, qui antea Saulus dicebatur,[19] ex tribu Beniamin
et oppido Iudaeae, Giscalis, originem ducebat; quo a Romanis
bello capto, cum parentibus suis Tharsum Ciliciae commigravit;
inde Hierosolymam ob studia legis missus a Gamaliele, viro doctissimo, eruditur. Acceptis deinde epistolis a pontifice templi, eos

that he drank no wine or fermented drink, never tasted meat, did not shave, bathe, or anoint himself, and wore only linen garments. In the Holy of Holies he would so incessantly pray for the welfare of the people on his knees that they became hardened like those of camels. When Festus was leaving the government of Judaea, but before Albinus succeeded him, the High Priest Avanus, son of Avanus, tried to force James publicly to deny that Christ was the Son of God and, when he refused, ordered him stoned to death. James was thrown headlong from a pinnacle of the Temple, but was still half alive and raising his hands to heaven and praying for his persecutors when he was at last struck dead with a fuller's club. Josephus reports that he was a man of such great sanctity that it was generally believed that his murder caused the destruction of Jerusalem. This is that James to whom the Lord appeared after His resurrection and, having blessed and broken bread, said, "Eat your bread, my brother, for the Son of Man has risen from death."[16] James presided over the church of Jerusalem for thirty years, that is, until the seventh year of Nero's reign. His sepulchre with an inscription was next to the temple from which he had been cast down; this was still standing in Hadrian's time.

Barnabas the Cypriot, surnamed Joseph the Levite, is also 9 known to have died before Peter's martyrdom. He was chosen as Apostle to the Gentiles along with Paul and wrote only one letter pertaining to the Church, although that too is considered apocryphal. He also disagreed with Paul on account of the disciple Mark and went with the latter to Cyprus, where he preached the faith of Christ and was crowned with martyrdom.[17]

Now Paul, formerly called Saul, was descended from the tribe 10 of Benjamin and came from a town of Judaea called Giscalis. After the Romans took the town in war, he went with his parents to Tarsus in Cilicia. From there Paul was sent to Jerusalem to study the law and was taught by the learned Gamaliel. After obtaining letters from the priest of the temple, Paul persecuted those who

persequens qui Christum verum Deum esse profiterentur, Stephani protomartyris neci interfuit. At vero, cum Damascum pergeret, spiritu divino ad fidem compulsus, vas electionis vocari meruit nomenque a Paulo proconsule Cypri accepit, quem praedicatione ad fidem redegerat. Una deinde cum Barnaba multis urbibus peragratis, Hierosolymam rediens, a Petro, Ioanne Iacoboque gentium apostolus eligitur. Hic autem post Christi mortem anno quinto et vigesimo, id est Neroniani imperii secundo, eodem tempore quo Festus procurator Iudaeae Felici successit, Romam vinctus, Plutarcho concaptivo comitante,[20] ut civis Romanus mittitur; ubi biennio in satis libera custodia manens, cum Iudaeis quotidie disputabat. Dimissus tandem a Nerone, et praedicavit multa et scripsit. Extant et eius decem ac quattuor[21] epistolae: ad Romanos una, ad Corinthios duae, ad Galatas una, ad Ephesios una, ad Philippenses una, ad Colossenses una,[22] ad Thessalonicenses duae, ad Timotheum duae, una ad Titum, ad Philemonem altera. Quae ad Hebraeos eius nomine fertur, incerta olim habebatur[23] propter stili sermonisque differentiam. Erant etiam[24] qui hanc et Lucae et Barnabae et Clementi ascriberent.

11   Scripsit et Petrus duas epistolas quae canonicae nominantur. Secunda a plerisque eius esse negatur, quod a stilo primae dissideat. Verum quia pluribus intentus esse non poterat, cum orationi et praedicationi vacaret, duos episcopos ordinavit, Linum scilicet et Cletum, qui sacerdotale ministerium Romano populo et advenis bene sentientibus exhiberent. His rebus intentus, vir sanctissimus tantum nominis sibi apud omnes comparaverat, ut iam fere pro Deo coleretur. Hanc ob rem indignatus Nero, mortem hominis quaerere; unde Petrus, monentibus amicis ad declinandam invidiam et iram principis, via Appia ab urbe discedens, ad primum lapidem[25] Christo, ut verbis Hegesippi utar, fit obviam, quem qui-

professed Christ as the true God and was present at the murder of Stephen the protomartyr. But as he was going to Damascus, he was compelled to convert by the Holy Spirit and gained the appellation of "the chosen vessel." He took his name from Paul, the proconsul of Cyprus, whom he had converted by his preaching. Having travelled through many cities together with Barnabas, Paul returned to Jerusalem, where Peter, John and James chose him as Apostle to the Gentiles. In the twenty-fifth year after the death of Christ and the second year of Nero's rule, at the same time that Festus succeeded Felix as procurator of Judaea, he was sent in chains along with Plutarch to Rome as a Roman citizen. For two years he remained in a rather free kind of custody and disputed daily with the Jews. Nero at length released him, and he preached and wrote much. Fourteen of his letters survive: one to the Romans, two to the Corinthians, one to the Galatians, one to the Ephesians, one to the Philippians, one to the Colossians, two to the Thessalonians, two to Timothy, one to Titus, and one to Philemon. The letter to the Hebrews which circulates under his name was formerly considered dubious because of its divergence in style and wording; there were some who would ascribe it to Luke, others to Barnabas, and others to Clement.[18]

Peter also wrote two canonical letters, though many deny that 11
the second letter is his as it differs in style from the first.[19] Since prayer and preaching kept him from attending to other matters, Peter ordained two bishops, Linus and Cletus, to minister as priests to the Roman people and right-thinking immigrants.[20] Owing to his care and ministry, this most holy man gained such a great reputation among all that he was worshipped almost as a god himself. Nero was enraged at this and planned his death. When his friends warned him to avoid the emperor's envy and anger, Peter departed from Rome on the Via Appia and (to use Hegesippus' words) at the first milestone met Christ. Adoring Him, Peter asked, "Lord, where are you going?" and Christ re-

dem adorans rogat: 'Domine, quo venis?' Tum Christus: 'Romam iterum crucifigi.' Extat sacellum eo loci ubi haec verba sunt habita. Tum vero[26] Petrus de martyrio sui ipsius dictum existimans, quod in se Christus passurus videretur, ad urbem rediit ac statim Clementem episcopum consecrat eique cathedram et ecclesiam Dei commendat his verbis: 'Eandem ego tibi potestatem ligandi et absolvendi trado, quam mihi Christus reliquit; spretis ac contemptis rebus omnibus tum corporis tum fortunae, oratione et praedicatione saluti hominum, ut bonum pastorem decet, consule.' Cum haec autem[27] ita disposuisset, non multo post una cum Paulo iussu Neronis necatur ultimo eius anno, diversis tamen cruciatibus. Petrus enim cruci affigitur capite in terram verso, elevatisque in sublime pedibus; ita enim voluit quod diceret se indignum esse qui mortem Salvatoris imitaretur. Sepultus est autem in Vaticano, via Aurelia, secus hortos Neronis, non longe a via Triumphali quae ad Apollinis templum ducit.

12   Sedit autem annis quinque et viginti. Paulus vero, eodem die capite mulctatus, funeratur via Ostiensi, anno post mortem Christi septimo et trigesimo. Hoc idem approbat Caius historicus in Proculum quendam Cataphrygum disputans: 'Ego,' inquit, 'trophaea apostolorum habeo quae ostendam; sive enim via Regali pergas quae ad Vaticanum ducit sive Ostiensi, trophaea eorum invenies qui hanc stabilivere ecclesiam.' Duo certe fuere, Petrus et Paulus.

13   Praeterea vero in eisdem Neronianis hortis multi cineres sanctorum martyrum reconditi sunt. Nam cum incendium tempore Neronis, a clivo Scauri ad Esquilias usque sex diebus vagatum, multas fortunas civium consumpsisset ac omnis culpa principi ascriberetur, ipse, ut ait Cornelius Tacitus, abolendo rumori intentus, falsos testes subornavit qui id factum a Christianis causarentur. Unde tot capti et interfecti sunt, ut ex eorum cadaveribus per

plied, "To Rome to be crucified again." There is still a chapel at the place where these words were spoken. Believing this to refer to his own martyrdom — that it was in himself that Christ looked like he was going to suffer — Peter returned to the city. He immediately consecrated Clement a bishop and entrusted the bishopric and the Church of God to him with these words: "I entrust to you the same power of binding and loosing that Christ left to me. Despise all goods of the body and fortune, and look to the salvation of men with prayer and preaching, as befits a good shepherd."[21] Not long after he had settled these matters, he was killed along with Paul by order of Nero in the last year of his reign, but by a different form of torture. Peter was crucified with his head towards the ground and his feet raised to the sky. He wanted to die this way, saying he was unworthy to imitate the death of the Saviour. He was buried in the Vatican on the Via Aurelia, next to Nero's gardens, not far from the Via Triumphalis which leads to the temple of Apollo.

He presided over the church for twenty-five years. Paul, who 12 was beheaded on the same day, was buried on the Via Ostiensis in the thirty-seventh year after the death of Christ.[22] The historian Gaius confirms this, when in arguing against a certain Proculus, a Cataphrygian,[23] he says: "I can show you the trophies of the Apostles. As you proceed either on the Via Regalis, leading to the Vatican, or the Via Ostiensis, you will find the trophies of those who founded this church."[24] The two trophies were surely Peter and Paul.

The ashes of many holy martyrs are buried in these same gar- 13 dens of Nero. For in Nero's time a fire lasting six days spread from the Scaurian street to the Esquiline and destroyed the fortunes of many citizens. When the entire blame for it was placed on the emperor, Tacitus says, Nero sought to quell the rumor and suborned false witnesses to allege that the Christians had done it. So many of them were arrested and put to death that the light from their

aliquot noctes lumina continuata dicantur. Sunt tamen qui dicant illud incendium ab eo excitatum fuisse vel ut Troiae ardentis similitudinem cerneret vel offensus deformitate veterum aedificiorum et angustiis flexibusque vicorum; homo libidinosus, intemperans, saevus et avunculo Calliculae[28] omnibus in rebus nequior ac sceleratior. Nam et magnam partem senatus interfecit et turpiter in scena videntibus omnibus cecinit ac saltavit. Tantae praeterea luxuriae fuit, ut frigidis lavaretur unguentis retibusque aureis piscaretur, quae attrahere funibus purpureis consueverat. Haec omnia vitia principio imperii sui ita occultavit, ut bonam spem omnibus prae se ferret. Nam cum admoneretur ut in supplicio cuiusdam capite damnati ex more subscriberet, 'Quam vellem,' inquit, 'nescire litteras.' Splendide tamen cum in urbe tum foris aedificavit. Nam et thermas suo nomine Romae et domum auream et porticum trium milium passuum mira celebritate perfecit et portum Antii, quem ego nuper mira cum voluptate inspexi, sumptuosissimis operis extruxit.

14   Ad saevitiam eius redeo, qua in Senecam praeceptorem, in Marcum Annaeum Lucanum poetam egregium, in matrem Agrippinam, in uxorem Octaviam, in Cornutum philosophum, praeceptorem Persii, quem in exilium egit, in Pisonem, in omnes denique qui aliquo in pretio apud cives suos erant, usus est. Tandem vero populi romani iram et odium ita in se concitavit, ut ad poenas quaesitus quam diligentissime sit. Quae tales profecto erant, ut vinctus in publicum sub furca duceretur et, virgis usque ad necem caesus, in Tiberim proiiceretur. Verum is fugiens ad quartum miliarium, in suburbano liberti sui inter Salariam et Nomentanam viam semetipsum interfecit, aetatis suae anno secundo et trigesimo, imperii vero quartodecimo.

burning corpses is said to have lasted for several nights.[25] But some say that Nero started the fire so that he might gaze upon a sight like that of burning Troy, or because he did not like the city's ugly old buildings and narrow winding streets. He was a lustful, intemperate, and savage man, more evil and wicked in all things than his uncle Caligula. He put to death a large part of the Senate and before everyone would shamelessly sing and dance on stage. His extravagance was so great that he bathed in cold perfumes and fished with golden nets, which he dragged with purple cords. At the beginning of his reign he hid all these vices so as to offer great hopes to all people. When he was urged to sign the usual execution papers of a condemned man, he said: "How I wish I were illiterate." Nevertheless, he was a splendid builder both within the city and beyond. In Rome he constructed the baths that bear his name, the Domus Aurea, and a three-mile-long portico of marvelous renown. At enormous expense he laid out the port of Antium which I recently viewed with marvelous pleasure.[26]

I come back to the cruelty with which he treated his teacher 14
Seneca, the famous poet Lucan, his mother Agrippina, his wife Octavia, the philosopher Cornutus — Persius's teacher, whom he banished — Piso, and all those esteemed by his citizens. In the end he so provoked the rage and hatred of the people against him that they sought with the utmost diligence to bring him to punishment. He was to be bound under a yoke and paraded in public, and then beaten to death with rods and thrown into the Tiber. He fled, however, to the country house of one of his freedmen and there, four miles from the city, between the Via Salaria and the Via Nomentana, he killed himself. He was thirty-two years old and in the fourteenth year of his reign.

: 2 :

Linus I

1   Linus, natione Tuscus, patre Herculaneo, ab ultimo Neronis anno[1] usque ad Vespasiani tempora pervenit,[2] a consulatu Saturnini
et Scipionis usque ad Capitonem et Rufum consules.

2   Hoc autem intervallo imperarunt, sed brevi tempore, Galba,
Otho, Vitellius. Galba enim, vir antiquissimae nobilitatis, in Hiberia[3] imperator a militibus creatus, ubi Neronis mortem comperit, Romam confestim venit. Verum cum omnes avaritia ac segni-
tia offenderet, insidiis Othonis Romae ad lacum Curtii iugulatur,
septimo imperii sui mense, cum Pisone nobilissimo adolescente,
quem in[4] filium per adoptionem susceperat. Vir certe fuit vita privata insignis militaribus ac domesticis in[5] rebus. Saepe tamen
consul, saepe proconsul, frequenter dux fuit gravissimis bellis.
Hunc ut laudem facit Marci Fabii Quintiliani doctrina, quem secum Galba ex Hispania Romam duxit.

3   Otho vero materno genere quam paterno nobilior, vita privata
mollis, quippe qui Neronis familiaris fuerat, inter tumultus, ut
dixi, caedesque invasit imperium. Cum autem civile bellum contra
Vitellium in Germania imperatorem creatum molitus, tribus levi-
bus proeliis superior fuisset, uno[6] ad Alpes, alio apud Placentiam,
tertio ad Castorem; quarto apud Bebriacum superatur, unde rerum desperatione sibimet manum iniecit, imperii sui mense tertio.

4   At Vitellius, familia magis honorata quam nobili, Romam veniens ac imperio potitus, in omnem nequitiam, saevitiam et inglu-

: 2 :

Linus I
[c. 66–c. 76]

Of Etruscan descent, with a father from Herculaneum, Linus was   1
pope from the last year of Nero's reign down to the time of
Vespasian, and from the consulship of Saturninus and Scipio to
that of Capito and Rufus.[1]

Galba, Otho, and Vitellius were all emperors for short periods   2
of time during these years. As soon as he learned of Nero's death,
Galba, a man of the most ancient nobility, was made emperor by
his soldiers in Spain and went immediately to Rome. But after
offending everyone by his avarice and sloth, through Otho's
treachery he had his throat cut in Rome at the "Lake of Curtius"
in the seventh month of his reign, along with his adopted son
Piso, a noble youth. As a private citizen he had certainly distinguished himself in both military and civic affairs. He was often
consul, often proconsul, and several times general in the most important wars. I praise him on account of the learning of Marcus
Fabius Quintilian, whom Galba brought with him out of Spain to
Rome.

Otho was nobler on his mother's side than his father's and in   3
his private life had been a voluptuary, as he had been an intimate
friend of Nero. He invaded the empire, as I said, amid tumult and
slaughter. While mounting a civil war against Vitellius, who had
been made emperor in Germany, he came out ahead in three small
skirmishes — near the Alps, at Placentia, and at Castor — but was
overpowered in a fourth battle at Bebriacum. In despair over this
loss, he committed suicide in the third month of his rule.

Vitellius, whose family was more honored than noble, came to   4
Rome, took power, and fell into every kind of wickedness, sav-

viem prolapsus est. Nam tantae voracitatis fuit ut et saepius in die comederet, et una cena suo iussu duo milia piscium et septem milia avium apposita sint. Verum ubi comperit Vespasianum, apud Iudaeam Palaestinae ab exercitu imperatorem creatum, cum legionibus adventare, primum deponere imperium constituit; postea vero, quibusdam animatus, sumptis armis Sabinum Vespasiani fratrem cum Flavianis in Capitolium compulit, quo quidem succenso omnes concremati sunt. Quare superveniente Vespasiano, cum nullum veniae locum sibi reliquisset, e cella palatii, in qua delituerat, turpissime tractus per viam sacram, nudus ad scalas Gemonias ducitur, ubi excarnificatus in Tiberim proiicitur.

5   Hoc itaque tempore Linus fuit Petri[7] successor. Sunt qui hunc locum Clementi ascribant et Linum ac Cletum praetermittant, quos non solum historia, verum etiam Hieronymi auctoritas reprehendit.[8] Quartus, inquit, post Petrum Romae episcopus Clemens fuit, siquidem Linus secundus,[9] Cletus tertius[10] sunt habiti, tametsi latinorum plerique post Petrum statim Clementem numerent. Quem certe constat (tantae modestiae fuit) coegisse Linum ac Cletum ante se munus[11] pontificatus obire, ne posteris haec principatus ambitio perniciosi exempli haberetur, licet eidem Petrus quasi ex testamento successionis locum tradiderit. Linus vero ex mandato Petri constituit ne qua mulier nisi velato capite templum ingrederetur. Praeterea vero ex sacris ordinibus bis in urbe habitis presbyteros decem et octo, episcopos undecim creat. Scripsit et res gestas Petri, maxime vero eius contentionem cum Simone Mago.

6   Huius autem temporibus fuit Philo Iudaeus, natione Alexandrinus, qui multa ita eleganter et graviter scripsit, ut dictum merito sit aut Plato Philonem sequitur aut Platonem Philo. Is autem sua doctrina et elegantia Appionis temeritatem contra Iudaeos ab

agery, and gluttony. For he was so voracious that he would eat several times a day, and at his orders two thousand fish and seven thousand fowl were placed on the table at the same time for dinner. When he heard that Vespasian had been made emperor at Palestine in Judaea and was advancing with his legions, Vitellius at first decided to give up the empire. But later, encouraged by certain men, he then took up arms and forced Vespasian's brother Sabinus with his Flavian soldiers into the Capitol, which was then set on fire, burning everyone to death. When Vespasian arrived on the scene, Vitellius, having no hope of pardon, hid in a small room of the palace, but was most ignominiously dragged out and brought naked along the Via Sacra to the Gemonian steps, where he was tortured and thrown into the Tiber.[2]

During this time Linus was successor to Peter. Some place 5 Clement here and leave out Linus and Cletus, but both history and Jerome's authority refute this. The fourth bishop of Rome after Peter, he says, was Clement, since Linus was considered the second and Cletus the third, although most Latins number Clement immediately after Peter. It is certainly true that, although Peter handed down his place in the succession to him as though by testamentary disposition, Clement (so great was his modesty) compelled Linus and Cletus to assume the pontifical office before him, so that the ambition to rule might not offer a corrupting example for future generations.[3] By Peter's mandate, Linus ordered that no woman should enter church without veiling her head. At two sacred ordinations held in the city, he ordained eighteen priests and eleven bishops. He wrote down Peter's deeds, especially his dispute with Simon Magus.[4]

During this period there lived Philo the Jew, born in Alexan- 6 dria, who wrote so elegantly and with so much dignity that it was deservedly said that either Plato follows Philo, or Philo Plato. By his learning and eloquence Philo checked the impetuous attacks of Apion, whom the Alexandrians had sent against the Jews. In

Alexandrinis missam compescuit. Romae vero imperante Claudio consuetudinem cum Petro habuit. Inde multa de laudibus Christianorum conscripsit. Iosephus quoque Matthiae[12] filius, ex Hierosolymis sacerdos, a Vespasiano captus ac cum Tito filio tantisper relictus donec Hierosolymae caperentur, Romam veniens, *Iudaicae captivitatis* libros septem patri ac filio obtulit Lini pontificatu, qui tum etiam in bibliothecam publicam repositi sunt, et auctor ipse ob ingenii gloriam statua, ac merito certe, donatus est. Scripsit et alios quattuor et viginti *Antiquitatum* libros, a principio mundi usque ad quartum decimum Domitiani Caesaris annum.[13]

7   Linus autem, cum sanctitate et moribus in pretio haberetur, daemones fugaret et mortuos in vitam reduceret, a Saturnino consule, cuius filiam a daemonibus liberaverat, capitali supplicio afficitur sepeliturque in Vaticano iuxta Petri corpus die XI Kalendas octobris, cum sedisset in pontificatu annos undecim, menses tres, dies duodecim. Sunt qui scribant Gregorium, episcopum Ostiensem, corpus sanctissimi pontificis Ostiam ex[14] voto transtulisse et in templo divi Laurentii magnifice collocasse.

: 3 :

Cletus I

1   Cletus, patria Romanus, de regione Vicopatricii, patre Aemiliano, adhortante Clemente pontificatus onus invitus suscepit, licet doctrina, moribus et dignitate plurimum apud suos valeret. Fuit autem temporibus Vespasiani et Titi, a consulatu Vespasiani septima

Rome during the reign of Claudius Philo befriended Peter and accordingly wrote many things in praise of the Christians. Also during Linus' pontificate Vespasian captured Josephus, who was the son of Matthias and a priest of Jerusalem, and left him with his son Titus until he captured Jerusalem. Vespasian then brought him to Rome, where Josephus presented father and son with his seven books on *The Captivity of the Jews*, which were placed in the public library. In recognition of his glorious genius a statue, and surely a well-deserved one, was erected to the author. Josephus also wrote twenty-four other books of *Antiquities*, spanning the period from the beginning of the world to the fourteenth year of Domitian's reign.[5]

Although Linus was revered for his sanctity and habits, cast out   7
devils and raised the dead, he was put to death by the consul Saturninus, whose daughter he had freed from demons. Linus was buried in the Vatican next to Peter's body on September 21. He had occupied the pontificate for eleven years, three months, and twelve days. Some write that in order to fulfill a vow, Gregory, Bishop of Ostia, moved the body of this most holy pontiff to Ostia and solemnly placed it in the Church of St. Lawrence.[6]

: 3 :

Cletus I
[c. 76–c. 91]

Cletus, son of Aemilianus, was born in Rome in the area around   1
the Vicus Patricius. At Clement's urging he unwillingly took up the burden of the pontificate, though his learning, character and dignity won him esteem among his friends. He lived in the time of Vespasian and Titus, from the seventh consulship of Vespasian

et Domitiani quinto usque ad Domitianum et Ruffum consules, ut Damasus scribit.

2   Vespasianus enim, ut antea dixi, Vitellio successit bellumque Iudaicum biennio ante protractum Tito filio commendavit, quod quidem biennio post constantissime absolvit. Nam capta Iudaea, eversis Hierosolymis temploque solo aequato, ad sexcenta milia hominum interfecta referuntur, licet Iosephus Iudaeus, eo bello captus ac vita donatus quod et mortem Neronis et Vespasianum imperatorem brevi futurum praedixerat, undecies centena milia ferro ac fame eo bello periisse scribat captaque ad centum milia ac publice venundata. Nec id vero dissonum videri, cum referat azymorum dies tum fuisse, quo tempore ex omni Iudaea Hierosolymam, tamquam in publicum carcerem, tum vel maxime die Paschae,[1] quo Christum occiderunt, sunt profecti, daturi poenas et frequentis contra populum Romanum defectionis et sceleris atque perfidiae qua Christum innocentem peremere.

3   Devictis itaque Iudaeis triumpharunt pater et filius, eodem curru vecti, subsequente Domitiano equo albo insidente. Extant adhuc in Via Nova huius triumphi monumenta; apparent insculpta candelabra, apparent tabulae veteris legis e templo ablatae et in triumphum ductae. Hac etiam in victos humanitate usus ut omnes qui ex familia David superfuissent, velut ex regia stirpe, conquisitos in pretio habuerit. Idem quoque[2] imperio semper[3] modestissime usus est. Tantae enim lenitatis et clementiae fuit, ut reos etiam maiestatis verbis tantum castigatos dimitteret; petulantium et loquacium dicta contemneret, offensarum et inimicitiarum immemor. Colligendarum tamen pecuniarum nimium studiosus habitus est, licet ex alieno non raperet, eis denique pecuniis ad liberalitatem et magnificentiam uteretur. Nam et templum Pacis

and the fifth of Domitian until the consulate of Domitian and Rufus, as Damasus writes.[1]

Vespasian, as I said before, succeeded Vitellius and entrusted 2 the Jewish War, which had been deferred two years before, to his son Titus, who most resolutely finished it two years later. When Judaea was conquered, Jerusalem destroyed, and the temple levelled to the ground, about six hundred thousand Jews were reportedly slain. But Josephus the Jew, who was captured in that war but whose life was spared because he foretold the death of Nero and that Vespasian would soon be Emperor, writes that eleven hundred thousand perished by sword and famine and that about a hundred thousand were taken prisoners and publicly sold as slaves. This is not improbable, since he tells us it was Passover, when people came from all over Judaea to Jerusalem, as into a public prison, and indeed on the very day of Passover when they killed Christ. They were now to be punished for their frequent revolts against the Roman government and for their treachery and wickedness in putting to death the innocent Jesus.[2]

After the Jews had been conquered, father and son rode in triumph on the same chariot, and Domitian followed them riding a white horse. The monuments of this triumph still remain in the Via Nova, where we see carved images of the candelabra and the tables of the old law which were taken out of the temple and carried in triumph. Vespasian, however, was so kind toward the conquered Jews that he esteemed all the survivors of the House of David as if they were royalty. He always wielded power with great moderation. He was so lenient and merciful that he dismissed with only a verbal warning even those guilty of treason, made light of the words of insolent and loquacious men, and overlooked offenses and injuries. Nevertheless, he was thought to be overly concerned with collecting money, though he never seized the property of others and he used the money in the end for liberal and magnificent ends. Thus he both finished the Temple of Peace

45

foro proximum divi Claudii coeptum perfecit, et amphitheatrum,[4] cuius partem cum admiratione adhuc[5] cernimus, incohavit.

4   Virtutem autem Titi filii tanti semper fecit, ut tumultuantibus quibusdam ob cupiditatem imperandi, dixerit aut neminem aut filium imperio potiturum — et merito quidem, cum ob virtutem et integritatem animi Titus 'amor et deliciae humani generis' haberetur. Nam et eloquentissimus in pace et fortissimus in bello et clementissimus in delinquentes est habitus; ita comis et liberalis ut nulli quicquam negaret.[6] Hoc cum reprehenderent amici, respondisse fertur, 'Neminem a vultu principis tristem discedere oportet.' Addidit et illud, recordatus quod nihil cuiquam muneris dedisset: 'Amici, diem perdidi.' Nemo ante se magnificentia maior fuit, absoluto atque dedicato amphitheatro thermisque, edita venatione ferarum quinque milium. Revocavit etiam ab exilio Musonium Ruffum, philosophum insignem, et Asconii Paediani viri doctissimi familiaritate delectatus est. Periit autem anno imperii sui secundo, delatusque ad sepulchrum est publico luctu ac si parente orbati omnes essent.

5   Sunt autem qui scribant anno secundo Vespasiani, qui annis decem imperium obtinuit, Cletum Lino successisse. Utcunque sit, constat Cletum virum optimum ac sanctissimum fuisse nihilque praetermisisse quod ad augendam ecclesiam Dei pertineret. Huius autem temporibus fuit Lucas, medicus Antiochensis, graeci sermonis apprime doctus, Pauli apostoli imitator[7] et omnis peregrinationis eius comes ac socius. Scripsit autem[8] Evangelium quod a Paulo laudatur.[9] Unde merito evangelium illud suum esse Paulus dicit. Apostolorum vero res gestae, quemadmodum viderat, conscripsit. Vixit annos tres et octoginta; uxorem habuit in Bithynia, sepultus est Constantinopoli, ad quam urbem vigentesimo Constantii anno eius ossa cum reliquiis Andreae apostoli de Achaia

next to the Forum, begun in the time of Claudius, and began the amphitheater whose remains we still admire today.³

He thought so much of his son Titus' ability that, when certain 4
men in their desire to rule raised a tumult, he told them that either his son or no one would succeed him to power. This was well said, since on account of his ability and integrity Titus was considered "the darling and delight of the human race."⁴ For he was held to be most eloquent in peace, brave in war, and merciful toward wrongdoers. He was so courteous and generous that he never denied anyone anything. When his friends criticized him for this, he reportedly answered: "No man should leave the prince's presence feeling depressed." He made another such remark when he remembered that he had not given any gifts one day and declared: "Friends, I have lost a day." No one surpassed him in magnificence: he finished and dedicated the Colosseum and baths and sponsored a hunt of five thousand wild beasts. He recalled the famous philosopher Musonius Rufus from exile and enjoyed conversing with the learned Asconius Pedianus. He died in the second year of his rule and was carried to his tomb with universal lamentation, as if everyone had lost a father.⁵

Some write that Cletus succeeded Linus in the second year of 5
Vespasian, who ruled for ten years. However that may be, it is certain that Cletus was a most holy and virtuous man, and that he left nothing undone that might contribute to the growth of the Church of God. In his time lived Luke, a physician of Antioch, who was especially learned in the Greek language. He was a follower of the Apostle Paul and a constant associate and companion in his travels. Luke wrote the gospel which Paul praises and rightly calls his own. He composed the Acts of the Apostles, being himself an eyewitness of them. Luke lived eighty-four years. He had a wife in Bithynia and was buried in Constantinople, where in the twentieth year of Constantius his bones, along with the remains of Andrew the Apostle, were brought from Achaea.⁶ During the

translata sunt. Philippus quoque eadem tempestate ex Scythia, quam viginti annis in fide, exemplo, praedicatione retinuit, in Asiam rediens, Hierosolymis[10] moritur.

6   Cletus autem, cum ecclesiam Dei optime pro tempore constituisset, redactis in ordinem ex mandato Petri quinque et viginti presbyteris, sub Domitiano martyrio coronatur ac sepelitur apud beati Petri corpus in Vaticano, V Kalendas maii. Affecti et alii multi martyrio, inter quos est habita et Flavia Domicilla, Flavii Clementis consulis ex sorore neptis, in insulam Pontiam relegata quia christianam se fassa est. Sedit autem Cletus annis duodecim, mense uno, diebus undecim. Sedes autem huius morte diebus viginti vacat.

: 4 :

Clemens I

1   Clemens, patria Romanus de regione Caelii montis, patre Faustino, Domitiani temporibus fuit, qui ab Augusto nonus Tito successit, Neroni aut Caligulae similior quam patri Vespasiano aut fratri. Moderatior tamen primis annis est habitus, mox in ingentia vitia prorupit libidinis desidiae iracundiae crudelitatis, quibus criminibus tantum odii in se concitavit ut paene patris ac fratris nomen aboleverit. Multos autem[1] ex nobilitate interfecit, plerosque exilium misit eoque in loco trucidari iussit. Tantae vero desidiae fuit, ut in cubiculo solus muscas praeacuto stilo configeret; unde quidam prodiens interrogatus, 'Essetne quispiam cum Caesare?'

same period Philip returned to Asia Minor from Scythia, which
he kept in the faith for twenty years by his example and preaching,
and died in Jerusalem.[7]

As for Cletus, after he had established the Church of God as   6
the circumstances of the time allowed and had ordained twenty-
five priests according to Peter's mandate, he was crowned with
martyrdom in the reign of Domitian and buried next to the body
of Peter in the Vatican on April 27. Many others also suffered
martyrdom, including Flavia Domicilla, the niece of the consul
Flavius Clemens, who was banished to the island Pontia for pro-
fessing Christianity. Cletus was pope for twelve years, one month,
and eleven days. After his death, the see was vacant for twenty
days.[8]

: 4 :

Clement I
[c. 91–c. 101]

Clement was born in Rome on the Caelian hill; his father was   1
Faustinus.[1] He lived in the time of Domitian, who succeeded Titus and was the ninth emperor after Augustus. Domitian was
more like Nero or Caligula than his father Vespasian or his
brother [Titus]. In the first years of his reign, nevertheless, he was
considered quite moderate; but soon fell into the great vices of
lust, indolence, anger and cruelty. These crimes made him so
hated that he almost completely effaced the good name of his father and brother. He killed many nobles, sending most of them
into exile with orders that they be slaughtered there. He was so in-
dolent that he would sit alone in his bedroom, impaling flies with
a sharp pen. Asked whether anyone was with Caesar, someone

respondit per iocum, 'Ne musca quidem.' Eo praeterea dementiae et iactantiae venit, ut se dominum ac deum vocari, scribi colique iusserit. Hic autem secundus post Neronem Christianos persequitur. Exquiri quoque quaestionibus et tormentis genus David inter Iudaeos mandavit conquisitumque funditus perdi ac deleri. Tandem vero divina superveniente ultione in palatio a suis interficitur anno imperii quinto decimo. Huius vero cadaver per vespillones delatum ignominiose sepelitur; Philix enim in suburbano suo Latina via illud funeravit.

2   Clemens autem quartus, ut dixi, tum erat Romae post Petrum episcopus; nam Linus secundus est habitus, tertius Cletus, tametsi plerique latinorum secundum post Petrum putaverint Clementem fuisse, quod etiam epistola ad Iacobum Hierosolymitanum episcopum plane significat: Simon Petrus, ubi finem vitae suae adesse sensit, in corona fratrum positus, apprehensa manu mea: 'Hunc,' inquit, 'Urbis episcopum constituo, qui mihi in rebus omnibus, postea quam Romam veni, comes fuit.' Subterfugiebam ego tantum onus. Tum ille: 'Tibi tantummodo consules, populum Dei in fluctibus ambulantem deseres, cum periclitanti subvenire possis?' Verum hic omnium modestissimus, ut dixi, Linum et Cletum sponte sibi in tanto honore praetulit. Scripsit item Romanae ecclesiae nomine ad Corinthios epistolam quidem perutilem nec characteri epistolae differentem quae sub Pauli nomine ad Hebraeos fertur; legitur haec publice a nonnullis. Extat et secunda eius nomine quam veteres non adeo probarunt. Disputationem quoque Petri et Apionis, longo sermone ab eodem conscriptam, Eusebius in tertio *Historiae* suae volumine coarguit.

3   Pervenisse autem ad haec usque tempora Ioannem apostolum constat, Zebedaei filium, Iacobi fratrem.[2] Hic vero[3] omnium novissimus evangelium scripsit ac ea confirmavit quae a Matthaeo,

leaving his room answered jokingly: "Not even a fly." He reached such a point of madness and arrogance that he ordered that he be addressed, written about and worshipped as lord and god. He was the second emperor after Nero to persecute the Christians. He also ordered a search for the descendents of David among the Jews using interrogation and torture, commanding that any who might be found should be utterly wiped out. In the end, however, divine vengeance caught up with him, and he was slain by his own servants in the palace in the fifteenth year of his reign. His body was carried out by common bearers and buried in dishonor by Philix in her villa on the Via Latina.[2]

Clement, as I have said, was the fourth bishop of Rome after 2 Peter. For Linus was considered the second and Cletus the third, though most of the Latins think Clement was second after Peter.[3] Clement's letter to James, the bishop of Jerusalem, clearly proves this: "When Simon Peter realized the end of his life was near, in the presence of the brothers he took my hand and said, 'I appoint this man bishop of Rome, for he assisted me in all matters after I came here.' When I tried to evade so great a burden, he said, 'Do you only care about yourself? Will you abandon God's people as they walk amid the waves, when you can help them in their danger?'" But Clement in his extreme modesty placed Linus and Cletus of his own accord before himself in this great honor, as I have said.[4] In the name of the Roman Church he wrote a very useful letter to the Corinthians, which differs little in style from the letter to the Hebrews ascribed to Paul. Some read this letter in public. There is also a second letter in his name which the ancients did not think authentic. In the third book of his *History* Eusebius also demonstrates that the long debate between Peter and Apion written by Clement is spurious.[5]

We know that the Apostle John, son of Zebedee and brother of 3 James, lived until this time. He was the youngest to write a gospel and confirmed what Matthew, Mark, and Luke had written. They

Marco, Luca conscripta fuerant. Ferunt et id ob eam rem a Ioanne postremo factum, quo Ebionitarum dogma consurgens infringeret, qui asserebant, et impudenter quidem, Christum ante Mariam non fuisse; eius enim divinam naturam Ioannes explicat. Scripsit et alia multa, tum vero Apocalypsim. Relegatus a Domitiano in Pathmon insulam, quo postea interempto et actis eius ob nimiam crudelitatem a senatu rescissis, imperante Nerva, Ephesum rediit ibique usque ad Traianum principem consilio et scriptis ecclesias Asiae sustentans, senio confectus, octavo et sexagesimo post passionem Christi anno in domino quievit.[4]

4   Clemens autem pietate, religione, doctrina multos ad fidem Christi quotidie traducebat. Quamobrem Publius Tarquinius sacrorum princeps cum Mamertino Urbis praefecto Traianum in Christianos concitat. Cuius imperio in insulam Clemens deportatur, ubi ad duo milia Christianorum ad secanda marmora damnatorum invenit. Dum ibi vero aquae penuria laboraretur quam sexto miliario repetebant, Clemens, collem haud longe positum conscendens, agnum vidit sub cuius dextro pede fons divinitus abundantem aquam scaturiebat, qua quidem et recreati omnes sunt et multi ad fidem Christi conversi. Hanc ob rem motus Traianus, ex satellitibus suis quosdam mittit qui Clementem in mare proiicerent, alligata ad collum anchora. Cuius sacratissimum corpus non ita multo post ad littus delatum est atque eo loci sepultum, extructo templo, unde fons divinitus emanaverat. Hoc autem factum narrant IX Kalendas decembris, anno tertio Traiani principis. Sedem vero Petri retinens annis novem, mensibus duobus, diebus decem, et regiones septem notariis divisit qui diligenter res gestas martyrum scriberent, et habitis quoque de more sacris ordinibus decembri mense presbyteros decem, diaconos duos, episcopos quindecim creat. Eius autem in morte dies duos et viginti sedes vacat.

say that John's gospel was written last in order to crush the rising heresy of the Ebionites, who shamelessly denied that Christ existed before Mary, while John explains his divine nature. He wrote many other things, including the Apocalypse. Domitian exiled him to the island of Patmos, but after Domitian was killed and his acts were rescinded on account of their cruelty, John returned to Ephesus under the emperor Nerva. John sustained the churches of Asia by his counsel and writings until Trajan became emperor, when worn out with age he rested in the Lord in the sixty-eighth year after the passion of Christ.[6]

Clement converted many to the Christian faith every day 4 through his piety, sanctity, and learning. On account of this, the high priest Publius Tarquinius, along with the city prefect Mamertinus, incited Trajan against the Christians, and by the emperor's order Clement was deported to an island where he found some two thousand Christians condemned to quarry marble. While everyone there was suffering from lack of water, which they had to go six miles to fetch, Clement climbed a nearby hill and saw a lamb under whose right foot a plentiful spring miraculously flowed. All the islanders were refreshed by this water and many converted to the faith of Christ. Enraged by this, Trajan sent out certain of his henchmen, who tied an anchor around Clement's neck and threw him into the sea. Soon thereafter, his most sacred body washed up onto shore and was buried in a church built at the place where the fountain had miraculously sprung up. They say this happened on November 23, in the third year of the reign of Trajan.[7] He held the chair of Peter for nine years, two months, and ten days. He divided the areas of the city among seven scribes, who diligently registered the acts of the martyrs. At the sacred ordinations, held according to custom in the month of December, he ordained ten priests, two deacons, and fifteen bishops. After his death, the see was vacant for twenty-two days.[8]

: 5 :

Anacletus I

1   Anacletus, natione Graecus, patria Atheniensis, Antiocho patre natus Clementi succedit, Nervae Traiani temporibus. Nerva enim, moderatae vitae tum publicae tum privatae princeps, aequissimum se atque utilem reipublicae praestitit. Praeterea vero eius opera ex senatus decreto Domitiani acta abrogata sunt, unde multi ab exilio rediere. Plerique vero bona sua, quibus antea spoliati fuerant, huius beneficio recepere. At Nerva cum iam senio premeretur et mors instaret, reipublicae cavens, Traianum principem in filium per adoptionem accipiens, secundo et septuagesimo aetatis anno moritur, imperii vero sui anno primo et mense quarto.

2   Nerva itaque Traianus, genere Hispanus, cognomento Ulpius Crinitus, imperium accipiens, militari gloria, urbanitate et moderatione omnes principes superavit. Nam fines imperii longe et late diffudit: Germaniam Transrhenanam in pristinum statum reduxit; Daciam et multas transdanubium gentes imperio Romano subegit; Parthos recepit; Albanis regem dedit; Euphratem et Tigrim provincias fecit; Armeniam, Assyriam, Mesopotamiam, Seleuciam, Ctesiphontem, Babylona vicit et tenuit usque ad Indiae fines et mare Rubrum accessit, in quo etiam classem constituit, qua Indiae fines vastaret.[1]

3   Anacletus autem,[2] institutis et moribus ecclesiam Romanam confirmaturus, constituit ne praesul neve clerici barbam vel comam nutrirent, neve episcopus a paucioribus quam a tribus episcopis ordinaretur, utque clerici publice, non privatim, ad sacros ordines asciscerentur. Omnibus quoque fidelibus praecepit ut peracta consecratione communicarent; qui vero nollent, e sacris aedibus eliminarentur. Augebatur hac ratione mirum in modum Christiana respublica.

ː 5 ː

Anacletus I

Anacletus, a Greek-born Athenian and son of Antiochus, suc- 1
ceeded Clement in the time of Nerva and Trajan.[1] Nerva led a life
of moderation both in public and in private. He showed himself
most favorable and beneficial to the State. Through him the acts
of Domitian were repealed by decree of the Senate, and many returned from exile. Through his kindness many recovered the
property that they had lost in exile. When he was suffering from
old age and death was drawing near, Nerva adopted Trajan out of
his concern for the state. He died in his seventy-second year and
in the first year and fourth month of his reign.

Surnamed Ulpius Crinitus, the Spaniard Trajan surpassed all 2
emperors in military glory, refinement, and moderation when he
took power. He extended the boundaries of the empire far and
wide: he reduced Germany beyond the Rhine to its pristine state,
subjugated Dacia and many peoples beyond the Danube for the
Roman empire, recovered Parthia, gave a king to the Albanians,
made the Euphrates and the Tigris into provinces, conquered and
held Armenia, Assyria, Mesopotamia, Seleucia, Ctesiphon, and
Babylon, and reached all the way to the borders of India and the
Red Sea, where he left a fleet to lay waste to the frontiers of
India.[2]

In order to strengthen the Roman Church in its precepts and 3
customs, Anacletus decreed that no prelate nor cleric grow a beard
or long hair, that no bishop be ordained by fewer than three bishops, and that clerics be admitted into holy orders in public, not in
private. He ordered all the faithful to receive communion after the
consecration; if they did not wish to, they should betake themselves out of the church.[3] In this way, the Christian republic was
wonderfully expanded.

4   Quare[3] Traianus, veritus ne quid detrimenti Romanum imperium inde caperet, tertiam persecutionem in Christianos concessit,
qua quidem multi interempti sunt; maxime vero Ignatius, Antiochenae ecclesiae tertius post Petrum episcopus, qui captus et damnatus ad bestias, dum Romam a satellitibus traheretur, quos decem leopardos vocat, omnes Christianos in itinere oratione vel
litteris in fide confirmabat, sic inquiens, 'ut[4] Iesum Christum inve-
niam, ignis, crux, bestiae, confractio ossium[5] et totius corporis
contentio et tormenta diaboli in me veniant, dummodo Christo
fruar.' Cum autem iam audiret leonum rugitum: 'Frumentum
sum,' inquit, 'dentibus bestiarum molar, ut panis mundus inveniar.'
Moritur autem undecesimo Traiani anno, eiusque reliquiae
Antiochiae iacent extra portam Daphnicam.

5   At vero Plinius Secundus, qui tum provinciam gubernabat,[6]
misericordia ob multitudinem interemptorum motus, ad Traianum scribit innumera hominum milia quotidie obtruncari, in quibus nihil omnino sceleris deprehenderetur aut aliquid quod Romanas leges offenderet, nisi hoc solum, quod antelucanos hymnos
Christo cuidam canerent Deo; adulteria vero aut huiusmodi cri-
mina apud eos illicita haberi. Unde permotus Traianus, rescribit
Christianos quidem non esse requirendos, oblatos tamen puniri
oportere. Periit etiam illo tumultu Simon, Domini consobrinus,
Hierosolymitanus episcopus, in cruce positus, filius Cleophae, qui
centum et viginti complevit annos.

6   Haec autem quae dixi sub hoc pontifice gesta sunt, non autem
sub Cleto, ut Eusebius in tertio historiae suae libro ostendit. Damasus enim Cletum ab Anacleto patria et genere mortis differre
ostendit. Nam Cletus, natione Romanus, sub Domitiano, Anacletus vero Atheniensis sub Traiano principe moritur. Hic autem et
memoriam patri composuit, et seorsum a plebe loca ubi martyres
sepelirentur assignavit, et sacris ordinibus semel mense decembri
habitis, presbyteros quinque, diaconos tres, episcopos diversis in
locis sex numero creavit; quo quidem ultimo supplicio perempto,

Fearing "lest the Roman Empire suffer any harm,"[4] Trajan al- 4
lowed a third persecution against the Christians.[5] Many were
slaughtered. Ignatius, the third bishop of the church of Antioch
after Peter, was captured and condemned to be killed by wild
beasts. While being taken to Rome by guards (whom he called his
"ten leopards"), in transit he made speeches and wrote letters to
strengthen all Christians in their faith, saying: "Let fire, the cross,
wild beasts, broken bones, the rack, and the tortures of the Devil
come upon me, so long as I find Christ and enjoy Him." When
yet he heard the lions roar, he said, "I am grain; let me be ground
in the teeth of these wild beasts, that I may be discovered to be
fine bread." He died in the eleventh year of Trajan's reign and his
remains lie in Antioch outside the gate of Daphne.[6]

Pliny the Younger, who was governor of the province, moved to 5
pity by the great numbers being executed, wrote to Trajan that every day thousands of men were being put to death who were guilty
of no crime and had not broken any Roman laws except that they
sang hymns in the morning to their God; indeed, they held adultery and other such offenses to be unlawful. Moved by this, Trajan
wrote in response that the Christians were not to be hunted down,
but only those who offered themselves were to be punished.[7] Simon, our Lord's cousin, son of Cleophas and bishop of Jerusalem,
was crucified in this persecution at the age of one hundred and
twenty.[8]

The things that I have recounted took place under this pontiff, 6
not under Cletus, as Eusebius shows in the third book of his history. For Damasus shows that Cletus differed from Anacletus in
his country of birth and manner of death: Cletus was Roman and
died under Domitian, while Anacletus was Athenian and died under Trajan.[9] Anacletus constructed a monument to Peter and assigned special burial places for the martyrs outside the city. At one
sacred ordination held in December he ordained five priests, three
deacons, and six bishops in different places. After his martyrdom,

vacat episcopatus diebus tredecim. Sedit autem annis novem, mensibus duobus, diebus decem.

: 6 :

Evaristus I

1 Evaristus, natione Graecus, patre Iudaeo, nomine Iuda, ex Bethlehem civitate ad Traiani tempora pervenit, cuius principis ob singularem iustitiam et humanitatem libenter mentionem facimus. Nam ubique terrarum ita se aequalem omnibus praebuit, ut usque ad Iustiniani tempora in creatione principum sit acclamatum,[1] 'felicior sit Augusto ac Traiano melior.' Praeterea vero tantae comitatis et humanitatis fuit in visendis aegrotis, salutandis amicis, celebrandisque passim festis diebus invitantiumque conviviis, ut ei tanta benignitas vitio daretur; unde dictum illud imperatore dignum prodiit, talem privatis imperatorem esse oportere, quales sibi privatos optat habere. Honores autem, divitias, facultates, praemia benemerentibus aeque distribuit. Nulli quicquam iniuriarum fecit augendi aerarii gratia. Immunitates civitatibus inopia laborantibus dedit. Fluminum traiectiones ac itinera periculosa tuto et[2] saluberrimo opere composuit. Portum Anconitanum ducto praealto et lato muro ad coercendos maris fluctus munivit. Nihil in vita agens, nihil cogitans, quod ad communem utilitatem non pertineret. Hac tanta gloria belli domique parta, apud Seleuciam Isauriae civitatem profluvio ventris periit, anno imperii eius decimo octavo, mense sexto; cuius ossa Romam postea delata sunt et in Urbe sepulta urna aurea in foro, quod ipse struxit, sub columna coclide[3] quam adhuc cernimus, cuiusque altitudo centum et quadraginta pedum est.

the bishopric was vacant for thirteen days. He was pope for nine years, two months, and ten days.[10]

: 6 :

Evaristus I
[c. 100–c. 109]

Evaristus was Greek and his father, Juda, was a Jew from the city 1 of Bethlehem.[1] He lived until the time of Trajan, whom I am happy to mention because of his outstanding justice and humanity. For throughout the earth he made himself second to none, so that down to the time of Justinian, at the creation of an emperor, people exclaimed: "let him be more prosperous than Augustus and better than Trajan." He was so courteous and kind in visiting the sick, greeting friends, celebrating feasts everywhere and attending the banquets of those who invited him that such great kindness was thought a vice in him. He used to say that an emperor ought to act towards his subjects as he wishes them to act toward him. He equally distributed honors, riches, opportunities and rewards to those who deserved them. He wronged no one to fill the treasury, granted immunities to poor cities, made dangerous rivers and highways safe and secure and fortified the port of Ancona against the waves of the sea with a long and high breakwater. Everything he did and thought in life contributed to public welfare. Having gained such great renown in war and at home, he died of diarrhaea in the Isaurian city of Seleucia in the eighteenth year and sixth month of his reign. His bones were brought to Rome and buried in a golden urn in the forum that he himself had built, under the one-hundred-and-forty-foot high spiral column that we still see.[2]

2   At Evaristus, ut Damasus ait, titulos in urbe Roma presbyteris divisit et septem diaconos in ordinem redegit, qui custodirent episcopum praedicantem propter stilum veritatis. Idem constituit ne plebis in episcopum accusatio reciperetur. Ordinationes ter habuit mense decembri ac presbyteros sex, diaconos duos, episcopos per diversa loca numero quinque creavit.

3   Huius tempore Papias fuit, Ioannis auditor, Hieropolitanus episcopus, qui non tantum historia[4] veterum discipulorum Domini, quantum voce Aristonis et senioris Ioannis adhuc viventis delectatus est. Unde apparet ex ipsa nominum dinumeratione, cum omnium fere apostolorum mentionem fecisset, alium esse Ioannem, qui inter apostolos locatur, alium seniorem Ioannem, quem post Aristonem numerat. Qui certe doctissimus est habitus, quemque etiam multi secuti ob doctrinam sunt, ut Irenaeus, Apollinaris, Tertullianus, Victorinus Pictaviensis, Lactantius Firmianus. Quadratus quoque apostolorum discipulus ecclesiam Dei tum periclitantem fide et industria sua, quoad fieri potuit, sustentavit. Nam cum Hadrianus, tum Athenis hiemem agens, symmystesque Eleusinae omnibus paene sacris initiatus, occasionem saeviendi in Christianos dedisset, Quadratus ipse librum Hadriano porrexit de honestate religionis Christianae compositum, plenum fidei et rationis. Idem fecit Aristides Atheniensis philosophus, sub pristino habitu Christi discipulus; volumen namque nostri dogmatis rationem continens eodem tempore quo et Quadratus Hadriano principi obtulit. His autem apologeticis libris factum est ut Hadrianus, iniustum fore existimans Christianos indicta causa ubique occidi, Minutio Fundano Asiae proconsuli scripserit neminem occidendum, nisi de accusatore et crimine constaret.

4   Evaristus autem, ut quidam tradunt, martyrio coronatur ultimo Traiani principis anno. Sed melius censent qui sub Hadriano, nondum in Christianos placato, id ei contigisse scribunt. Annis enim novem sedit, mensibus decem, diebus duobus. Sepultus est

Evaristus, as Damasus says, divided up the titular or parish   2
churches of Rome among the priests and organized seven deacons
into an order to watch over the bishop while he preached near the
pillar of truth. He did this to prevent any accusations of the people against the bishop. He held three December ordinations and
appointed six priests, two deacons, and five bishops for different
areas.[3]

In his time lived Papias, bishop of Hierapolis and disciple of   3
John, who delighted not so much in the history of the old disciples
of the Lord as in the conversation of Ariston and the elder John,
who was still alive. It is clear from his accounting of names (and
he mentioned nearly all the apostles), that there were two Johns,
one the Apostle and the other the elder, whom he numbers after
Ariston. This John was certainly considered very learned and
had many disciples, including Irenaeus, Apollinaris, Tertullian,
Victorinus Pictaviensis and Lactantius Firmianus. Quadratus, a
disciple of the Apostles, supported the Church of God with his
faith and diligence as much as possible in dangerous times. When
the emperor Hadrian, wintering in Athens, had been initiated into
almost all the Eleusinian mysteries and had begun to persecute the
Christians, Quadratus gave him a book he had composed, full of
faith and reason, on the moral worth of the Christian religion.
The Athenian philosopher Aristides did the same thing as a newly
converted Christian. He presented to the emperor Hadrian a volume containing an account of our religion at the same time as
Quadratus.[4] These apologetical books convinced Hadrian that it
was unjust to kill Christians without reason, and he wrote to the
proconsul of Asia Minor, Minutius Fundanus, that no Christian
should be executed unless prosecuted and convicted of a crime.[5]

Some say that Evaristus was martyred in the last year of   4
Trajan's reign, but others, judging more correctly, write that he
died during Hadrian's reign, before the emperor was reconciled to
the Christians. He was pope for nine years, ten months, and two

autem Evaristus in Vaticano apud beati Petri corpus VI Kalendas
novembris. Vacat tum sedes dies undeviginti.

: 7 :

Alexander I

1   Alexander, patria Romanus, patre Alexandro, ex regione Capite-
tauri, iuvenis aetate, moribus senior, usque ad Aelii Hadriani tempora pervenit. Hadrianus enim, consobrinae Traiani filius, imperium accipiens, primo quidem Christianis adversatus est; postea,
ut deinceps dicetur, cognita eorum religione et pietate, in eos admodum beneficus fuit. De populo Romano benemeritus, pater
patriae statim appellatur, eiusque uxor Augustae nomen suscepit.
Utraque vero lingua eruditissimus, et leges multas composuit
et bibliothecam insignem Athenis retulit, Plutarchi Cheronaei,
Sexti, Agathoclis et Oenomai philosophi doctrina ac familiaritate
delectatus. Atheniensibus autem leges petentibus ex Draconis et
Solonis sententia iura composuit. Idem quoque sacris Eleusinae
initiatus, multa Atheniensibus dona contulit eorumque pontem
restituit quem Cephysus fluvius inundans alluvione dissolverat.
Fecit etiam Romae sui nominis pontem, qui adhuc extat, et sepulchrum in Vaticano apud Tiberim, quo nunc pontifices pro arce
utuntur. Tiburtinam quoque villam miro sumptu aedificavit, quae
quidem hodie Tibur vetus appellatur, in eaque provinciarum et locorum celeberrima nomina inscripta erant. Pelusium autem veniens, Pompeii tumulum magnificentius extruxit; murum duxit in
Britannia octoginta milia passuum, qui barbaros Romanosque di-

62

days. Evaristus was buried in the Vatican next to Peter's body on October 27 and the see was vacant for nineteen days.[6]

: 7 :

Alexander I
[c. 109–c. 116]

Alexander, a Roman, son of Alexander, was from the Caput Tauri 1 region in the city.[1] Although young, he was wise in his ways and held the pontificate into the time of Hadrian. When Hadrian, the son of Trajan's cousin, came to power, he at first opposed the Christians, then (as we shall see) after learning of their religion and devotion, he became a great benefactor. For his good deeds to the Roman people, he was quickly called the father of his country, and his wife received the name Augusta. He was very learned in both Latin and Greek, made many laws, erected a famous library at Athens, and delighted in the learning and friendship of Plutarch, Sextus, Agathocles, and Oenomaus the philosopher. At the request of the Athenians, he made laws in the tradition of Dracon and Solon. After being initiated into the Eleusinian mysteries, he gave many gifts to the Athenians and repaired a bridge over the Cephisos which a flood had destroyed.[2] In Rome he also built a bridge named after himself, which still stands, and a tomb in the Vatican by the Tiber, which the popes now use as a fortress. At extravagant expense he built the villa at Tivoli, which is today called Vecchia Tivoli, and inscribed in it the names of the most famous provinces and places. He went to Pelusium and magnificently adorned Pompey's tomb, and in Britain built a wall eighty miles long to separate the barbarians and the Romans. [He replaced] the captain of his Praetorian Guard, Septius [sc.

63

videret. Septio Claro praetorii sui tum praefecto et Suetonio Tran-
quillo epistolarum magistro <*lac.*>.

2   At vero Alexander Romanus pontifex, primus ob memoriam
passionis Christi in sacrificio addidit 'Qui pridie quam pateretur'
usque ad hanc clausulam,[1] 'Hoc est corpus meum.'[2] Instituit item
ut aqua, quam sanctam appellamus, sale admixta interpositis sacris orationibus et in templis et in cubiculis ad fugandos daemones
retineretur. Voluit quoque aquam admisceri vino in consecratione
sanguinis et corporis Iesu Christi, quo significatur Christum ecclesiae coniunctum esse. Oblationem quoque ex azymo, non autem ex fermentato, ut antea, fieri mandavit, quia hoc modo purior
ac potior haberetur et Ebionitis haereticis calumniandi occasio au-
ferretur.

3   Huius vero temporibus fuit Agrippa, cognomento Castoris, qui
Basilidis haeretici volumina in evangelium scripta sua doctrina mirifice confutavit, Barrabam et Barthecab, eius prophetas, conficta
scilicet ad terrorem nomina, et deum maximum eiusdem, Abraxas,
deridens. Mortuus est autem ea tempestate Basilides qua etiam
Chocebas, dux Iudaicae factionis, Christianos variis suppliciis per-
secutus est. Huius vero atque Iudaeorum omnium pertinaciam
Hadrianus imperator ultima caede perdomuit praecepitque ne cui
Iudaeo facultas introeundi Hierosolymam daretur, Christianis
tantummodo civitate permissa, quam moenibus et aedificiis in-
staurans, de suo nomine Aeliam appellavit. In eadem vero civitate
Marcus ex gentibus primus episcopus constituitur, cessantibus his
qui fuerant ex Iudaeis. Huius quoque pontificis tempore[3] martyrium pro fide Christi Saphyra Antiochena et Sabina Romana mulier passae sunt, et Favorinus, Palaemon, Herodes Atheniensis,
Marcus Byzantius rhetores insignes habentur.

Septicius] Clarus, and his secretary Suetonius Tranquillus [for acting too familiarly with the empress Sabina, and would have divorced his wife too for her petulance and difficult ways, he used to say, had he been a private person].[3]

The Roman pontiff Alexander was the first to add, for the re- 2 membrance of Christ's passion, the words spoken at Communion, from "Who on the day before his passion" down to the sentence, "This is my body."[4] He likewise ordained that what we call holy water should be mixed with salt and consecrated with prayers, and kept in churches and bedrooms to guard against demons. At the consecration of the body and blood of Jesus Christ, he caused water to be mixed with wine to signify Christ's union with the Church. He also ordained that the Eucharist be made from unleavened bread, not from leavened bread as before, as this was held to be purer and better, and would silence the slander of the Ebionite heretics.[5]

In his time lived Agrippa, surnamed Castor, who by his learn- 3 ing marvelously refuted the books that the heretic Basilides wrote against the Gospel. Agrippa mocked his prophets, Barrabas and Barthecab, and his great god Abraxas, whose names Basilides had invented in order to excite terror.[6] Basilides died at a time when Cochebas, the head of the Jewish faction, was persecuting Christians with various tortures. The emperor Hadrian, however, thoroughly repressed his obstinacy and that of all Jews with a final massacre and commanded that no Jew be allowed to enter Jerusalem, but that only Christians be given access to the city. He repaired its walls and buildings and renamed the city Aelia after himself.[7] In the same city Marcus became the first gentile bishop, the Jewish ones having come to an end. In the time of this pope, Sapphira of Antioch and the Roman matron Sabina suffered martyrdom for the faith of Christ, and Favorinus, Palaemon, Herodes Atticus, and Marcus of Byzantium were famous rhetoricians.[8]

4   At Alexander, post ordinationes tres quas habuit mense decembri, quibus presbyteri quinque, diaconi tres, episcopi per diversa loco quinque creati sunt, martyrio coronatur cum Eventio et Theodoro diaconis sepeliturque in via Nomentana, ubi interfectus est, septimo ab urbe miliario V Nonas maii. Sedit annis decem, mensibus septem, diebus duobus. Vacavit autem sedes dies quinque et viginti.

: 8 :

Sixtus I

1   Sixtus, natione Romanus, patre Pastore, vel, ut alii volunt, Helvidio, fuit Hadriani tempore usque ad Verum et Anniculum consules. Quem quidem Hadrianum inter bonos principes numerandum censuimus. Liberalis enim, splendidus, magnificus ac clemens fuit. Nam et stultum[1] in se gladio furentem medicis curandum tradidit et aegrotos bis terve in diem invisit et Alexandriam a Romanis eversam sua instauravit impensa; Romae Pantheon restituit ac munera aromatica populo dedit. Moriens hos versus fecisse dicitur:

> Animula, vagula, blandula,
> hospes comesque corporis,
> quo nunc abibis in loca,
> pallidula, rigida, nudula,
> nec, ut soles, dabis iocos?

Moritur autem morbo intercutaneo, secundo et vigesimo imperii sui anno, ac sepelitur Puteolis in villa Ciceroniana.

As for Alexander, after ordaining five priests, three deacons, 4
and five bishops in three December ordinations, he was crowned
with martyrdom along with his deacons Eventius and Theodore.
He was buried on the Via Nomentana, in the place where he was
killed, seven miles from the city on May 3. He was pope for ten
years, seven months, and two days. The see was then vacant for
twenty-five days.[9]

: 8 :

Sixtus I
[c. 116–c. 125]

Sixtus, a Roman, the son of Pastor or (as others will have it) of 1
Helvidius, lived in the time of Hadrian until the consulship of
Verus and Anniculus.[1] We have decided to number Hadrian
among the good emperors, since he was generous, illustrious, magnificent and clement. For even when a raving fool attacked him
with a sword he saw to it that he received medical attention. He
visited the sick two or three times a day, and at his own expense
repaired Alexandria after the Romans had destroyed it. At Rome
he restored the Pantheon, and gave free sweets to the masses. On
his deathbed he is said to have composed these verses:

> Little soul, wandering and gentle,
> guest and companion of my body,
> for what places do you now depart,
> pale, stiff, naked little thing;
> why don't you make jokes as once you did?

He died of dropsy in the twenty-second year of his reign and was
buried at Pozzuoli in Cicero's villa.[2]

2   Sixtus autem rei divinae, ut par erat, curam gerens, constituit ne a quoquam nisi a ministris sacrorum mysteria et vasa sacra tangerentur, maxime vero a feminis, neve quod sacerdotes corporale vocant ex alio quam ex lineo panno et quidem purissimo fieret. Idem censuit ne episcopi, ad sedem apostolicam vocati, redeuntes a suis reciperentur nisi secum deferrent literas pontificis plebem salutantis. In celebratione vero mandavit ut 'Sanctus, Sanctus, Deus Sabaoth' cantaretur.

3   Nuda primo haec erant et omnia simpliciter tractabantur. Petrus enim, ubi consecraverat,[2] oratione 'Pater noster' usus est. Auxit haec mysteria Iacobus episcopus Hierosolymitanus; auxit et Basilius; auxere et alii. Nam Celestinus missae introitum dedit, Gregorius 'kyrie eleyson,' 'gloria in excelsis Deo' Telesphorus,[3] collationes Gelasius primus, epistolam et evangelium Hieronymus; 'alleluia' vero sumptum est ex ecclesia Hierosolymitana, symbolum in concilio Niceno; mortuorum autem commemorationem Pelagius invenit, thus Leo Tertius, osculum pacis Innocentius Primus. Ut caneretur 'agnus Dei' Sergius pontifex instituit.

4   Cum vero Sixti temporibus propter frequentes caedes pauci reperirentur qui nomen Christi profiteri auderent, et Galli Christiani praesulem sibi[4] deposcerent, eo Peregrinum Romanum civem misit, qui confirmatis in fide Gallis Romam rediens, ultimo supplicio afficitur in via Appia, eo loci ubi Christus discedenti Petro apparuit. Eius corpus in Vaticanum per fideles delatum, apud sepulchrum Petri reconditur. Aquila quoque Iudaeus, natione Ponticus, cum Priscilla uxore edicto Claudii discedens, usque ad haec tempora, ut nonnulli aiunt, supervixit, secundus Mosaicae legis interpres post illos Septuaginta qui Philadelphi temporibus fuere.

5   At vero Sixtus, ubi ordinationes ter mense decembri habuisset quibus presbyteros undecim, diaconos undecim, episcopos per di-

In his just concern for the worship of God, Sixtus ordained 2
that the mysteries and vessels of the altar should not be touched
by anyone except the ministers, and especially not by women; and
that what priests call the corporal should only be made out of the
purest linen cloth. He decreed that no bishops called before the
Apostolic See should upon their return be received by their flocks
unless they carried with them a letter of greeting from the pope.
He commanded that the Sanctus be sung at Mass.[3]

At first, all such things were devoid of ornament and performed 3
with simplicity. After the consecration, Peter prayed the Our
Father; James the bishop of Jerusalem added to the rites, Basil
added more, and others added still more. Celestine brought in the
Introit of the Mass, Gregory the Kyrie Eleison, Telesphorus the
Gloria, Gelasius I the Collects, and Jerome the Epistle and Gos-
pel. The Alleluia was taken from the church of Jerusalem and the
Credo instituted at the Council of Nicaea. Pelagius introduced the
Commemoration of the Dead, Leo III the incense, Innocent I
the kiss of peace, and pope Sergius instituted the singing of the
Agnus Dei.

In Sixtus's time, owing to frequent persecutions, few dared to 4
profess the name of Christ, and the Christian Gauls were asking
Sixtus for a bishop. He sent them Peregrine, a Roman citizen,
who, after he had confirmed the Gauls in the faith, returned to
Rome and suffered martyrdom on the Via Appia at the place
where Christ appeared to Peter as he was leaving the city. The
faithful brought his body to the Vatican and buried it near Peter's
tomb.[4] Some say that Aquila, a Jew of Pontus, survived until this
time. Along with his wife Priscilla he had been banished by an
edict of Claudius. Aquila was the second translator of the Old
Testament, after the Seventy who lived at the time of Ptolemy
Philadelphus.[5]

As for Sixtus, after ordaining eleven priests, eleven deacons, 5
and four bishops for different places in three December ordina-

versa loca quattuor creavit, martyrio coronatur et in Vaticano apud Petrum sepelitur. Sedit autem annis decem, mensibus tribus, diebus unis et viginti. Vacat tum sedes biduo tantum.

: 9 :

Telesphorus I

1 Telesphorus, natione Graecus, ex patre anachoreta, Antonini Pii temporibus fuit, cuius quidem imperatoris paternum genus e Gallia Cisalpina originem habuit. Imperavit autem cum filiis Aurelio et Lucio annis duobus ac viginti, mensibus tribus, tanta cum modestia et benignitate ut merito Pii cognomentum adeptus sit ac pater patriae appellatus. Nulli enim unquam tum privatim, tum publice acerbus fuit aut in redimendis pecuniis aut exactione tributi, quod quidem interdum ita remisit ut cautionibus incensis omnium debita relaxaret. Quid plura de hoc principe dicam? Qui religione, pietate, gratia, humanitate, clementia, iustitia, modestia cum Numa Pompilio bonorum omnium sententia comparari potest. Is praeterea cum Tiberis inundatione plurima Romae vexasset aedificia tum privata tum publica, sua impensa cives in restituenda[1] Urbe liberalissime iuvit. Tarracinensem quoque et Caietanum portum miris operibus,[2] ut nunc etiam apparet, restituit. Eius quoque impensa erectam esse columnam illam cochleam putarim, a qua Urbis celeberrima regio nomen accepit.

2 Telesphorus autem, quem diximus Sixto successisse, constituit ut septem hebdomadibus ante Pascha ieiunium observaretur utque in natali Iesu Christi noctu tres missae celebrarentur: prima in di-

tions, he was crowned with martyrdom and buried in the Vatican near Peter. He was pope for ten years, three months, and twenty-one days. The see was then vacant for only two days.[6]

: 9 :

Telesphorus I
[c. 125–c. 136]

Telesphorus was a Greek and the son of an anchorite.[1] He lived   1
in the time of the emperor Antoninus Pius, who on his father's side came from Cisalpine Gaul. Antoninus ruled with his sons Aurelius and Lucius for twenty-two years and three months with such great moderation and kindness that he deservedly gained the name of Pius, and Father of his Country. For he was never severe to anyone either in private or in public, either in collecting money or in exacting taxes, which he sometimes remitted to the point where he burned the bonds and relieved everybody's debt. What more may I say of this emperor? In the opinion of all good men, in religion, devotion, kindness, culture, clemency, justice, and moderation he can be compared to Numa Pompilius. When the Tiber flooded and damaged most of the private and public buildings in Rome, at his own expense he most generously helped the citizens to restore the city. With amazing building projects he restored the harbors of Tarracina and Gaeta, as one may still see today. It was at his expense, I believe, that that spiral column was erected, from which the most populous area of the City takes its name.[2]

Telesphorus, who (as we said) succeeded Sixtus, ordained that   2
a fast be observed for seven weeks before Easter, and that on the eve of the Nativity of Jesus Christ three masses should be cele-

midio noctis, quo Christus in Bethleem nascitur; secunda illuces-
cente aurora, quando a pastoribus cognitus est; tertia, eadem hora
diei qua nobis dies redemptionis et veritatis illuxit, cum omni reliquo tempore ante horam tertiam celebrare interdictum esset, qua
hora[3] Dominus noster in crucem ponitur, ut Marcus ait. Constituit item ut ante sacrificium hymnus ille caneretur, 'Gloria in excelsis Deo.'

3   Huius temporibus multum elaboravit pro fide Christi Iustinus
philosophus ex Neapoli urbe Palestinae, qui et Antonino Pio principi ac filiis eius librum dedit contra gentes scriptum et dialogum
contra Tryphonem, principem Iudaeorum, habuit. Invectus est et
in Marcionem, qui Cerdonis dogma secutus, alterum bonum, alterum iustum Dominum asseruit, tamquam duo contraria principia
creationis et bonitatis. Impugnavit et Crescentem Cynicum ut gu-
losum, mortis timidum, luxuriaeque ac libidinum appetentissi-
mum[4] Christique blasphemum, cuius insidiis ad extremum circumventus pro dignitate Christiani nominis sanguinem fudit.
Hunc autem Iustini hostem non philosophum fuisse, sed philo-
pompum, id est amatorem arrogantiae, scribit Eusebius. Eodem
quoque tempore invaluisse Valentinianam haeresim constat. Ii quidem Valentiniani,[5] cuiusdam Platonici[6] sectatores, dicebant Christum de corpore Virginis nil sumpsisse, sed per eam tamquam per
fistulam quandam purum transiisse. Photinus autem, tum Lugdunensis episcopus, vir certe singularis virtutis et doctrinae, ut ait
Isidorus, iam nonagenarius martyrii coronam constanti animo per-
pessus est.

4   At vero Telesphorus, cum ordinationes quattuor mense decembri habuisset creassetque presbyteros quindecim, diaconos octo,
episcopos tredecim martyrium subiens, apud beati Petri corpus in
Vaticano sepelitur. Sedit annis undecim, mensibus tribus, diebus
duobus et viginti. Vacat tum sedes dies septem.

brated: one at midnight, when Christ was born in Bethlehem; the second at dawn, when the shepherds recognized him; and the third at the hour when the day of redemption and truth dawned for us, since at all other times the celebration of the Mass was forbidden before the third hour, when our Lord was crucified, as Mark says. He also ordained that the hymn *Gloria in excelsis Deo* be sung before the sacrifice.[3]

In this period a philosopher from the city of Neapolis in Pales- 3 tine named Justin [Martyr] wrote much in defense of Christ's faith. He gave the emperor Antoninus Pius and his sons a book he had written against the Gentiles, and had a debate against Tryphon, the leader of the Jews. He also inveighed against Marcion, who followed the heresy of Cerdo and asserted that there were two gods, one good and one just, as two contrary principles of creation and goodness. He attacked Crescens the Cynic as gluttonous, fearful of death, utterly besotted with luxury and lusts, and a blasphemer of Christ; and it was through his plottings that Justin in the end poured out his life's blood for the honor of the Christian name. Eusebius writes that this enemy of Justin was not a philosopher, but a philopomp, a lover of presumption.[4] At the same time, as is well known, the Valentinian heresy was growing strong. They followed a certain Valentinian, a Platonist, and declared that Christ took nothing from the Virgin's body but passed clean through her, as through a pipe. Also at that time, Photinus, the bishop of Lyons, a man of singular virtue and learning, as Isidore relates, suffered martyrdom with resolute spirit. He was ninety years old.[5]

As for Telesphorus, after ordaining fifteen priests, eight dea- 4 cons, and thirteen bishops in four December ordinations, he suffered martyrdom and was buried in the Vatican near the body of Saint Peter. He was pope for eleven years, three months, and twenty-two days. The See was then vacant for seven days.[6]

∶ 10 ∶

Hyginus I

1   Hyginus, natione Graecus, patria Atheniensis, patre philosopho, Antonino Pio imperante Telesphoro successit. Addere vero aliquid etiam de laudibus Pii, antequam ad Higinum[1] veniam, hominis virtus me cogit, qui adeo moderatae gloriae fuit in re militari ut defendere magis provincias quam augere studeret, utque hanc Scipionis sententiam saepius usurparet ac diceret, malle se unum civem servare quam mille hostes occidere, contra Domitiani institutum, qui populi Romani exercitum hostibus obiiciebat, quo rarior in patriam reverteretur, adeo multitudinem oderat et reformidabat ob eius saevitiam. Tantae autem iustitiae Pius fuit ut multi reges multaeque nationes, positis eius iussu armis, ad hominem controversias suas litesque deferrent eiusdemque[2] sententiae statim parerent. Ob haec autem merita, quae maxima sunt, populus Romanus mortuo et flaminem et circenses et templum et sodales Antonianos lacrymantibus omnibus constituit.

2   At Hyginus, urbis Romae episcopus, tum maxime clerum prudenter in ordinem redegit, gradus distribuit instituitque ne templa sine celebratione dedicarentur neve augerentur diminuerenturque sine arbitratu metropolitani vel episcopi. Vetuit item ne ligna[3] reliquave materies ad aedificanda templa congesta in profanos usus converteretur; posse tamen ad structuram alterius templi vel coenobii concedente episcopo transferri. Voluit item unum saltem patrimum unamve matrimam baptismo interesse; sic enim eos appellant qui infantes tenent dum baptizantur, licet re vera patrimus et

Hyginus I
[c. 138–c. 142]

Hyginus, a Greek from Athens and a philosopher's son, succeeded 1
Telesphorus during the reign of Antoninus Pius, whose virtue
compels me to add to his praises before coming to Hyginus.[1]
Antoninus Pius was so moderate in his desire for military glory
that he sought more to defend the provinces than to increase
them, adopting and often repeating the saying of Scipio, that he
would rather save one citizen than kill a thousand enemies. In this
he followed the opposite of Domitian's practice, who because of
his cruelty so hated and feared the multitude that he would expose
the army of the Roman people to enemies so that their ranks
might return home thinner. Pius' sense of justice was so great that
many kings and countries laid down their arms at his command,
brought their quarrels and disputes to him, and immediately
obeyed his decision. Because of these great qualities, everyone
wept at his death, and the Roman people set up a priesthood, held
games, built a temple, and established an Antonine fellowship.[2]

At this time Hyginus, the bishop of Rome, prudently reorga- 2
nized the clergy and apportioned them into ranks. He ordained
that churches should not be dedicated without a solemn celebration and that their number should not be increased or diminished
without the decision of the metropolitan or bishop. He likewise
forbade that timber and materials used to build churches be converted to profane uses; but said that they could be used for building another church or religious house with the bishop's consent.
He ruled that at least one godfather or one godmother should be
present at a baptism. (For such they call those who hold infants
during baptism, although godfather and godmother really mean

matrima aliud significent. Est enim patrimus, teste Festo, qui cum pater sit, patrem adhuc habeat; idem de matrima dicetur.⁴ Instituit praeterea ne metropolitanus episcopum provinciae suae alicuius criminis reum faceret et damnaret, nisi prius a provincialibus episcopis causa discussa et cognita fuisset. Sunt tamen qui hoc postremum Pelagio pontifici ascribant.

3   Huius quoque tempore fuit et Polycarpus, Ioannis apostoli discipulus, Smyrnaeus episcopus ab eo creatus ac totius Asiae religione et doctrina tum facile princeps. Is autem Romam veniens, plurimos fidelium Marcionis et Valentini falsa persuasione deceptos ad fidem reduxit. Cum autem Marcion forte huic obviam factus diceret, 'Me ne cognoscis?' respondit: 'Cognosco quidem primogenitum diaboli.' Negabat enim patrem Christi Deum esse creatorem qui per filium mundum fecerat.⁵ Postea vero, imperante⁶ Marco Antonino et Lucio Aurelio Commodo, quarta post Neronem persecutione, Smyrnae sedente proconsule, igni crematus est. Melito quoque Asianus, Sardensis episcopus Frontinisque oratoris discipulus, librum de doctrina Christiana Marco Antonino tradidit. Huius ingenium Tertullianus mirum in modum laudat dicitque a plerisque nostrorum prophetam habitum esse. Scripsit et Theophilus Antiochenae⁷ ecclesiae episcopus librum contra Marcionem, imperante Marco Antonino; scripsit et librum contra Hermogenis haeresim, qui materiam, non naturam introducens, Deo, non autem naturae eandem comparavit, materiam elementorum et Deum appellans.⁸

4   Hyginus autem bene de ecclesia Dei meritus, cum ordinationes ter decembri mense habuisset creassetque presbyteros quindecim, diaconos quinque, episcopos sex, moritur et apud beati Petri corpus in Vaticano sepelitur III Idus ianuarii. Sedit annos quattuor, menses tres, dies quattuor. Sedes autem quadriduo tum vacat.

something else. As Festus attests, he is a godfather who both is a father and has a father still living; and the same is said about a godmother.) He likewise ordained that no metropolitan should accuse or condemn a bishop of his province for any offense until the provincial bishops should have heard and discussed the cause, though some ascribe this ruling to Pope Pelagius, not to Hyginus.[3]

In his time lived Polycarp, a disciple of John the Apostle, who made him bishop of Smyrna. At that time he was easily the most noble in religion and learning of all Asia Minor. On his way to Rome he led many back to the faith who had been deceived by the false beliefs of Marcion and Valentinus. When he chanced to meet Marcion, the latter said: "Do you not recognize me?" Polycarp answered: "I recognize that you are the first-born of the devil." For he denied that the father of Christ was God the creator who had made the world through His Son. Later, during the reign of Marcus Antoninus and Lucius Aurelius Commodus, Polycarp was burnt at Smyrna by order of the proconsul in the fourth persecution after Nero.[4] A man from Asia Minor named Melito, who was the bishop of Sardis and a disciple of Fronto the orator, also presented Antoninus with a book about the Christian faith. Tertullian wonderfully praises his genius and says that most Christians considered him a prophet.[5] Also in the reign of Antoninus, Theophilus, the bishop of Antioch, wrote a book against Marcion and one against the heresy of Hermogenes, who put forward matter, not nature, and compared the same to God, not nature, calling the matter of the elements God as well.[6]

Hyginus served God's Church well. After ordaining fifteen priests, five deacons, and six bishops in three December ordinations, he died and was buried in the Vatican next to the body of blessed Peter on January 11. He was pope for four years, three months, and four days. The See was then vacant for four days.[7]

: II :

Pius I

1   Pius, natione Italus, patria Aquileiensis, patre Ruffino, Marci
Antonini Veri tempora attigit, qui tum una cum Lucio Aurelio
Commodo fratre annis undeviginti imperium aequo iure adminis-
travit. Bellum autem contra Parthos simul susceptum admirabili
virtute et felicitate gesserunt de hostibusque triumpharunt. Verum
non ita multo post, apoplexiae morbo e medio sublato[1] Commodo
fratre, Antoninus solus imperium obtinet, quem certe ob eius
praestantem in omni genere virtutis animum mirari facilius quam
laudare licet. Hic enim et quia a teneris annis eiusdem animi eiusdemque vultus in quavis fortuna semper est habitus, et quia benignitas naturae cum[2] doctrina a Colatino Frontone oratore habita
in eodem viro[3] certabat, ab omnibus Philosophus merito appellatus est. Platonis sententia, quam semper Capitolino teste in ore
habuit, saepius repetita:[4] tum[5] demum florere civitates, si aut philosophi imperarent aut imperantes philosopharentur. Adeo autem
doctrinae avidus fuit ut imperator etiam Apollonium philosophum
et Sextum, Plutarchi nepotem, legentem audiverit. Frontonis
quoque praeceptoris statuam honoris causa in senatu collocavit.

2   Hoc tempore Pius pontifex consuetudinem et quidem magnam
cum Hermete habuit, qui librum scripsit titulo *Pastoris* insignitum,
quo quidem in libro angelus pastoris personam induens, ei mandat
ut omnibus persuadeat Pascha die dominico celebrari, quod etiam
fecit. Constituit item Pius ne haereticus quispiam ex Iudaeorum
haeresi susciperetur et baptizaretur. Rogatu vero Praxedis, sanctissimae feminae, thermae Novati in Vico Patricii honorem sororis
suae divae Pudentianae dedicavit. Multaque dona huic templo obtulit ac saepius eadem in loco sacrificium Deo praestitit. Ubi et[6]

∷   II   ∷

Pius I
[c. 142–c. 155]

Pius, an Italian of Aquileia and son of Rufinus, lived into the time   1
of Marcus Antoninus Verus, who together with his brother
Lucius Aurelius Commodus justly ruled the empire for nineteen
years.[1] These emperors waged war against the Parthians with
wonderful courage and success, and triumphed over their enemies.
Soon after, however, Commodus died of apoplexy, and Antoninus
ruled alone. Antoninus's soul so excelled in every kind of virtue
that it is easier to admire than to praise him. Since from an early
age he always maintained the same outlook and composure in any
change of fortune, and since the kindness of his temper competed
with the learning he had obtained from the orator Colatinus
Fronto,[2] everyone deservedly called him the Philosopher.
Antoninus, as Capitolinus attests, used to repeat always the saying
of Plato that cities would flourish if either philosophers ruled, or
rulers philosophized.[3] He loved learning so much that even as emperor he listened to the lectures of Apollonius the philosopher and
Sextus, Plutarch's nephew. He also erected a statue of Fronto in
the Senate in honor of his teacher.[4]

At this time Pope Pius had a great friendship with Hermas,   2
who wrote a remarkable book entitled *The Shepherd*. In this book,
an angel disguised as a shepherd commands him to persuade
all Christians to celebrate Easter on Sunday, which Pius did. He
likewise ordered that no heretic from the heresy of the Jews be
taken in and baptized. At the request of Praxedes, a very holy
woman, he dedicated a church to her sister Saint Pudentiana at
the baths of Novatus in the Vicus Patricius. He made many donations to this church and often celebrated Mass there. He also

fontem baptismi constituit ac benedicens consecravit multosque
venientes ad fidem in nomine Trinitatis baptizavit. Illis quoque
poenam constituit, qui negligentes sunt in attrectando Christi sanguine et corpore. Poenitentiam, inquit, agant quadraginta[7] diebus,
quorum negligentia in terram aliquid deciderit; si super altare, tribus diebus; si super linteum, quattuor; si in aliud linteum, novem
diebus. Ubicumque[8] deciderit, si recipi potest, lambatur; sin secus,
aut lavetur aut radatur, lotum et rasum aut comburatur aut in sa-
crarium reponatur.

3   Huius tempore in pretio est habitus Apollinaris, Asiae Hiera-
politanus episcopus, qui insigne volumen de fide Christi Marco
Antonino Secundo tradidit. Scripsit et in Kataphrygas, qui tunc
etiam cum Prisca et Maximilla insaniebant vaticinantes, incipiente
tamen Montano, quorum omnium haec erat opinio: adventum
Spiritus Sancti non in apostolis, sed in se traditum fuisse. Illis
quoque temporibus laudabatur et Tatianus vir doctissimus, quam-
diu ab opinione Iustini Martyris praeceptoris sui non discessit.
Nam postea, inflatus[9] opinione sui,[10] novam haeresim condidit,
quam postea Severus auxit, unde Severiani appellati. Ii vinum non
bibunt, carnes fastidiunt et Vetus Testamentum ac resurrectionem
non recipiunt. Praeterea vero Philippus Cretensis episcopus praeclarum contra Marcionem librum hoc tempore edidit. Nam, sicuti
dixi, Marcionistae Cerdonis dogma sequebantur. Scripsit et Musanus librum contra quosdam qui ad Eucratiatarum[11] haeresim de-
clinabant; horum quidem opinio cum Severianis convenit.
Omnem enim coitum spurcum putabant cibosque damnabant
quos Deus generi humano proposuisset.[12]

4   At vero Pius, ubi in ordinationibus suis, quae quinque fuere,
mense decembri presbyteros decem et novem, diaconos unum et
viginti, episcopos decem creasset, moritur et apud beati Petri cor-

built, blessed, and consecrated a font there, and in it baptized many proselytes in the name of the Trinity.[5] He decreed punishments for those who were negligent in handling the body and blood of Christ. If they carelessly dropped some of it on the ground, they should do penance for forty days; if it fell on the altar, for three days; if on the altar cloth, four days; and, if on any other cloth, nine days. Wherever it fell, they should lick it up, if possible; otherwise, the surface it fell on should be washed or scraped, and the recovered material either burned or placed in a shrine.[6]

In his time, Apollinaris, bishop of Hierapolis in Asia Minor, was highly esteemed. He presented an excellent book on the faith of Christ to Marcus Antoninus the Second.[7] He also wrote against the Cataphrygians [i.e., Montanists] who at that time with the prophetesses Prisca and Maximilla were ranting and raving. Following Montanus, they believed that the Holy Spirit descended, not upon the Apostles, but upon themselves.[8] At this time the learned Tatian was also held in high esteem, so long as he did not stray from the doctrine of his teacher Justin Martyr. For afterwards, inflated by self-conceit, he founded a new heresy, which Severus then propagated, so that its followers became known as Severians. They drank no wine, ate no flesh, and rejected the Old Testament and the Resurrection.[9] At this time Philip, the bishop of Crete, published an outstanding book against Marcion, whose followers, as I said, believed in the heresy of Cerdo. Musanus also wrote a book against those who fell into the Encratites' heresy. They agreed with the Severians that all sexual intercourse was unclean, and condemned the food that God had given to mankind.[10]

As for Pius, after ordaining nineteen priests, twenty-one deacons, and ten bishops in five December ordinations, he died on

pus in Vaticano sepelitur, V Idus iulii. Sedit vero annis undecim, mensibus quattuor, diebus tribus. Vacavit tum sedes dies tredecim.

∶ 12 ∶

Anicetus I

1 Anicetus, natione Syrus, patre Ioanne de Vicomurco vel (ut Damaso placet) Humisia, eiusdem Antonini Veri tempore fuit, de quo in Pio diximus, quem quidem Antoninum philosophia nequaquam a rebus in bello gerendis retardavit. Nam Germanos, Marcomannos, Squados, Sarmatas ingenti virtute et felicitate una cum filio Commodo Antonino superavit ac triumphum egit. Iturus autem ad hoc bellum, cum non haberet unde stipendia militibus praeberet, exhausto aerario, omnem imperatoriam supellectilem omnemque ornatum uxoris in foro Traiani hastae subiecit. Verum, cum postea superato hoste in patriam redisset, emptoribus pretia restituit; nemini tamen molestus fuit, qui reddere empta noluisset; parta victoria, in omnes de republica meritos liberalis fuit. Tributa quibusdam provinciis remisit. Fiscalium titulorum monumenta in foro congesta cremari iussit. Leges severiores novis constitutionibus temperavit. His rebus gestis factum est, ut ab omnibus ita diligeretur amareturque, ut sacrilegi nomen incurreret qui eius imaginem domi non habuisset.

2 Anicetus autem ecclesiae Romanae consulens, ne moribus petulantium quorundam labefactaretur, instituit ne clericus ullo modo comam nutriret secundum apostoli praeceptum, neve episcopus

July 11 and was buried in the Vatican next to the body of Saint Peter. He was pope for eleven years, four months, and three days. The See was then vacant for thirteen days.[11]

: 12 :

Anicetus I
[c. 155–c. 166]

Anicetus was a Syrian and the son of John of Vicomurcus or, as 1 Damasus prefers, of Emesa.[1] He lived in the time of Antoninus Verus, about whom we spoke in the life of Pius. The study of philosophy in no way kept Antoninus from waging war. For together with his son Commodus Antoninus, he conquered with great courage and success the Germans, the Marcomanni, the Quadi, and the Sarmatians, and held a triumph. When he was about to embark on this war, since he had no money to pay the troops and the treasury was empty, Antoninus auctioned off all the imperial furniture and his wife's jewels in Trajan's forum. After he had conquered the enemy and returned home, however, he bought back what he could, but did no harm to anyone who did not want to return the goods. After victory was achieved, he was generous to all who had served the republic. He relieved some provinces of paying tribute, and ordered the records of public debt to be piled up and burned in the Forum. He moderated the more severe laws with new constitutions. These actions made him so loved by the people that anyone who did not have a statue of the emperor in his house acquired a reputation for sacrilege.[2]

Looking after the Roman Church, lest it be weakened by the 2 wanton habits of a few men, Anicetus ordained that according to the Apostle's precept no cleric should by any means have long hair;

consecrari posset a paucioribus quam a tribus eiusdem ordinis viris, quod postea Nicaena synodus confirmavit. Ubi vero metropolitanus consecrandus est, omnes provinciales interesse debent. Statuit praeterea, ut Ptolomaeus ait, ne episcopus crimen metropolitani sui ad alium quam ad primatem aut ad sedem apostolicam deferret, quod et dicta synodus et auctoritas summorum pontificum deinceps confirmavit. Eiusdem etiam institutum fuit ne archiepiscopi nisi ex singulari titulo primates nominarentur. Ii autem merito patriarchae vocantur; ceteri autem archiepiscopi nominentur vel (ut quidam volunt) metropolitani.[1]

3   Huius temporibus Hegesippus, laudator fidei nostrae, fuisse dicitur, qui omnem a passione Domini usque ad suam aetatem ecclesiasticorum operum texuit historiam sermone simplici, ut quorum vitam quam diligentissime observavit, eorum quoque dicendi genus imitaretur. Affirmat autem se Romam Aniceti tempore, decimi post Petrum episcopi, pervenisse ac perseverasse usque ad Eleutherium, qui Aniceti quondam diaconus fuerat. Multa vero in idololatras[2] scripsit, quod tumulos mortuis templaque facerent, ut Hadrianus, qui in honorem Antinoi servi, quem in deliciis habuerat, gymniacum agona constituit apud Antinoum civitatem, quam de nomine ipsius conditam vocavit ac prophetas in templo statuit. Sunt qui et Dionysium huius aetate fuisse dicant. Variantur hoc loco tempora, cum alii Pium, alii Anicetum praeponant; variantur et historiae. Utcunque sit, in tam remota historia tantaque maiorum negligentia satius erit res ipsas paulo ante vel post[3] gestas aliqua ex parte attingere quam eas[4] omnino praetermittere.

4   Anicetus autem, ubi ex ordinationibus quinque, quae mense decembri habuit, presbyteros unum de viginti, diaconos quattuor, episcopos novem creasset, martyrio coronatus ac sepultus est in Callisti coemiterio via Appia XV Kalendas maii. Sedit annos un-

that no bishop could be consecrated by less than three men of the same order, a ruling which the Council of Nicaea later confirmed; and that all the provincials had to be present at the consecration of a metropolitan. He also ordained, as Ptolemy reports, that a bishop should lodge an accusation against his metropolitan only before the primate or the Apostolic See, an ordinance which the Council of Nicaea and the authority of the popes later confirmed. He laid it down that archbishops should not be called primates unless by particular title: primates are deservedly called patriarchs, but the rest are called archbishops or, as some prefer, metropolitans.[3]

Hegesippus, encomiast of our faith, is said to have lived in his 3 time. He wrote a history of the Church from the passion of the Lord until his own age in a plain style so as to imitate the manner of speaking of those whose life he most respected. He says that he arrived in Rome in the time of Anicetus, the tenth bishop after Peter, and that he stayed until the time of Eleutherius, who was at one time the deacon of Anicetus. He greatly criticized idolaters for building monuments and temples to the dead, citing Hadrian who, in honor of his darling companion Antinous, instituted games in the city he built and named after him, and appointed priests in a temple for his worship.[4] Some say that Dionysius lived in the pontificate of Anicetus, but chronologies and histories differ on this point, as some place Pius before Anicetus and others viceversa. However this may be, given the remoteness of this history and the great negligence of our ancestors, it will be better to discuss to some extent events a little before or after they occurred rather than ignore them altogether.[5]

As for Anicetus, after ordaining nineteen priests, four dea- 4 cons, and nine bishops in five December ordinations, he was crowned with martyrdom and on April 17 was buried in the catacombs of Calixtus on the Via Appia. He was pope for eleven

decim, menses quattuor, dies tres. Sedes vero dies tres de viginti post eius mortem vacat.

: 13 :

Soter I

1 Soter, natione Campanus, patria Fundanus, ex patre Concordio, Lucio Antonino Commodo imperante fuit. Hic enim omnibus incommodus, ut Lampridius ait, nil commune cum patre habuit, nisi quod et ipse contra Germanos adiuvantibus Christianis militibus feliciter pugnavit. In eo bello, cum exercitus Commodi penuria aquae laboraret, ferunt precibus christianorum militum aquam divinitus e caelo missam pluraque fulmina in Germanos et Sarmatas cecidisse, quod etiam imperator ipse accidisse literis suis testatus est. Ceterum ad Urbem rediens, in omnia luxuriae et obscenitatis dedecora prolabitur, nihil virtutis et pietatis habens. Gladiatoriis quoque armis in ludo, Neronem imitatus, depugnavit. In amphitheatro feris sese frequenter obiecit. Plurimos quoque senatores interfecit, et eos maxime quos nobilitate industriaque excellere animadvertit.

2   Soter autem a tantis malis animum ad rem divinam convertens, instituit ne monacha ulla pallam attrectaret, neve thus in acerram poneret dum sacrificia fierent. Eius extabat epistola hac de re scripta ad episcopos Italiae. Instituit item ne legitima haberetur uxor, nisi cui sacerdos ex instituto benedixisset, et quam parentes solemni pompa more christiano marito collocassent quamque etiam paranymphae de more custodivissent. Hoc autem constituit, multa pericula reiiciens quae in novas nuptias cadere solent ex

86

years, four months, and three days. After his death the see was vacant for seventeen days.[6]

Soter I
[c. 166–c. 174]

Soter, a Campanian from Fundi and son of Concordius, lived in   1
the reign of Lucius Antoninus Commodus.[1] Commodus, as
Lampridius says, was incommodious to everyone. He had nothing
in common with his father except that he fought successfully
against the Germans with the help of Christian soldiers. In that
war, when Commodus' army was suffering from a lack of water,
they say that at the prayers of Christian soldiers water was divinely sent from heaven and many lightning bolts fell upon the
Germans and Sarmatians. The emperor himself testified that this
happened in his letters. When he returned to Rome, however, he
slipped into every kind of disgraceful extravagance and obscenity,
having nothing of virtue or piety. He imitated Nero and fought in
gladiatorial games and frequently challenged wild beasts in the
amphitheatre. He put many senators to death, especially those
whom he noticed excelling in nobility and industry.[2]

Turning his attention away from such great evils toward church   2
affairs, Soter decreed that no nun should touch the altar-cloth or
put incense into the censer during Mass. His epistle about this
matter to the bishops of Italy is extant. He likewise ordained that
a wife should be held to be legitimate only if a priest had formally
blessed her, her parents had solemnly given her to her husband in
the Christian manner, and bridesmaids had watched over her in
the customary way. He decreed this to eliminate the many dangers

praestigiis et magicis artibus quorundam improborum. Gratianus
tamen hoc decretum Evaristo ascribit. Utri vero sit attribuendum
legentes diiudicent. Non enim multum refert illi ne an huic attri-
buatur.

3   Soteris temporibus fuisse Dionysium Corinthiorum episcopum
scribit Eusebius, qui tantae eloquentiae et industriae fuit, ut non
solum suae civitatis et provinciae populos, verum etiam aliarum
urbium ac provinciarum episcopos suis epistolis erudiret. Instruc-
tus enim Pauli apostoli doctrina,[1] facillime potuit sanctitate et eruditione[2] alios in officio continere. Multa et Theodocion, genere
Asianus, Tatiani discipulus, ad laudem religionis nostrae tum
scripsit. Maxime vero Appellem haereticum scriptis suis percom-
mode irridet, quod Deum, quem coleret, ignorare se diceret.
Affirmabat enim Christum non Deum in veritate, sed hominem in
phantasia apparuisse.[3] Non desunt qui dicant Kataphrygarum
haeresim hoc tempore ortam, auctore Montano. Clemens praeterea, Alexandrinae ecclesiae presbyter, multa conscripsit, e quibus
illa sunt *Stromatum*, id est varietatum libri octo, *Hypotyposeon*, id est
informationum libri totidem, *Contra gentes* unus. Huius autem discipulum Origenem fuisse constat. Huius quoque aetati et Piny-
tum Cretensem, virum eloquentissimum, Oppianum, qui *Alieutica*
scripsit, poetam insignem, et Herodianum, grammaticum quidam,
ascribunt.

4   Soter autem, ubi per ordinationes quinque, mense decembri ha-
bitas,[4] presbyteros octo, diaconos novem, episcopos undecim
creasset, moritur ac sepelitur via Appia in coemiterio Calixti. Sedit annos novem, menses tres, dies unum et viginti. Vacat tum sedes dies totidem.[5]

that usually befall newlyweds from the trickery and magical arts of the wicked. Gratian ascribes this decree to Evaristus. Let my readers decide to whom it should be attributed, since it makes little difference whether the former or the latter.[3]

Eusebius writes that Dionysius, the bishop of Corinth, lived in the time of Soter. He was so eloquent and industrious that he not only taught the peoples of his own city and province, but through his epistles the bishops of other cities and provinces. As he had been instructed in the teaching of the Apostle Paul, he could very easily encourage others in their duty by his sanctity and learning. Theodocion, a follower of Tatian from Asia Minor, wrote much in that time in praise of our faith. In his writings he especially ridiculed very aptly the heretic Apelles for saying that he did not know the God he worshipped. For Apelles denied that Christ was truly God and asserted that He was a man only in appearance. Some say that the Cataphrygian heresy began at this time under Montanus.[4] Clement, a priest of the church of Alexandria, moreover, wrote many works then, including the *Stromata*, a miscellany in eight books, the *Hypotyposeis*, eight books of sketches, and one *Against the Gentiles*. It is well-known that Origen was his student. Some say that Pinytus the Cretan, a most eloquent man, Oppian, a famous poet who wrote the *Halieutica*, and a certain grammarian named Herodian all lived in his lifetime.[5]

As for Soter, after ordaining eight priests, nine deacons, and eleven bishops in five December ordinations, Soter died and was buried in the catacombs of Calixtus on the Via Appia. He was pope for nine years, three months, and twenty-one days. After his death the see was vacant for twenty-one days.[6]

: 14 :

Eleutherius I

1   Eleutherius, natione Graecus, patria Nicopolitanus, patre Abundio, temporibus Lucii Antonini Commodi fuit, cuius flagitiosae vitae Urbs ipsa poenam tulit. Nam Capitolium fulmine ictum una cum egregia illa bibliotheca, maiorum cura parata, concrematur. Aedes quoque in proximo sitae eandem calamitatem sensere. Exortum est deinde aliud incendium, quo et aedes Vestae et Palatium bonaque Urbis pars exusta est ac solo aequata. Tantae praeterea temeritatis fuit ut et suae imaginis caput colosso permagno et egregio, priore detracto, imponi iusserit, et mensem decembrem ad imitationem Augusti Caesaris Commodum appellari voluerit. Quae omnia post mortem eius abrogata sunt, ipseque mortuus etiam humani generis hostis adiudicatus est, adeo eius vita flagitiis contaminata omnibus erat odio. Strangulatus in domo Vestalium duodecimo imperii sui anno et mense septimo, e medio sublatus est.

2   Eleutherius autem, quem diximus Soteri successisse, inito pontificatu statim epistolam accepit a Lucio rege Britanno, qua rogabatur ut se ac suos in Christianorum numerum reciperet. Quare Fugatium et Damianum, viros optimos, eo misit, qui regem ipsum ac populum baptizarent. Erant tum in Britannia pontifices quinque et viginti quos flamines vocabant. Inter hos autem tres archiflamines habebantur, quorum in loco archiepiscopi tres constituti sunt, ut Ptolomaeus ait.[1] Protoflaminum vero loco primitiva ecclesia patriarchas instituit.

: 14 :

Eleutherius I
[*c. 174–c. 189*]

Eleutherius, a Greek of Nicopolis and son of Abundius, lived in   1
the time of Lucius Antoninus Commodus, for whose disgraceful
life the city of Rome paid the penalty.[1] For the Capitol was struck
by lightning and was consumed in fire along with its famous library that had carefully been built over generations. Nearby
houses also suffered the same calamity. Then another fire broke
out in which the temple of Vesta, the Palatine, and a good part of
the city were burnt to the ground. Commodus was so foolhardy
that he ordered the head of a huge and famous colossal statue to
be removed and one in his own likeness put in its place. In imitation of Augustus Caesar he had the month of December renamed
Commodus. All these things were abrogated after his death and
he was adjudged an enemy of the human race — so much was his
life poisoned with disgrace and hated by all. He was strangled to
death in the house of the Vestals in the twelfth year and seventh
month of his reign.[2]

    Immediately after starting his pontificate, Eleutherius (who   2
succeeded Soter, as I said) received a letter from Lucius, the king
of Britain, in which he petitioned the pope to accept him and his
people into the Christian fold. Eleutherius accordingly sent two
excellent men, Fugatius and Damianus, to baptize the king and
his people. In Britain at that time there were twenty-five priests
called flamens, and among them three were held to be
archflamens, in whose place three archbishops were set up, as
Ptolemy says. The early Church put patriarchs in the place of
protoflamens.[3]

3   Idem etiam statuit ne quis ob superstitionem cibi genus ullum
respueret, quo humana consuetudo vesceretur. Noluit praeterea
quempiam de gradu suo deiici, nisi accusatus, reus criminis
convinceretur, exemplo Salvatoris, qui errorem Iudae, licet rei,
nondum tamen convicti, ita aequo animo tulit, ut quicquid interim egisset, pro dignitate apostolatus ratum firmumque manserit.
Prohibuit etiam ne absente eo, quem accusator reum facit, ulla in
causa decerneretur, quam quidem sententiam et Damasus pontifex
et ius pontificum postea confirmavit. Huius autem pontificatu et
ecclesiis pax[2] data est ac quies, et nomen Christianum per omnem
terram mirum in modum auctum, Romae potissimum, ubi multi
ex nobilitate Romana cum coniugibus et liberis in fidem recepti,
baptismi charactere notati sunt. Solus vero Apollonius, orator insignis, martyrium tum passus est, habita prius oratione de laudibus
christianae fidei, quod illis temporibus capitale habebatur.

4   Mortuo Apollonio multae haereses invaluere. Marcionis quippe
secta varie divisa est. Alii enim unum principium fatebantur, alii
duo, alii tria, et tres naturas confirmantes, fidem prophetis abroga-
bant. Florinus quoque et Blasco nova contra veritatem machina-
bantur figmenta, Deum[3] creasse mala, contra illud 'Deus omnia
bona fecit.' Contra hos sensere Quolitiani, affirmantes Deum non
creasse mala, contra id quod scriptum est: 'Ego sum Deus creans
malum.'

5   Sunt qui dicant et Galenum Pergamenum, medicum insignem,
et Iulianum legum latorem et Frontonem rhetorem his temporibus
fuisse, quod ego in tanta perturbatione temporum et historiae nec
affirmo nec refello. De Modesto vero et Bardesane affirmare au-
sim, quorum alter in Marcionem scripsit, alter vero in Valenti-
num. Nam cuius primum sectator fuerat, eius postea confutator
factus est. Hunc Hieronymus concitatissimum in dicendo fuisse
affirmat, cum eius scripta ex Syria lingua in Graecam conversa vi-

Eleutherius ordained that no one out of superstition should ab- 3
stain from any kind of commonly eaten food. Furthermore, he did
not want anyone to be degraded, unless he were accused and convicted of a crime. In this he followed our Savior, who patiently
bore Judas' wrongdoing, since, although guilty, he had not yet been
convicted, so that whatever Judas did in the meantime remained
firm and valid because of the dignity of his apostleship. He also
prohibited the sentencing of any accused person in absentia, which
Pope Damasus and pontifical law later confirmed.[4] In his
pontificate, the Church enjoyed peace and tranquillity, and Christianity wonderfully spread throughout the entire world—especially in Rome, where many Roman nobles with their wives and
children received the faith and were baptized. Only the famous orator Apollonius suffered martyrdom after delivering a speech in
praise of Christianity, which at that time was a capital crime.[5]

After Apollonius died, many heresies flourished. Indeed, 4
Marcion's sect divided into several parties: some professed one
principle, some two, others three, and as they confirmed three natures, they annulled the faith of the prophets.[6] Florinus and
Blastus devised new fantasies against the truth, asserting that God
had created evil things, which goes against the Biblical text: "God
made all things good."[7] The Quolitiani believed the opposite of
this, declaring that God did not create evil things, which contra-
dicts the Biblical text: "I, God, create evil."[8]

Some say that Galen, the famous physician of Pergamum, 5
Julian the legislator, and Fronto the rhetorician lived at this time;
but amid such a confusion of dates and of history I neither con-
firm nor deny this.[9] I am rather more willing to make assertions
about Modestus, who wrote against Marcion, and Bardesanes,
who wrote against Valentinus. For they who at first were followers, later became refuters. After seeing his works translated from
Syriac to Greek, Jerome declared Bardesanes' prose extremely vig-

disset: 'Et si,' inquit, 'tanta vis est in interpretatione, quantam pu-
tabimus esse in sermone proprio?'

6   Eleutherius autem, ubi ex tribus ordinationibus mense decembri habitis presbyteros duodecim, diaconos octo, episcopos quindecim creasset, moritur et apud beati Petri corpus sepelitur VII
Kalendas iunii. Sedit autem annos quindecim, menses tres, dies
duos. Vacat tum[4] sedes dies quinque.

:   15   :

Victor I

1   Victorem, natione Aphrum, patre Felice, fuisse Helii Pertinacis
tempore crediderim, qui quidem Helius, cum grandis natu esset
(septuagesimum enim agebat annum) ex praefecto urbis, quem
magistratum tum gerebat, senatus consulto[1] imperator creatur.
Rogatus deinde ut et uxorem Augustam faceret et filium Caesarem
appellaret, id facere recusavit, testatus sufficere quod ipse impera-
ret invitus. At vero, quoniam in imperatore nihil avaritia turpius
est, cum illiberalis ac sordidus haberetur quod dimidiatas lactucas
et cardos convivis apponeret, nemine contradicente a Iuliano iuris-
perito in palatio occiditur, imperii sui mense sexto. Hic est ille Iulianus qui perpetuum edictum composuit quique septimo mense
postea quam imperare coeperat, apud pontem Milvium victus a
Severo civili bello et interfectus est.

2   At Victor pontifex reipublicae Christianae, ut par erat, curam
gerens, constituit ut Pascha dominico die celebraretur ex Eleuthe-
rii sententia, ut Damasus ait, a decima quarta luna primi mensis
usque in una et vicensima. Cuius decretis obtemperans, Theophilus, Palestinae urbis episcopus, contra eos scripsit qui decima

orous. "And if," he says, "there is so much power in the translation, how great shall we think it is in the original?"[10]

As for Eleutherius, after ordaining twelve priests, eight dea- 6
cons, and fifteen bishops in three December ordinations, he died
and was buried next to Saint Peter's body on May 26. He was
pope for fifteen years, three months, and two days. The see was
then vacant for five days.[11]

: 15 :

Victor I

[189–98]

Victor, an African and son of Felix, lived in the time of Aelius 1
Pertinax, as I am inclined to believe.[1] After being prefect of the
city, Aelius became emperor by decree of the Senate when he was
seventy years old. When asked to make his wife "Augusta" and call
his son "Caesar," he refused, saying it was enough that he himself
ruled unwillingly. But since there is nothing more disgraceful in an
emperor than avarice, and he was considered ungenerous and mi-
serly, as he would serve half-heads of lettuce and thistle at banquets, no one protested when the lawyer Julian killed him in his
palace in the sixth month of his reign. This is the Julian who composed the perpetual edict, and in the seventh year of his reign
Severus vanquished and killed him at the Milvian bridge in the
civil war.[2]

Caring for the Christian church, as was right, Pope Victor de- 2
creed that, according to Eleutherius' decree, as Damasus writes,
Easter should be celebrated on a Sunday between the fourteenth
and the twenty-first day from the new moon of the first month.
Theophilus, the bishop of the city of Palestine, obeyed these de-

quarta luna cum Iudaeis Pascha celebrabant. In hanc vero opinionem invectus est Polycrates Ephesiorum episcopus, qui ex vetere consuetudine decima quarta luna[2] cum Iudaeis Pascha celebrabat. Se enim Apostoli Ioannis et veterum auctoritatem secutum ostendit: 'Nos,' inquit, 'inviolabilem celebramus diem, neque addentes quicquam nec diminuentes. Hanc vero[3] opinionem secutus est Philippus, Hierapoli mortuus; hanc Ioannes, qui supra pectus Domini recubuit, et pontifex eius fuit, auream laminam in fronte portans; hanc Polycarpus, Thraseas, Melito et Narcissus, Hierosolymitanae ecclesiae episcopus.' Idem quoque Victor decrevit ut in quavis aqua baptismum[4] petentes, baptizarentur, si necessitas instaret; hanc ob rem quidam aestimant concilium in Palaestina habitum esse, cui Theophilus, Irenaeus, Narcissus, Polycarpus, Bacchylus, Asianae provinciae insignes episcopi, interfuere. Res tamen integra in Nicaeum concilium translata, in quo etiam constitutum est ut Pascha post decimam quartam lunam celebraretur, ne Iudaeos imitari[5] videremur.

3   Fuere huius pontificis tempore multi doctissimi viri. Nam et Apion tum *Hexameron* fecit, et Paulus Samosatenus una cum Theodoto Coriario aestimavit Salvatorem purum hominem fuisse, et Sextus de resurrectione conscripsit, et Arabianus opuscula edidit ad christianam doctrinam pertinentia. Iudas quoque christoriographiam superiorum temporum usque ad decimum Severi annum conscripsit, in qua tamen erroris arguitur, quod adventum[6] Antichristi suis temporibus futurum dixerit. In quem errorem ideo incurrisse putamus quod et vitia hominum et crudelitatem eo pervenisse cernebat ut diutius tolerari humanum genus a Deo non posset, quae res et Lactantium postea et Augustinum fefellit.

4   Victor autem, compositis etiam quibusdam de religione voluminibus, moritur et apud beatum[7] Petrum in Vaticano sepelitur, cuius diem festum V Kalendas augusti celebramus. Sedit autem annis decem, mensibus tribus, diebus decem. At sedes dies duodecim tum vacat.

crees and wrote against those who celebrated Easter with the Jews on the fourteenth day from the new moon.[3] But Polycrates, the bishop of Ephesus, inveighed against this decision and celebrated Easter, according to ancient custom, with the Jews on the fourteenth day. For he maintained that he followed the authority of the Apostle John and the ancients, and said, "We celebrate the exact day, neither adding nor subtracting anything. Philip, who died at Hierapolis, followed this; as did John, who laid upon the Lord's breast, and his pontiff, who carried a gold plate in front; and so did Polycarp, Thraseus, Melito, and Narcissus, bishop of Jerusalem."[4] Victor also decreed that those seeking baptism could, if necessary, be baptized in any kind of water.[5] It was for this reason, some say, that a council was held in Palestine, at which were present Theophilus, Irenaeus, Narcissus, Polycarp and Bacchylus, all distinguished bishops from the province of Asia. The whole matter was, nevertheless, referred to the Council of Nicaea, in which it was decreed that Easter should be celebrated thirteen days after the new moon, lest we appear to imitate the Jews.[6]

Many very learned men lived in the time of this pope. Apion 3 wrote the *Hexameron*, and Paul of Samosata together with Theodotus Coriarius believed the Savior to have only been a man. Sextus wrote about the Resurrection, and Arabianus published short works on Christian doctrine. Judas wrote a christoriography of earlier times until the tenth year of Severus' reign, in which he erred in declaring that the Antichrist would come in his time. He fell into this error, I think, because he believed that the vices and cruelty of men had gone so far that God could no longer tolerate mankind. Lactantius and Augustine were similarly misled.[7]

As for Victor, after writing certain volumes about religion, he 4 died and was buried next to Saint Peter in the Vatican. We celebrate his feast on 28 July. He was pope for ten years, three months, and ten days. The see was then vacant for twelve days.[8]

:   16   :

Zepherinus I

1   Zepherinus, natione Romanus, ex patre Habundo,[1] Severi temporibus fuit, qui genere Afer ex oppido Lepti una cum imperio cognomentum Pertinacis a Iuliano caeso accepit. Is enim fisci procurator, mox tribunus militaris, per gradus alios usque ad imperium pervenit. Parcus admodum, natura saevus, multis bellis lacessitus, fortissime quidem rempublicam, licet laboriosissime, gubernavit. Ad bellicam gloriam laudem quoque litterarum addidit,[2] philosophiae admodum studiosus. Foris Parthos et Adiabenos[3] superat; Arabas autem interiores ita cecidit ut regionem eorum provinciam Romanam faceret. Hanc ob rem triumphans, ut in eius arcu sub Capitolio posito adhuc apparet, Parthicus Arabicus Adiabenicus cognominatur. Aedificiis praeterea publicis Urbem exornavit. Nam et thermas Severianas et Septizonium extruxit non longe a Circo Maximo Palatinum inter et Coelium montem. Paulum autem abfuit quin Pauli Secundi[4] pontificis iussu lapicidae quidam superioribus annis eam partem Septizonii, quae adhuc extat, demolirentur.

2   At Zepherinus pontifex rei divinae magis quam humanae intentus, constituit ut astantibus clericis et laicis fidelibus et levita et sacerdos ordinaretur; quod postea in Chalcedonesi concilio confirmatum est. Statuit item ut consecratio divini sanguinis in vitreo vase, non autem in ligneo, ut antea, fieret. Haec quoque institutio sequentibus temporibus immutata est; vetitum enim est ut neque in ligna fieret propter raritatem,[5] qua sacramentum imbibitur, neque in vitro propter fragilitatem, neque ex metallo ob tetrum saporem quem inde concipit, sed fieri voluere ex auro argentove aut

: 16 :

Zephyrinus I
[198/9–217]

Zephyrinus, a Roman and son of Abundius, lived in the time of 1
Severus, who was an African by birth from the town of Leptis.[1]
Severus took the name of Pertinax, along with the empire, from
the murdered Julian. He was first an officer of the exchequer, then
a military tribune, before gaining the empire by other steps. He
was very frugal and cruel by nature. Assailed by many wars, he
governed the empire with great bravery albeit with great effort. In
addition to his military glory he also gained praise for letters, as he
was devoted to philosophy. Abroad he conquered the Parthians
and the Adiabeni, and cut down the Arabs of the interior, making
their region a Roman province. On this account he celebrated a
triumph, and on the arch set up below the Capitoline, which still
stands, he was given the titles of Parthicus, Arabicus, and
Adiabenicus. He also adorned the City with public buildings. He
built the baths of Severus and the Septizonium not far from the
Circus Maximus between the Palatine and Caelian hills. It was
only a little while ago that stone-cutters at the command of Pope
Paul II demolished the last surviving part of the Septizonium.[2]

Intent more on divine than human affairs, Pope Zephyrinus 2
decreed that deacons and priests should be ordained in the presence of the faithful, both clergy and laity, as was later confirmed at
the council of Chalcedon. He likewise decreed that the Divine
Blood at communion should be consecrated in a glass chalice, not
a wooden one as before. This regulation, however, was changed in
later times. Wood was forbidden on account of its porousness,
which would soak up the sacrament; glass because of its fragility;
and metal because of the foul taste it imparts. Instead they de-

ex stamno, ut in Triburiensi[6] et Remensi concilio scriptum apparet. Idem praeterea instituit ut omnes Christiani annos pubertatis
attingentes singulis annis in solemni die Paschae publice communicarent. Quod quidem institutum Innocentius Tertius deinceps
non ad communionem solum, verum etiam ad confessionem[7] de-
lictorum traduxit. Mandavit item ne episcopus vel a patriarcha vel
a primate vel a metropolitano suo in iudicium vocatus, sine auctoritate apostolica damnaretur. Voluit postremo presbyteros omnes
adesse celebrante episcopo, quod etiam, ut dictum est, Evaristo
placuit.

3   Huius autem temporibus fuere et Heraclitus, qui in Apostolum
commentarios scripsit, et Maximus, qui famosam quaestionem insigni volumine discussit, et Candidus, qui *Hexaemeron* composuit,
et Origenes, qui decimo Severi Pertinacis anno persecutione in
Christianos mota, Leonida patre interempto, quem ipse adolescens
ad martyrium adhortatus est, cum sex fratribus et matre vidua
pauper relinquitur, redactis in fiscum paternis bonis, quod Christum verum Deum profiterentur, unde grammatica sibi ac suis victum quaesivit. Discipulum autem Plutarchum habuit, qui postea
martyrio coronatus est. Totus deinde ad religionem conversus, ca-
techizandi, hoc est praedicandi, officium habuit. Tanti autem ingenii fuit ut nulla eum lingua, nulla litteratura latuerit. Mira utebatur continentia in cibo et potu, abstinentia in rebus alienis. Nam
et paupertatem Christi imitatus est et multis annis nudis ambula-
vit pedibus. Illud quoque, quod in evangelio dicitur, secutus est,
etsi puerile habetur, quia sunt eunuchi qui seipsos castraverunt
propter regnum Dei. Huius virtutem plerique imitati, martyrium
pro fide Christi aequo animo passi sunt: maxime vero Potamiena
mulier, calida pice in caput eius[8] fusa.

cided that gold, silver, or pewter vessels should be used, as appears in the canons of the councils of Triburia and Reims. Moreover he ordained that all Christians after the age of puberty should publicly receive communion every year on the solemn day of Easter. Innocent III later expanded this to include also the confession of sins. Zephyrinus likewise commanded that no bishop put on trial either by his patriarch, primate or metropolitan should be condemned without apostolic authority. Finally, he ordered that all the priests should be present when the bishop celebrated Mass, which Evaristus also decreed, as I said before.[3]

In his time lived Heraclitus, who wrote a commentary on the Apostle [Paul]; Maximus, who discussed a famous question in an outstanding volume; and Candidus, who composed the *Hexaemeron*. Origen also lived then. As a youth, he had encouraged to martyrdom his father Leonidas, who was killed in the tenth year of Severus Pertinax's persecution against the Christians. After this, Origen was left poor with his six brothers and widowed mother, his father's estate having been confiscated because they professed Christ as the true God. He then made a living for himself and his family by teaching grammar school. He had as a student Plutarch, who was later crowned with martyrdom. After this, Origen turned his attention entirely to religion and took up the office of catechizer or preacher. So great was his intellect that no language or literature remained hidden from him. He was wonderfully temperate and abstemious in food, drink, and other things. He imitated the poverty of Christ and walked on his bare feet for many years. Although it was considered puerile, he followed the Gospel passage that says "there are eunuchs who have castrated themselves for God's kingdom."[4] Many imitated his virtue and patiently suffered martyrdom for Christ's faith, especially a woman named Potamiena, upon whose head scalding pitch was poured.[5]

4   Zepherinus autem, cum ex ordinationibus quattuor mense decembri habitis presbyteros tredecim, diaconos septem, episcopos tredecim creasset, moritur Severi tempore ac in via Appia, non longe a
coemiterio Calixti, sepelitur VII Kalendas septembris. Sedit autem
annos octo, menses septem, dies decem. Vacat tum sedes dies sex.

: 17 :

Calixtus I

1   Calixtus, natione Romanus, patre Domitio, ex regione Urbis Ra-
vennatum, usque ad Severi tempora pervenit, cuius cum animo
fortuna mutata est. Nam ubi quintus a Nerone persecutionem in
Christianos movet, continuo variis periculis et bellis distrahitur:
hinc a Pescennio Nigro, qui magnos in Syria motus concitaverat;
hinc a Clodio Albino, quem tamen in Gallia non incruento proelio
superavit. Inde vero in Britanniam profectus, deficientibus fere so-
ciis omnibus, variis casibus afflictatus, apud Eburacum Galliae
moritur, anno imperii sui secundo et viginti, duobus filiis relictis,
Bassiano[1] et Geta, quorum Geta hostis publicus iudicatus est ac
interfectus, cum ob vitam eius omnibus probris contaminatam
tum vel maxime quia Papinianum, iuris civilis alterum asyllum,
sua manu necaverat. At Bassianus, sumpto a senatu Antonini nomine, imperio potitus est ac Caracallae cognomentum accepit a genere vestis quam populo dono dedit. Is autem patre asperior et
omnium libidine intemperantior, nullum genus facinoris in vita
praetermisit. Nam et fratrem Getam occidisse putatur, licet Geti-
cum triumphum eius nomine duxerit, et novercam suam in uxorem duxit. Nihil egregium de se reliquit praeter thermas Antonianas,[2] quas ipse incohavit et Alexander perfecit; munivit et viam
Novam. Eos praeterea capitali poena affecit qui remedia quartanis

As for Zephyrinus, after ordaining thirteen priests, seven dea-   4
cons and thirteen bishops in four December ordinations, he died
in the time of Severus and was buried on the Via Appia not far
from the catacombs of Calixtus on August 26. He was pope for
eight years, seven months, and ten days. The see was then vacant
for six days.[6]

: 17 :

Calixtus I
[217–22]

Calixtus, a Roman and son of Domitius, from the region called   1
Urbs Ravennatium, lived until the time of emperor Severus.[1]
Severus' fortune changed with his mind. For when he launched
the fifth persecution of the Christians after Nero, he was dis-
tracted by various dangers and wars. On the one side was
Piscennius Niger, who caused great commotions in Syria, and on
the other side Clodius Albinus, whom he vanquished in a bloody
battle in Gaul. After he went to Britain, almost all of his allies
abandoned him and, plagued by various setbacks, he died in York
[of Gaul] in the twenty-second year of his rule. He left behind
two sons, Bassianus and Geta. Geta was indicted as a public enemy and executed, both because of his shameful life and especially
because he had killed Papinian, that bastion of civil law, with his
own hand. After obtaining the name of Antoninus from the Senate, Bassianus took over the empire. He gained the surname of
Caracalla from a type of garment that he gave to the people as a
gift. More cruel than his father and more uncontrollably lustful
than anyone else, he neglected no kind of crime in his life. He is
even thought to have killed his brother Geta, although he held a

ac tertianis colla gestarent; damnati praeterea ab eo sunt qui ad
statuas minxissent. Hic postremo, dum bellum in Parthos movet,
inter Edessam et Caras ab hostibus circumventus, occiditur septimo imperii sui anno, dum levandae vesicae causa ex equo descen-
disset.

2   Calixtus autem pontifex in tanta rerum perturbatione tamque
sceleratis imperatoribus nequaquam ab instituto suo discedens,
constituit ut ter in anno ieiunaretur die sabbati, praesertim fru-
menti vini et olei gratia secundum prophetam, videlicet quarto
mense, septimo et decimo, incohando annum Hebraeorum more.
Verum postea mutata sententia id in quattuor anni tempora transtulit, invernale scilicet, aestivale, autumnale et hiemale, quibus
temporibus deinceps ratio sacrorum ordinum habita est, cum antea id quidem tantummodo decembri mense fieri consuevisset.
Idem quoque instituit ne clericorum delatores et accusatores vel
infames vel suspecti vel inimici in accusationibus et iudiciis reciperentur. Eos vero haereticos putavit, qui arbitrantur sacerdotes post
crimen admissum, etiam si dignam paenitentiam subiissent, ad
pristinos honores redire non posse.

3   Hunc aedificasse basilicam in Transtiberina regione in honorem
beatae Virginis Damasus scribit. Non tamen crediderim hanc illam esse quam hodie tam celebrem et amplam cernimus, cum ea
tempestate ob[3] crebras persecutiones occulta essent omnia, et sacella potius atque eadem abdita et plerumque subterranea quam
apertis in locis ac publicis fierent. Coemeterium quoque de suo
nomine condidit via Appia, eo loci ubi multorum martyrum cineres antea repositi fuerant. Unde mirum cuipiam videri non debet,
si prius multos eisdem in locis sepultos diximus, cum nomen illud
postea a notiore persona traxerit. Invisi ego haec loca cum amicis
quibusdam religionis causa. Visuntur adhuc cineres et ossa marty-

triumph in Geta's name, and he married his stepmother. He left behind nothing illustrious, except the Antonine baths, which he began but Alexander finished, and he paved the Via Nova. He made it a capital offense to wear amulets on the neck against fever, and condemned people for urinating on statues. Finally, while battling in Parthia, he was overtaken by his enemies between Edessa and Charrae, and in the seventh year of his reign he was slain when he got off his horse to relieve his bladder.[2]

During such times of great tumult and wicked emperors, Calixtus in no way deserted his office. He decreed that there should be three fasts from grain, wine, and oil, following the Prophet's authority, on the Sabbath during the year in the fourth, seventh, and tenth month, beginning the year in the Jewish style. But afterwards he changed his mind and moved the fast to four times a year, spring, summer, fall, and winter, at which times holy orders were thereafter conferred, as formerly they were usually only done in December. He also established that people should not be allowed to accuse the clergy in court if they were notoriously hostile or otherwise suspect witnesses. He considered heretics those who believed that priests could not restore criminals to their former honors, even if they had done suitable penance.[3]

Damasus writes that Calixtus built a basilica in Trastevere in honor of the Blessed Virgin. But I do not believe that this is the same famous and large church that we see today, since at that time frequent persecutions caused everything to be hidden; chapels were concealed and most often built underground rather than in open and public places. He also built a cemetery on the Via Appia and called it by his name, where the ashes of many martyrs had formerly been deposited. No one ought to think it strange if I said earlier that many were buried in the cemetery of St. Calixtus, since it received its name later from this better known person. Out of devotion, I have gone to see this place with some friends. The ashes and bones of martyrs are still seen, as are the chapels where

rum; visuntur sacella ubi privatim sacrificia fierent, quae publice quorundam imperatorum edicto exhiberi Deo non poterant.

4   Huius temporibus fuit Tertullianus Afer, centurionis proconsularis filius, quem Hieronymus primum post Victorem et Apollonium inter doctos latinos commemorat. Acris enim ingenii fuit; multa volumina scripsit. 'Vidi ego,' Hieronymus inquit, 'Paulum quendam Concordiae, quod oppidum Italiae est, qui se beati Cypriani notarium, cum ipse admodum adolescens esset, Romae vidisse diceret referretque⁴ Cyprianum nunquam absque Tertulliani lectione unam diem praeteriisse.' Is vero, cum usque ad mediam aetatem presbyter mansisset, invidia deinceps et contumeliis clericorum Romanae urbis ad Montani doctrinam lapsus, contra ecclesiam volumina composuit, maxime vero *De pudicitia, De monogamia, De ieiuniis*. Scripsit et *Contra Apollonium* libros sex.

5   Eisdem quoque temporibus multa praeclare gessit Origenes. Nam et Hebioneorum haeresim impugnavit, qui et Christum ex Ioseph et Maria natum purum esse hominem dicebant et legem iudaico ritu servandam praedicabant. Hoc idem et Symmachus sentiebat. Traduxit etiam sua doctrina ad veram fidem Ambrosium quendam Valentiniani⁵ dogmatis, ut ait Eusebius, imitatorem⁶ vel, ut Hieronymo placet, Marcionitem, cui pro Theochristo presbytero liber Origenis *De martyrio* inscribitur. Hunc quidem, etsi hostem sibi Porphyrius desumpserit, Christiani nominis acerrimus persecutor, ita tamen interdum laudat ut nunc doctissimum, nunc⁷ philosophorum principem vocet, et cum dicat eum omnia Platonis secreta consecutum, carpit tamen quod religioni Christianae se addixerit. Scripsisse Origenem ad sex milia volumina librorum Hieronymus ipse refert. Erravit tamen, ut eidem et Augustino placet, in plerisque, maxime vero in libro *De principatu*, quem *Periarchon* appellavit. Hunc vero et Pamphilus martyr et Eusebius et Rufinus Aquileiensis presbyter mirifice commendant.

the sacraments were privately performed, which by the edict of some emperors could not be shown to God in public.[4]

In Calixtus' time lived the African Tertullian, son of a procon- 4 sular centurion. Jerome places him first among the Latin doctors after Victor and Apollonius. He had a sharp mind and wrote many volumes. "In Concordia," Jerome says, "which is a town in Italy, I saw a certain Paul, who said that when he was a young man he saw an assistant of the blessed Cyprian in Rome and reported that Cyprian never let a day pass without reading Tertullian." He was a priest until his middle years, when the envy and reproaches of the Roman clerics drove him to embrace Montanist doctrine. He composed volumes against the Church, especially *On Shame*, *On Monogamy*, and *On Fasts*. He also wrote six books *Against Apollonius*.[5]

In these same times Origen did many excellent things. He 5 attacked the heresy of the Ebionites, who believed that Christ was entirely human, born of Joseph and Mary, and who preached that Jewish rites should be observed, which Symmachus also believed. By his teaching, Origen brought over to the true faith a certain Ambrosius, who, as Eusebius says, was a Valentinian, or, as Jerome thinks, a Marcionite. At the request of the priest Theochristus, Origen dedicated his book *On Martyrdom* to Ambrosius. Although Porphyry, that most bitter persecutor of the Christian name, chose Origen as his enemy, he nevertheless occasionally praises him, calling him sometimes the most learned and other times the prince of philosophers. Although he says that Origen understood all the secrets of Plato, Porphyry carps at him for devoting himself to the Christian religion. Jerome himself reports that Origen wrote almost six thousand volumes of books.[6] Nevertheless, according to Jerome and Augustine, he erred in most of his works, especially in his book *On First Principles*, which in Greek he called *Peri archon*. Still, Pamphilus the martyr, Eusebius and Rufinus, the priest of Aquileia, highly commend Origen.[7]

6   At Calixtus, ubi ex ordinationibus quinquies per mensem decembrem actis presbyteros sedecim, diaconos quattuor, episcopos octo creasset, martyrio coronatus est ac sepultus in coemiterio Calepodii[8] via Aurelia, tertio ab Urbe miliario, pridie[9] Idus octobris. Sedit annos sex, menses decem, dies decem. Vacat tum sedes dies sex.

: 18 :

Urbanus I

1   Urbanus, natione Romanus, patre Pontiano, Marco Aurelio Antonino imperante fuit, anno Christi ducentesimo vicensimo sexto, ab Urbe vero condita noningentesimo et septuagesimo. Hic autem, ut putatur, Caracallae filius—erant enim qui dicerent eum vulgo conceptum—Romam veniens, magna[1] omnium expectatione imperium adeptus, Heliogabali nomen sumpsit a sole, cuius sacerdos erat edito templo. Phoenices enim Heliogabalum solem vocant. Verum ita praeter expectationem is vixit, ut nullam de se nisi flagitiorum totiusque obscenitatis memoriam reliquerit. Nam et in virgines Vestales incestum commisit et probrosas mulieres semper domi habuit et iracundia incitatus Sabinum consularem virum, ad quem Ulpianus scripsit, e media tolli iussit. Dignitates autem et honores malis ac flagitiosis committebat, quos quidem ita aliquando deridebat, ut cum secum accubuissent, stratis follibus in cena eisdemque reflatis, subito sub mensa omnes reperirentur. Ita autem inhoneste ridebat, ut publice in theatro solus audiretur.

As for Calixtus, after ordaining sixteen priests, four deacons, 6
and eight bishops in five December ordinations, he was crowned
with martyrdom and buried in the cemetery of Calepodius three
miles from the city on the Via Aurelia on October 14. He was
pope for six years, ten months, and ten days. The see was then vacant for six days.[8]

: 18 :

Urban I
[222–23]

Urban, a Roman and son of Pontian, lived during the reign of 1
Marcus Aurelius Antoninus in the year of Christ 226 (in the year
of Rome 970).[1] Antoninus is thought to be the son of Caracalla,
but some said he was a bastard. After coming to Rome and taking
possession of the empire amid universal great expectations, he
adopted the name of Heliogabalus, which is what the Phoenicians
call the sun, built a temple to the sun, and made himself its priest.
His life ran so counter to expectation that he left no memory of
himself, except for his disgraceful deeds and every kind of inde-
cency.[2] For he defiled Vestal virgins and always had disgraceful
women in the palace. In a rage, he commanded the execution of
Sabinus, a man of consular rank and a correspondent of Ulpian.
He conferred dignities and honors on wicked criminals, whom he
would sometimes subject to mockery by making them lie with him
at supper, having placed deflated bellows beneath them; these
would suddenly inflate, throwing everyone under the table. His
laugh was so indecent that he alone would be heard in a public
theater.

2   Primus Romanorum holoserica veste, mensis ac capsis argenteis usus est. Admonentibus amicis caveret ne ad inopiam redigeretur, respondit: 'Quid melius, quam ut ipse mihi haeres sim et uxori meae?' Eo vesaniae interdum provectus est ut decem milia pondo arachnearum collegerit, qua ex re dicebat magnitudinem urbis Romae comprehendi posse. Exhibuit praeterea decem milia murum, mille mustellas, mille sorices. Hac vero insania adeo contemni coeptus est, ut tumultu militari exorto, ipse cum matre necaretur. Aiunt, cum ei a sacerdotibus Syriis dictum esset vi moriturum, eum parasse funem serico et cocco intortum, quo vitam laqueo finiret. Moritur autem quarto imperii sui anno, quo tempore in Palaestina Nicopolis urbs, quae prius Emaus dicebatur, condita est, legationis industriam eius rei gratia suscipiente Africano rerum ac temporum scriptore.

3   Urbanus vero, qui huius monstri tempore fuit (non autem Diocletiani, ut quidam volunt), multos sanctitate vitae et doctrina singulari ad fidem traduxit; inter hos autem Valerianum virum praestantissimum,[2] beatae Caeciliae sponsum, et Tyburtium eiusdem Valeriani[3] fratrem, qui postea martyrium constanti animo tulere. Quam conditionem etiam virgo ipsa subiit in domo paterna, iam antea suo rogatu ab Urbano Deo dicata. Eiusdem quoque Urbani institutum fuit ut ecclesia praedia ac fundos a fidelibus oblatos reciperet partiaretur que proventus clericis omnibus viritim, nihilque cuiuspiam privatum esset, sed in commune bonum—quod hodie obsolevit, tanta est hominum rapacitas et libido. Sunt qui huic attribuunt distinctionem quattuor temporum ac ieiunii, quae antea confundebantur[4] hominum imperitia.

4   Huius temporibus Tryphonem Origenis auditorem fuisse constat, qui librum praecipue composuit de vacca ruffa in Deuteronomio. Minutius item Felix, insignis tum Romae causidicus, dialo-

Heliogabalus was the first of the Romans to wear velvet and use 2
silver trays and receptacles. When his friends warned him not to
let himself be reduced to poverty, he answered: "What could be
better than that I should be heir to myself and to my wife?" Once
his madness was so great that he collected ten thousand pounds of
spiders, from which, he said, the size of Rome could be understood. Furthermore, he put on show ten thousand mice, weasels
and shrews. Thanks to his madness he became so despised that a
military tumult arose, and he and his mother were slain. They say,
when Syrian priests had predicted to him that he would die a violent death, that he prepared a twisted rope of silk and scarlet as a
noose with which to end his life. He died in the fourth year of his
reign, when the Palestinian city of Nicopolis, formerly called
Emmaus, was founded, which the historian Africanus undertook
an embassy to promote.[3]

Urban lived in the time of this monster and not that of 3
Diocletian as some would have it. By the holiness of his life and
his remarkable teaching, Urban brought many to the faith, including the excellent Valerian, the husband of the blessed Caecilia,
and his brother Tiburtius, who later endured martyrdom with a
constant spirit. The virgin Caecilia also suffered martyrdom in her
father's house, which Urban had previously made into a church at
her request. Urban ordained that the Church might receive estates
and lands donated by the faithful and that this revenue should be
divided among all clerics individually and that nothing should be
owned privately by anyone, but for the common good. This custom has become outdated today, so great is the lust and greed of
men. Some attribute to this pope the distinction of the four an-
nual times of fasting, which before this were confused due to
men's ignorance.[4]

It is well established that Trypho, a disciple of Origen, lived at 4
this time. He composed a book about the red heifer in Deuteron-
omy. Likewise, Minucius Felix, a famous advocate in Rome at that

gum scripsit quo christianum et ethnicum disputantes inducit. Scripsit et contra mathematicos, cuius etiam Lactantius meminit. Alexander quoque Hierosolymitanus episcopus bibliothecam illam Hierosolymis tum instituit, unde tantum laudis consecutus est.

5   At ubi ex ordinationibus quinquies mense decembri habitis presbyteros novem, diaconos quinque, episcopos novem creasset, martyrio coronatus est et sepultus in coemiterio Praetextati via Tiburtina.[5] Sedit annos quattuor, menses decem, dies duodecim. Sedes autem dies triginta tum vacat.

: 19 :

Pontianus I

1   Pontianus, natione Romanus, patre Calphurnio, temporibus Alexandri imperatoris fuit, anno ab Urbe condita nongentensimo septuagensimo quarto, anno vero Christi ducentensimo et quadragensimo quinto. Inter imperium vero Heliogabali et Alexandri tres imperatores sunt habiti, Diadumenus, Macrinus[1] et Albinus, quorum nomina praetermittere institui, cum quia parum imperarunt, tum vel maxime quia nihil memoria dignum gessere. Solus tamen Albinus ob edacitatem nomen aliquod apud posteros consecutus est, ut ait Cordus, qui centum persica campana, decem melones ostienses, quingentas ficos passarias, quadringenta ostrea una cena comedebat.

2   Sed omittamus haec monstra; ad Alexandrum venio, unicum virtutis exemplar, qui senatus ac militum studio imperator creatus, ad componendam rempublicam, vitio superiorum principum labefactatam, animum adiecit. Adiutores autem ad hanc rem habuit[2]

time, wrote a dialogue in which a Christian and a pagan debate. He also wrote against the mathematicians, a book Lactantius mentions. Alexander, the bishop of Jerusalem, at this time founded the famous library at Jerusalem for which he earned so much praise.[5]

As for Urban, after ordaining nine priests, five deacons, and 5
nine bishops in five December ordinations, he was crowned with martyrdom and buried in the cemetery of Praetextatus on the Via Tiburtina. He was pope for four years, ten months, and twelve days. The see was then vacant for thirty days.[6]

: 19 :

Pontian I
[230–35]

Pontian, a Roman and son of Calpurnius, lived in the time of the 1
emperor Alexander in the year of Rome 974 and of Christ 245.[1] Between the reigns of Heliogabalus and Alexander, there were three emperors: Diadumenus, Macrinus, and Albinus. I decided to leave these emperors out because they reigned for so little time but mostly because they did nothing worthy of memory. Albinus alone achieved some notoriety in later times on account of his gluttony, as Cordus says. For he would eat one hundred Campanian peaches, ten Ostian melons, five hundred dried figs, and four hundred oysters at one dinner.[2]

But let us omit these monsters; I come to Alexander, a unique 2
exemplar of virtue, who became emperor by the efforts of the military and the Senate. He applied himself to settling the government, which had been weakened by the vices of earlier emperors. In this, he had the assistance of Julius Frontinus, a most learned

Iulium Frontinum, virum doctissimum, Ulpianum et Paulum, viros in iure civili praestantissimos. Iusticiam vero ita coluit ut nemo unquam de illata ab eo iniuria questus sit. Procul omni pompa et ambitione vixit, unde semel tantum, dum consul esset, picta toga usus est. Si quis autem inter salutandum caput flexisset aut blandius aliquid dixisset, ut adulator reiiciebatur. Erat praeterea tantae prudentiae ut a nemine decipi posset, unde Turinum, qui munera accipiebat quod magnae esse auctoritatis apud imperatorem videretur, in foro Transitorio ad palum alligatum fumo necari iussit, praecone clamante 'Fumo punitur qui fumum vendidit.'

3   Pecunias autem, quarum mater Mammea ut mulier studiosa fuit, omnino contempsit. Gemmas reiecit ut res muliebres, dictitans in Virgilio, quem Platonem poetarum vocabat, plures et meliores gemmas esse. Lenonum vectigal et meretricum et exoletorum in sacrum aerarium inferri vetuit idque sumptibus publicis assignandum censuit, quo et theatrum et circus et amphitheatrum et stadium instaurarentur. Statuas summorum virorum undique conquisitas in foro Transitorio locavit. Thermas vero Antonini Caracallae, quae hodie Antonianae vocantur, perfecit et ornavit. Templum Christo aedificare voluit eumque inter deos recipere. Habuit praeterea Christum ipsum, Abraham et Orpheum in lario suo. Alexander igitur, tot virtutibus insignis, iuvenis admodum imperator creatus, bellum statim contra Persas suscepit ac Xerxem eorum regem constantissime vicit. Disciplinae vero militaris adeo severus emendator fuit ut quasdam etiam integras legiones exauctoraverit. Qua severitate factum est ut militari tumultu apud Maguntiacum in Gallia occideretur.

4   Pontianus autem pontifex Romanus, instigantibus sacrificulis idolorum, mandato principis ab urbe Roma in Sardiniam insulam cum Philippo presbytero deportatur, eo potissimum tempore quo

man, and Ulpian and Paul, outstanding jurists of civil law. He cultivated justice to such an extent that no one ever complained of any injury inflicted by him. He was so far from all pomp and ostentation that he wore the embroidered toga only once when he was a consul. Whenever someone bowed his head in greeting him, or said something unctuous, he was dismissed as a flatterer. Furthermore, he was so prudent that no one could deceive him. When Turnus, for example, accepted bribes because of the great influence he appeared to have with the emperor, Alexander ordered him to be bound to a pole in the Forum Transitorium and suffocated to death with smoke. The herald cried out: "The man who sold smoke is punished with smoke."

Alexander completely despised money, although his mother 3 Mammea,[3] being a woman, was fond of it. He refused gems as feminine trifles, often saying that there were more and better gems in Virgil, whom he called the Plato of poets. He forbade storing the revenue of pimps, prostitutes, and catamites in the sacred treasury; but used it for public expenses, to restore the theater, the circus, the amphitheater, and the stadium. He collected statues of famous men from everywhere and placed them in the Forum Transitorium. He completed and embellished the baths of Antoninus Caracalla, which are today called the Antonian. He planned to build a temple to Christ and receive Him among the gods. Besides Christ, he had Abraham and Orpheus in his domestic chapel. Distinguished by so many virtues, Alexander became emperor very young and immediately embarked on a war against the Persians, conquering their king Xerxes with great determination. He was such a severe reformer of military discipline that he discharged entire legions. It was this severity that led to his murder in a military uprising at Mainz in Gaul.[4]

Pontian, the Roman pontiff, at the instigation of the idolatrous 4 priests was deported along with the priest Philip to the island of Sardinia by emperor's decree.[5] It was at this time that Origen led

Origenes Germanum presbyterum Antiochenum et Beryllum Arabiae episcopum ab haeresi ad veritatem reduxit. Negabat Beryllus Christum ante incarnationem fuisse. Aliqua opuscula hic scripsit, maxime vero epistolas aliquot quibus Origeni pro sana doctrina gratias agit; extat et dialogus Origenis et Berylli in quo Beryllum haereseos arguit. Tanti autem ingenii fuit Origenes et doctrinae, ut septem notarii sibi invicem succedentes homini vix sufficerent; librarios habuit totidem et puellas apprime eruditas, quos omnes ingenii copiam et ubertatem effundendo defatigabat. Ab Antiochia vero accersitus Romam a Mammea Alexandri matre, in quam filius unice pius fuit, in pretio habitus, Origenes, mulierem christianam fidem edoctam relinquens, Antiochiam rediit.

5 Pontianus vero, multas calamitates et gravia tormenta pro fide Christi in Sardinia passus, tandem moritur, cuius corpus postea a Fabiano pontifice[3] Romam cum magna veneratione ac totius cleri supplicationibus reportatum est ac sepultum via Appia in Calixti coemiterio. Hic autem ex sacris ordinibus bis mense decembri habitis, sex presbyteros, diaconos quinque, episcopos sex creavit. Vixit autem in pontificatu annis novem, mensibus quinque, diebus duobus. Vacat tum sedes a martyrio eius dies decem.

: 20 :

Antherus I

1 Antherus, natione Graecus, patre Romulo, pontifex creatur Maximino imperante, qui anno ab Urbe condita nongentensimo octogensimo septimo ex corpore militari, posteaquam bellum in Germania prospere gesserat, sine ulla senatus auctoritate imperator

back to the faith two heretics, Germanus, a priest of Antioch, and Beryllus, the bishop of Arabia. Beryllus had denied that Christ existed before the Incarnation. He wrote some short works and especially some letters in which he thanked Origen for his sound doctrine. A dialogue between Origen and Beryllus exists in which the former accuses Beryllus of heresy. Origen had such genius and learning that seven scribes taking turns scarcely sufficed for this man. He had just as many copyists, and especially learned young women, all of whom he exhausted by pouring forth the abundance and richness of his genius.[6] Alexander's mother, Mammea, who was held in great reverence by her son, esteemed Origen and summoned him to Rome. After instructing her in the Christian faith, Origen then returned to Antioch.[7]

As for Pontian, after enduring many calamities and grave tor- 5 ments in Sardinia for his faith in Christ, he at length died. With great veneration and the prayers of the entire clergy, Pope Fabian later brought his body back to Rome and buried it in the cemetery of Calixtus on the Via Appia. Pontian ordained six priests, five deacons, and six bishops in two sacred December ordinations. He was pope for nine years, five months, and two days. The see was vacant for ten days after his martyrdom.[8]

: 20 :

Antherus I

[235–6]

Antherus, a Greek and son of Romulus, became pope when 1 Maximinus was emperor.[1] After Maximinus had successfully waged war in Germany, he was elected emperor by the army, without the Senate's approval, in the year of Rome 987. He was a man

electus est. Fuit autem ingentis staturae vir, adeo ut pedes octo ex-
cederet. Pedem habuit tantae magnitudinis ut postea in proverbii
locum cesserit, cum de longis et ineptis hominibus loquimur,
Maximini caligam requirit. Pro anulo autem uxoris dextrocherio
utebatur. Tantae vero[1] bibacitatis erat ut vini amphoram una cena
biberet. Verum cum sextus a Nerone Christianos caedibus persequeretur, tertio anno posteaquam regnare coeperat, a Pupieno
Aquileiae quam obsidebat una cum filio Maximino interfectus,
persecutioni simul et vitae[2] finem imposuit, Mammeae mulieris
christianae et Origenis mortem permaxime cupiens. Ferunt in ea
obsidione Aquileiensis feminas funes ex capillis suis fecisse cum
nervi deessent aut funes ad emittendas sagittas. Unde in honorem
matronarum templum Veneri Calvae senatus dedicavit.

2   Antherus autem primus statuit ut res gestae martyrum diligenter exquisitae a notariis scriberentur. Conscriptas recondi in aerario ecclesiae mandavit propter Maximum quendam qui[3] martyrio
coronatus est, ne[4] una cum vita bene agentium memoria abolere-
tur. Censuit item episcopum,[5] omisso primo episcopatu, ad alium
necessitatis causa et utilitatis, non sui ipsius sed creditarum
ovium posse transferri, interposita summi pontificis auctoritate.
Quod hodie a plerisque contra fit: ad utilitatem enim propriam
respicientes, immo voluptatem, ut habeant unde expilent, ad ube-
riorem semper respiciunt, non quot oves et qua ratione pascendae
sint quaerentes, quod est officium boni pastoris, sed sciscitantes
quantum singulis annis inde excerpi possit. De cura animarum
parva fit mentio, de augendis proventibus magna, quo multa iu-
menta et plures servos, ac eos quidem ignavos et stolidos, domi
alant.

3   Huius autem temporibus Iulius Africanus fuit inter scriptores
nobilis, constituta etiam, ut Eusebius ait, Caesareae suo nomine
insigni bibliotheca. Hic sub Marco Aurelio Antonino legationem
suscepit pro instauratione Emaus, quae postea Nicopolis appellata
est, ut ante diximus. Scripsit item epistolam ad Origenem, qua os-

of huge stature, over eight feet tall. He had a foot of such great size that it became proverbial when we talk of tall and gangling men to say "he needs Maximinus' boot." He used his wife's bracelet for a ring. His desire for drink was so great that he drank an amphora of wine at one meal. He was the sixth emperor to persecute the Christians after Nero. But in the third year of his reign, along with his son, Maximinus, he was killed by Pupienus while besieging Aquileia. Although Maximinus greatly desired the death of the Christian woman Mammea and Origen, his own death brought an end to the persecution. They say that during the siege, when bowstrings were needed, the women of Aquileia made them from their hair. In honor of these matrons, the senate dedicated a temple to Bald Venus.[2]

Antherus was the first to order that the deeds of the martyrs 2 should be diligently investigated and recorded by scribes. On account of a certain Maximus, who was crowned with martyrdom, he ordered their recorded deeds preserved in the Church treasury, lest the memory of the virtuous perish along with their lives. He likewise decreed that bishops should be allowed to leave their first bishopric for another only to meet the needs of the flocks entrusted to them, not for their own benefit, and only with the pope's approval. Today most bishops do the opposite; considering their own advantage, or rather pleasure, they always look upon a richer bishopric as a source of plunder. They don't ask how large the flock is or how to feed them, but inquire how much the see brings in every year. Little mention is made of the care of souls, but much of increasing revenues, so that they may support more horses and more lazy and stupid servants in their homes.[3]

The eminent writer Julius Africanus lived in Antherus' time 3 and founded a famous library in his name at Caesarea. Under Marcus Aurelius Antoninus, he led an embassy for the restoration of Emmaus, which afterwards was called Nicopolis, as we said before. He likewise wrote a letter to Origen in which he showed that

tendit fabulam Susannae apud Hebraeos non haberi, contra quem postea Origenes ob hanc rem grandem epistolam scripsit. Geminus quoque Antiochenae ecclesiae presbyter, et Heraclias, Alexandrinae ecclesiae pontifex, tum quidem in pretio sunt habiti.

4 Antherus vero, uno tantummodo episcopo creato, martyrium subiens, in coemiterio Calixti via Appia sepelitur III Nonas ianuarii. Sedit annis undecim, mense uno, diebus duodecim. Vacat tum sedes dies tredecim.

: 21 :

Fabianus I

1 Fabianus, natione Romanus, ex patre Fabio, a Gordiano et Philippo usque ad Decium imperatorem pervenit. Gordianus enim imperium adeptus, cum Parthos iam erumpentes ingenti clade superasset, ad triumphum rediens, a Philippis necatur. Cuius haec fuit praecipua laus, quod ad sexaginta duo milia librorum in bibliotheca habuisse dicitur. Philippus autem anno ab Urbe condita noningentesimo nonagesimo septimo reductis militum copiis[1] e Syria, in Italiam una cum filio Philippo annos quinque imperat. Hunc autem primum imperatorem Christiani habuere, qui quidem mysteria adire nunquam est ausus nisi confessus. Post tertium vero imperii sui annum millesimus ab Urbe condita annus impletus est, unde et saeculares ludi celebrati sunt, qui centesimo quoque anno repetebantur; instituti a Valerio Publicola post exactos reges, a saeculo nomen ducentes, quod est[2] humanae vitae spatium. Hi tamen Decii fraude, licet diversis in locis, interfecti sunt, nam Philippus pater[3] Veronae, Romae filius occiditur.

the Jews didn't know the story of Susanna. Later Origen wrote a sublime letter against Julius on this topic. Geminus, a priest of the church of Antioch, and Heraclias, pontiff of the Alexandrian church, were also held in great esteem at that time.[4]

As for Antherus, after ordaining only one bishop, he suffered 4 martyrdom and was buried in the cemetery of Calixtus on the Via Appia on January 3. He was pope for eleven years, one month, and twelve days. The see was then vacant for thirteen days.[5]

: 21 :

Fabian I
[236–50]

Fabian, a Roman and son of Fabius, lived from the reigns of 1 Gordian and Philip until that of the emperor Decius.[1] Gordian gained the empire after conquering the restive Parthians in a great defeat. He returned home to a triumph, but was killed by the two Philips. His chief fame was that he is said to have had sixty-two thousand books in his library. In the year of Rome 997, Philip moved his army from Syria to Italy and together with his son Philip ruled for five years. He was the first whom the Christians considered their emperor. He never dared to approach the sacred mysteries without first confessing. The third year of his reign was the thousandth year of Rome's founding, and the Secular Games were celebrated, which were repeated every hundred years. (Valerius Publicola instituted them after the expulsion of the kings; they take their name from the word *saeculum*, which is the space of a human life.) Both Philips were killed by the treachery of Decius, but in different places: the father in Verona and the son in Rome.[2]

2   Fabianus autem pontifex septem diaconis regiones divisit, qui a notariis martyrum res gestas colligerent ad ceterorum exemplum qui Christi fidem profitebantur. Idem quoque in coemeteriis pro dignitate martyrium aedificavit. Statuit praeterea ut singulis quibusque annis in cena Domini chrisma renovaretur ac vetus in ecclesia combureretur.

3   Huius tempore exorta est Novatiana haeresis. Novatianus enim, urbis Romae[4] presbyter, ob cupiditatem episcopatus divina omnia atque humana miscebat, ne in manus Cornelii, qui Fabiano successit, pontificatus deveniret. Ab ecclesia enim separatus, semet ac suos καθαρούς, id est mundos, appellabat. Negabat apostatas, etiam paenitentes, recipiendos esse. Hanc ob rem Romae concilium sexaginta episcoporum, totidem presbyterorum, cum diaconis pluribus habitum est, quo Novatiani[5] opinio ut falsa[6] improbatur, quod Salvatoris exemplo nemini paenitenti deneganda sit venia.

4   Eisdem quoque temporibus Origenes haeresim quorundam sustulit, affirmantium animas hominum una cum corporibus interire rursumque in *anastasi*, quam nostri resurrectionem vocant, una cum corporibus suscitari. Substulit et haeresim Helchesatarum, qui Paulum apostolum omnino respuunt quique asserunt negantem in tormentis Christum nihil criminis habiturum, modo integri et recti sit cordis. Scripsit etiam idem auctor in Celsum epicureum Christianos impugnantem. Litteras quoque de fide ad Philippum et Severam eius uxorem dedit. Ad Fabianum postremo de ordine fidei multa conscripsit.

5   Alexander vero Cappadociae episcopus, cum desiderio sacrorum locorum Hierosolymam perrexisset, cogitur a Narcisso, eiusdem urbis episcopo iam sene, administrationem episcopatus secum suscipere. Verum sub Decio ardente persecutione, quo

Pope Fabian divided the regions of the city among seven dea- 2
cons, who were to collect from scribes the acts of the martyrs for
the benefit of others who professed the faith of Christ. He also
built monuments in the cemeteries in honor of the martyrs. Furthermore, he ordained that every year the chrism at the Lord's
Supper should be renewed and the old burnt in the church.[3]

In his time the Novatian heresy arose. Out of desire for a bish- 3
opric, a priest of the city of Rome named Novatian confounded
everything human and divine to prevent the pontificate from falling into the hands of Cornelius, who succeeded Fabian. He separated himself from the Church and called himself and his followers the *Katharoi*, that is, the Pure. He said that even repentant
apostates should not be received back into the Church. On this account a council of sixty bishops and priests and many deacons was
convened in Rome which condemned Novatian's teaching as false,
since by the example of the Savior no repentant sinner should be
denied forgiveness.[4]

At the same time, Origen refuted the heresy of those who 4
affirmed that human souls died together with their bodies, and
would be resuscitated again with their bodies at the *anastasis*,
which we call the Resurrection. He also refuted the heresy of the
Elkesaites, who completely rejected the Apostle Paul and asserted
that a man who denies Christ while being tortured commits no
offense, provided his heart is pure and upright. The same author
also wrote against Celsus, an Epicurean who was attacking the
Christians. He sent a letter concerning the faith to Philip and his
wife, Severa, and wrote a great deal about the order of faith to Fabian.[5]

Now Alexander, the bishop of Cappadocia, had gone to Jerusa- 5
lem out of a desire to see the holy places, and was compelled by
Narcissus, the elderly bishop of that city, to assist him in the administration of the bishopric. But, as the persecution under
Decius was heating up, when Babylas suffered martyrdom at

tempore Babylas Antiochiae martyrium passus est, Caesaream ductus, ob confessionem Christi necatur.

6   At Fabianus pontifex, cui dum Anthero successor quaereretur, columba, ut creditum est,[7] supra caput astitit eiusdem formae qua illa visa est[8] quae Spiritum Sanctum supra caput Iesu apud Iordanem detulit, martyrio coronatur, ubi ex quinque ordinationibus mense decembri habitis presbyteras duos et viginti, diaconos septem, episcopos undecim creasset. Sepultus est autem in coemiterio Calixti via Appia XIIII Kalendas februarii. Sedit annos quattuordecim, menses undecim, dies undecim. Vacat autem sedes diebus sex.

⁝ 22 ⁝

Cornelius I

1   Cornelius, natione Romanus, patre Castino, Decii temporibus fuit, qui Pannonia inferiore Budaliae natus, interfectis Philippis imperium sumpsit, odio in Christianos exardens propter Philippos, eiusdem sectae imitatores. Verum, cum postea biennio cum filio Caesare imperasset, a barbaris opprimitur, adeo ut eius cadaver nusquam repertum sit. Digno certe damnatus iudicio, qui septimam post Neronem persecutionem in Christianos movens, multos sanctissimos viros interemit.

2   At vero sub episcopatu Cornelii, qui apostatas recipiendos censebat, paenitentes praesertim, Novatus Novatianum extra ecclesiam ordinavit et in Africa Nicostratum. Quamobrem confessores qui a Cornelio secesserant, cum Maximo presbytero ac Moyse sentientes, ad ecclesiam reversi, veri confessoris nomen adepti sunt. Verum postea instantibus haereticis Cornelius Centumcellas in

Antioch, he was brought to Caesarea and executed for his faith in Christ.[6]

As for pope Fabian, when they were looking for a successor to Antherus, a dove is believed to have stood above his head, just like the one that carried the Holy Spirit over Jesus' head in Jordan.[7] Fabian was crowned with martyrdom, after ordaining twenty-two priests, seven deacons, and eleven bishops in five December ordinations. He was buried in the cemetery of Calixtus on the Via Appia, January 19. He was pope for fourteen years, eleven months, and eleven days. The see was vacant for six days.[8]

: 22 :

Cornelius I

[251–53]

Cornelius, a Roman and son of Castinus, lived in the time of Decius.[1] Decius was born at Buda in Lower Hungary. After the Philips were murdered, he took over the empire and seethed with hatred against the Christians on account of the Philips' support for this religion. But after ruling with his son for two years, he was slaughtered by barbarians, and his body was never found—a worthy end for one who led the seventh persecution after Nero against the Christians and killed many holy men.[2]

During the pontificate of Cornelius, who thought that apostates, especially repentant ones, should be received back into the Church, Novatus ordained, outside the Church, Novatian and, in Africa, Nicostratus. Because of this, those believers who had separated from Cornelius and agreed with Maximus the priest and Moses, returned to the Church and obtained the name of true believer. But later, at the urging of heretics, Cornelius was sent in ex-

exilium mittitur, ad quem Cyprianus Carthaginensis episcopus, in carcerem coniectus,[1] litteras mittit quibus intellexit et amici calamitatem et exilii sui confirmationem. Extant et aliae Cypriani ad Cornelium epistolae, plenae religionis et fidei, sed illa potissimum elegans habetur qua Novatum, discipulum quendam suum, accusat et damnat. De eadem quoque haeresi et Dionysius, Alexandrinae urbis episcopus, Origenis olim auditor, ad Cornelium scripsit. Novatianum[2] praeterea alia epistola reprehendit quod a communione Romanae ecclesiae discessisset quodque etiam se invitum ad pontificatum obeundum diceret esse deductum. Tum ille: 'Si invitus, Novatiane,[3] ut dicis, designatus[4] es, probabis, cum volens secesseris.'

3   Cornelius autem priusquam in exilium mitteretur, instante Lucina matrona sanctissima, corpora Petri et Pauli e cathecumbis, ubi minus tuta esse videbantur, noctu levavit. Paulum Lucina in praedio suo via Ostiensi collocat, eo loci ubi interfectus fuerat. Petrum vero Cornelius apud locum reponit ubi crucis martyrium subierat, in templo Apollinis ad radices aurei montis III Kalendas iulii.

4   At vero Decius, ubi intellexit Cornelium litteras a Cypriano accepisse, eum a Centumcellis Romam perduci iubet, quem ita in Telluris templo,[5] astante Urbis prefecto, alloquitur: 'Sic,' inquit, 'obstinate vitam ducere instituisti ut neque deos cures neque praecepta vel minas principum timeas et contra rempublicam litteras accipias ac mittas?' Huic Cornelius: 'De laudibus Christi, de ratione redimendorum animorum, non de imminutione imperii[6] litteras accepi et reddidi.' Tum Decius iratus, sanctissimum virum plumbatis caedi (genus id flagelli est) atque deinceps ad templum Martis duci iubet, ut simulacrum eius adoraret; id si iacere abnueret, poena capitali afficeretur. At vir sanctus, dum ad supplicium duceretur, omnia bona sua Stephano archidiacono commisit. Post

ile to Civitavecchia. Cyprian, the bishop of Carthage, who had been thrown into prison, wrote letters to him in which he acknowledged both the calamity of his friend and the confirmation of his own exile.[3] Other letters of Cyprian to Cornelius on religious topics are also extant, but the one is considered especially choice in which he accuses and condemns Novatus, one of his disciples.[4] Dionysius, the bishop of Alexandria and once a follower of Origen, wrote to Cornelius about this same heresy. In another letter, moreover, he chastises Novatian for leaving the communion of the Roman Church and for saying that he was unwillingly chosen to take up the pontificate. To this, Dionysius replies: "If, as you say, you were chosen unwillingly, Novatian, prove it by voluntarily leaving it."[5]

Before he was sent into exile, Cornelius, at the urging of 3 Lucina, a most holy matron, removed at night the bodies of Peter and Paul from the catacombs, where they seemed unsafe. Lucina placed Paul in her estate on the Via Ostiense, in the place where he had been killed, and Cornelius laid Peter near the place where he had suffered the martyrdom of the cross, in the temple of Apollo at the foot of the golden mountain on June 30.

When Decius found out that Cornelius had received letters 4 from Cyprian, he had him moved from Civitavecchia to Rome, and in the temple of Tellus, in the presence of the city prefect, he addressed him: "Have you decided to conduct your life with such obstinacy that you neither regard the gods nor fear the commands or threats of emperors, and receive and send letters against the state?" Cornelius answered: "I have received and sent letters about the excellences of Christ and the redemption of souls, not about the subversion of the empire." Decius then became angry and ordered this most holy man to be scourged with a cat-o-nine tails, then brought to the temple of Mars to worship the god's idol; if he refused to do this, he was to be executed. While he was being led out to his punishment, the holy man entrusted all of his goods to

hoc vero III Nonas maii[7] obtruncatur. Huius corpus beata Lucina una cum quibusdam clericis noctu sepelivit in arenario praedii sui via Appia, non longe a coemiterio Calixti. Sunt qui scribant hunc pontificem sub Gallo et Volusiano passum. At ego multo magis Damaso credo,[8] qui Decii iussu hoc factum affirmat. Cornelius autem mense decembri sacrorum initiandorum potestatem bis fecit, unde presbyteros quattuor, diaconos quattuor, episcopos septem creavit. Sedit annis duobus, mensibus duobus, diebus tribus. Sedes autem diebus quinque et triginta tum vacat.

: 23 :

Lucius I

1   Lucius, natione Romanus, patre Porphyrio, imperante Gallo Hostiliano pontifex eligitur. Gallus enim cum Volusiano filio imperium obtinuit, quorum temporibus in ultionem Christiani nominis tanta pestis exorta est, ut paucae domus, nedum civitates et provinciae extiterint, quae non tantam calamitatem senserint. Verum Gallus et Volusianus, dum contra Aemilianum res novas agitantem bellum civile moliuntur, Interamne necantur, nondum completo imperii sui biennio. Aemilianus vero, obscuro loco natus, tertio mense occupatae[1] tyrannidis opprimitur. Mox autem Valerianus in Rhetiis et Norico ab exercitu, Gallienus Romae a senatu imperatores eliguntur. Quorum imperium perniciosum Romano nomini fuit principum ignavia et in Christianos saevitia. Nam et Germani Ravennam usque pervenere, ferro ac flamma omnia vastantes, et Valerianus in Mesopotamia bellum gerens, a Parthis cap-

Stephen the archdeacon. Cornelius was then beheaded on May 5. Together with some clerics the blessed Lucina buried his body at night in a catacomb on her estate, on the Via Appia not far from the cemetery of Calixtus.[6] Some write that he suffered under Gallus and Volusianus, but I put more trust in Damasus, who affirms that this was done at the command of Decius.[7] Cornelius ordained four priests, four deacons, and seven bishops in two December ordinations. He was pope for two years, two months, and three days. The see was then vacant for thirty-five days.[8]

: 23 :

Lucius I
[253–54]

Lucius, a Roman and son of Porphyry, was elected pope during   1
the reign of Gallus Hostilianus.[1] Gallus held the empire along
with his son Volusianus. In their time, so great a plague arose to
avenge the Christian name that there were few houses, let alone
cities and provinces, that did not experience calamity. While
Gallus and Volusianus were waging a civil war against Aemilianus,
who was fomenting revolution, they were killed at Teramo before
completing the second year of their reign. A person of obscure
birth, Aemilianus was killed in the third month of his usurped
tyranny. Then Valerian was chosen as emperor by his army in
Rhetia and Noricum, and Gallienus by the Senate in Rome. Their
rule was ruinous for Rome owing to their lack of spirit and their
cruelty toward the Christians. For the Germans had descended as
far as Ravenna, laying waste to everything with sword and fire;
and, while waging war in Mesopotamia, Valerian was captured by
the Parthians and lived in servitude and shame. For the king of

tus, in servitute turpiter vixit, eo enim ut scabello Paratus, Persarum rex, equum inscensurus utebatur, ac merito quidem, cum
statim ubi imperium arripuit, octavus a Nerone adigi tormentis
Christianos, idola colere abnegantesque interfici ubique iusserit.
Territus autem tam claro Dei iudicio, Gallienus pacem ecclesiis
tribuit. Sero tamen: iam enim Dei voluntate barbari omnes in
fines Romanos eruperant, et tyranni quidam pernitiosi exorti sunt
qui, quod domi relictum erat ab externo hoste, pessundarent. Gallienus vero, cum rempublicam deseruisset ac Mediolani libidinibus
operam daret, occiditur.

2   Lucius igitur, mortuo Volusiano, exilii poena liberatus, Romam
veniens, constituit ut duo presbyteri, diaconi tres, ubique locorum
episcopum comitarentur, eius vitae et actionis testes. Huius autem
temporibus martyrium passus est Cyprianus, qui primo rhetoricam docuit, deinde, suadente presbytero Caecilio, ut Hieronymus
ait, a quo et cognomen sortitus est, ad Christianos transiens, omnes facultates suas pauperibus erogavit. Presbyter primo, deinde
Carthaginensis episcopus creatus, sub Gallo et Volusiano martyrii
poena afficitur. Cuius vitam et martyrium Pontius, eiusdem Cypriani presbyter et exilii comes, egregio volumine composuit. Ante
vero quam moreretur Cyprianus, venerat in sententiam ecclesiae
Romanae[2] non esse rebaptizandos haereticos, sed sola manus im-
positione in gratiam recipiendos. Hac enim de re inter Cyprianum
et Cornelium magna fuerat olim contentio.

3   Lucius vero, antequam ad martyrium iubente Valeriano duceretur, omnem potestatem ecclesiae Stephano archidiacono suo per-
misit. Ter autem dandis ordinibus sacris vacavit decembri mense,
unde presbyteros quattuor, diaconos quattuor,[3] episcopos septem
creavit. Sepultus est in coemiterio Calixti via Appia VIII Kalendas septembris. Sedit annis tribus, mensibus tres, diebus tres.
Dies quinque et triginta sedes tum vacat.[4]

the Persians, Pacorus, used him as a stool to mount his horse. He deserved this fate, since as soon as he came to power Valerian was the eighth emperor after Nero to command that the Christians be tortured and forced to worship idols, and, if they refused, be put to death. Gallienus, however, was terrified by God's manifest judgment and made peace with the churches. It was nevertheless too late, since by the will of God the barbarians had already burst through the Roman borders, and certain pernicious tyrants arose who destroyed whatever the foreign enemy had left. While abandoning the state and dedicating himself to the pleasures of Milan, Gallienus was slain.[2]

After the death of Volusianus, Lucius was freed from exile and   2 returned to Rome. He ordained that two priests and three deacons should accompany a bishop wherever he went as witnesses of his life and actions. In his time Cyprian suffered martyrdom. Cyprian first taught rhetoric, and then, as Jerome says, at the persuasion of Caecilius the priest, from whom he took his surname, he joined the Christians and gave all his wealth to the poor. He was priest first, then bishop of Carthage, and suffered martyrdom under Volusianus and Gallus. His priest and companion in exile Pontius wrote about Cyprian's life and martyrdom in an outstanding book. Before he died, Cyprian came to agree with the Roman Church that heretics should not be rebaptized, but should be received back into grace only by the laying on of hands — this had once been a point of contention between Cyprian and Cornelius.[3]

As for Lucius, before his martyrdom at the command of Va-   3 lerian, he gave all the power of the Church to his archdeacon Stephen. Lucius ordained four priests, four deacons and seven bishops in three December ordinations. He was buried in the cemetery of Calixtus on the Via Appia on August 25. He was pope for three years, three months, and three days. The see was then vacant for thirty-five days.[4]

: 24 :

Stephanus I

1   Stephanus, natione Romanus, patre Iulio, cum iam de imperio
Romano actum videretur, pontifex eligitur, eo potissimum tempore quo Posthumus in Gallia tyrannidem occupat cum maximo
rei publicae emolumento. Nam annis decem ingenti moderatione
usus, pulsis hostibus provinciam in pristinam formam redegit.
Huic deinde militari tumultu apud Magunciacum interfecto, Victorinus successit, vir quidem in re militari strenuus, sed, dum
nimiae libidinis esset et aliena matrimonia corrumperet, Agrippinae occiditur.

2   Stephanus autem ad ordinandam ecclesiam conversus, instituit
ne sacerdotes et levitae vestibus sacris alibi quam in ecclesia et per-
agendis sacris uterentur, ne, si secus facerent, poenam Balthassar
regis Babylonis subirent, qui vasa sacra profanis manibus attigerat.
De rebaptizandis autem his qui ad fidem rediissent, eadem sensit
quae Cornelius pontifex, neque ullo modo his communicandum[1]
esse qui rebaptizarent. Unde Dionysius, qui antea hac de re cum
Carthaginiensibus et Orientalibus[2] senserat, mutata sententia ad
Stephanum scribens, eum bono esse animo iubet, cum ecclesiae
tam Asianae quam Africanae, mutata opinione, in sententiam Romanae sedis iam venissent. Iuvit et ecclesiam Dei illa tempestate
Malchion, eloquentissimus Antiochenae ecclesiae presbyter. Hic
enim contra Paulum Samosatenum episcopum Antiochenum
scripsit, quod dogma Artemonis instaurare conaretur, affirmantis
Christum communis naturae hominem tantummodo fuisse,[3] nec
semper fuisse, sed a Maria sumpsisse principium. Quae opinio
postea in Antiocheno concilio omnium consensu improbata est.

: 24 :

Stephen I
[254–57]

Stephen, a Roman and son of Julius, was chosen to be pope[1] when   1
the Roman empire appeared already to be finished, and at a time
when Postumus usurped power and ruled in Gaul with great
profit to the state. Postumus exercised great moderation for ten
years, expelled enemies, and restored the province to its pristine
form. He was then slain in a military revolt at Mainz. Victorinus
succeeded him, who was well-versed in military matters, but he
was exceedingly lustful and destroyed many marriages, and was
slain in Cologne.[2]

Turning his attention to church discipline, Stephen ordained   2
that priests and ministers should not wear sacred vestments and
perform sacred rites outside church, lest they suffer the punishment of Balthasar, king of Babylon, who touched holy vessels with
profane hands. Concerning the rebaptism of those who returned
to the faith, he felt the same way as pope Cornelius, that one
should hold no sort of communion with those who rebaptized.
Whereupon Dionysius, who had before agreed with the
Carthaginians and the Eastern Church, changed his mind, wrote
to Stephen, and told him to be of good cheer, since the Asian and
African churches had changed their belief and now agreed with
the Roman See.[3] At that time, Malchion, the most eloquent priest
of the church of Antioch, also assisted God's church. He wrote
against Paul of Samosata, the bishop of Antioch, for trying to revive the teaching of Artemon, who asserted that Christ was only a
man, and that He did not always exist, but began life in Mary.
This opinion was later condemned with universal consent at the

Hac autem de re idem Malchion grandem epistolam nomine synodi ad Christi fideles scripsit.

3   Stephanus autem, cum opere[4] et verbis multos gentiles ad fidem Christi convertisset, conquisitus a Gallieno, ut quidam volunt, vel ab his qui ex Deciano edicto Christianos persequebantur, una cum plerisque suorum ad martyrium rapitur. Capite enim mulctatus, in Calixti coemiterio via Appia sepelitur, IIII Nonas augusti, cum iam ex ordinibus sacris bis mense decembri propositis presbyteros sex, diaconos quinque, episcopos tres creasset. Sedit annis septem, mensibus quinque, diebus duobus. Sedes autem ad dies duos et viginti tum vacat.

: 25 :

Sixtus II

1   Sixtus Secundus, natione Graecus, patria Atheniensis, ex philosopho Christi discipulus factus est, durante adhuc Deciana et Valeriana persecutione. Sed non erit a re nostra alienum reliquos tyrannos, ut coepimus, sparsim scribere, quoad verum principem attigerimus. Nam Victorino in Gallia interempto, Tetricus senator, qui tum Aquitaniam gubernabat, absens a militibus imperator creatur. At vero, dum haec in Gallia agerentur, per Odenachum Persae victi, defensa Syria, Mesopotamia usque ad Ctesiphontem recepta est.

2   Ea quoque[1] tempestate exorta doctrina est apud[2] Ptolemaidem, quae olim Barcae vocabatur, Pentapoleos civitatem, plena blasphemiis in Deum patrem et in Christum, quem summi Dei filium

council of Antioch, and Malchion wrote a sublime letter on it in
the name of the Synod to Christ's faithful.[4]

As for Stephen, after he had converted by his words and deeds 3
many gentiles to the faith of Christ, Gallienus, as some will have
it, or those who were persecuting the Christians after Decius'
edict, arrested him and along with many followers carried him off
to martyrdom. After he had been beaten to death on the head,
Stephen was buried in the cemetery of Calixtus on the Via Appia
on August 2. He ordained six priests, five deacons, and three bishops in two December ordinations. He was pope for seven years,
five months, and two days. The see was then vacant for about
twenty-two days.[5]

: 25 :

Sixtus II

[257–58]

Sixtus II, a Greek from Athens, was converted from a philosopher 1
to a disciple of Christ during the persecutions of Decius and
Valerius.[1] But as we have begun doing so, it will be relevant to our
theme to give accounts here and there of the remaining tyrants,
before arriving at the true successor. For after Victorinus was
killed in Gaul, a senator named Tetricus, who at that time was
governing Aquitaine, was declared emperor by the soldiers in absentia. But while this was going on in Gaul, Odenatus vanquished
the Persians, defended Syria, and seized Mesopotamia as far as
Ctesiphon.[2]

At this time in Ptolomais, formerly called Barce, a city of the 2
Pentapolis, a doctrine arose full of blasphemies against God the
Father and Christ. It denied that Christ was the son of the highest

esse negabat primogenitumque omnis creaturae, simul etiam Spiritus[3] Sancti intellectum auferebant; ii Sabelliani a Sabellio auctore, tam perversae[4] sectae inventore, vocati sunt. Quid dicam de spurcissimo Cherinti dogmate, qui post mille annos futuram *anastasim* et regnum Christi in terris dicebat, unde *chiliastos* a Graecis vocatus est? Is autem, quia libidinum et cupiditatum impatiens erat, voluptates ipsas in promissionibus futuri regni sanctis proponebat, abundantiam[5] ciborum et mulierum copiam. Idem sentiebat et Nepos, in partibus Aegypti episcopus. In deliciis enim corporis et voluptatibus omnibus regnaturos in terra sanctos cum Christo dicebat. Hinc Nepotiani, tam turpis sectae imitatores, vocati sunt.

3   Confutare et extinguere has opiniones Sixtus aliquando meditabatur, verum accusatus quod Christi fidem contra imperatorum decreta praedicaret, captus, ad Martis templum ducitur, ut aut Marti sacrificet[6] aut, si id facere noluerit, poenam capitis subeat. Euntem ad supplicium Laurentius archidiaconus ita alloquitur: 'Quo,' inquit, 'progrederis sine filio, pater? Quo, sacerdos optime, sine ministro properas?' Cui Sixtus: 'Ego te non desero, fili; maiora tibi pro fide Christi supersunt certamina. Post triduum me sequeris sacerdotem levita. Interim autem, si quid in thesauris habes, id pauperibus distribue.' Eodem vero die una cum Sixto diaconi sex interficiuntur: Felicissimus, Agapitus, Ianuarius, Magnus, Innocentius, Stephanus, VI Idus augusti. Laurentius vero triduo post, una cum Claudio subdiacono et Severo presbytero et Crescentio lectore et Romano hostario, variis cruciatibus necatur IIII Idus augusti. Exustum igni Laurentium ferunt. Vincentius vero, quem Sixti discipulum fuisse constat, in Hispaniam profectus, huic martyrio interesse non potuit.

God and the firstborn of all creation, and at the same time did away with the knowledge of the Holy Spirit. They were called Sabellians, after Sabellius, who founded this utterly perverse sect. What shall I say about the most foul teaching of Cerinthus? He said that the resurrection would come after a thousand years and Christ's kingdom would be on earth; hence in Greek he was called a "chiliast." Since he was intolerant of lusts and desires, he held out the prospect of sensual pleasures, an abundance of food and plenty of women, in the holy promises of the kingdom to come. Nepos, a bishop in parts of Egypt, also believed this. He said that the saints would reign on earth with Christ amid every delight and pleasure of the body. The followers of this filthy sect were called Nepotians.[3]

Sixtus was planning to refute and extinguish these beliefs some day, but he was accused of preaching the faith of Christ against the emperors' decrees, arrested, and taken to the temple of Mars, to sacrifice to Mars or else endure capital punishment. As he was going to his punishment, the archdeacon Lawrence addressed him: "Where are you going without your son, father? Where are you hurrying without your attendant, noble priest?" Sixtus answered him: "I am not deserting you, son; greater battles are left to you for your faith in Christ. After three days you, minister, will follow me, your priest. In the meantime, if you have anything in your treasury, give it to the poor." Six deacons, Felicissimus, Agapitus, Januarius, Magnus, Innocentius, and Stephen, were killed along with Sixtus on the same day, August 8. On the third day after this, August 10, Lawrence, together with the subdeacon Claudius, the priest Severus, the lector Crescentius, and the gatekeeper Romanus, were all tortured to death in different ways. Lawrence, they say, was roasted on an open flame. Vincent, who is said to have been a follower of Sixtus, had gone to Spain and so could not share in this martyrdom.[4]

3

4   Sixtus autem in pontificatu suo sacrorum ordinum potestatem
bis fecit mense decembri, unde et presbyteros quattuor, diaconos
septem, episcopos duos creavit. Sixti corpus in coemiterio Calixti
via Appia sepelitur. Reliqui vero martyres iacent in coemiterio
Praetextati in agro Veranio via Tiburtina. Sedit autem Sixtus annos duos, menses decem, dies tres et viginti. Vacat tum sedes dies
quinque et triginta.

: 26 :

Dionysius I

1   Dionysius, cuius originem Damasus inveniri potuisse negat, ex
monacho pontifex creatus, presbyteris ecclesias et coemiteria in
urbe Roma statim divisit. Parochias et dioeceses foris distribuit,
quo quisque finibus[1] suis limitibusve contentus esset.
2   Huius temporibus fuisse Claudium existimaverim, qui, ubi ex
voluntate senatus imperium suscepit, Gothos annis iam quindecim
Illyricum Macedoniamque vastantes bello adortus, incredibili
clade superavit. Hanc ob rem in curia aureus clipeus, in Capitolio
aurea statua eidem a senatu decreta est. Morbo autem correptus
apud Sirmium moritur, nondum expleto biennio in imperio. Quo
mortuo statim Quintilius frater ab exercitu imperator eligitur, vir
quidem unicae moderationis et qui solus fratri praeferri posset. Is
quoque decimo septimo imperii die interficitur.
3   Dionysii vero temporibus Paulus Samosatenus, ab orthodoxa
fide desciscens, Artemonis haeresim suscitavit. Nam in demortui

During his pontificate Sixtus ordained four priests, seven dea- 4
cons, and two bishops in two December ordinations. His body is
buried in the cemetery of Calixtus on the Via Appia. The other
martyrs lay in the cemetery of Praetextatus in the Veranian field
on the Via Tiburtina. Sixtus was pope for two years, ten months,
and twenty-three days. The see was then vacant for thirty-five
days.[5]

: 26 :

Dionysius I
[260–68]

Dionysius, whose ancestry Damasus says cannot be found, was a 1
monk when he became pope. He immediately divided the
churches and cemeteries in the city of Rome among the priests
and distributed the parishes and dioceses outside Rome, so that
each would be satisfied with his borders and limits.[1]

I believe that Claudius was emperor in Dionysius' time. After 2
taking over the empire with the Senate's consent, he waged war on
and vanquished with incredible slaughter the Goths, who had
been devastating Illyricum and Macedonia for fifteen years. Because of this, the Senate decreed that a golden shield should be
erected for him in the Curia and a golden statue on the Capitol.
But before the end of his second year of rule, he fell ill and died in
Sirmium. Upon his death, his brother Quintilius was immediately
chosen emperor by the army. He was a man of singular moderation, the only one who could be more esteemed than his brother.
But he was killed on the seventeenth day of his rule.[2]

In the time of Dionysius, Paul of Samosata left the orthodox 3
faith and revived the heresy of Artemon. After replacing as bishop

139

locum Antiochenus episcopus creatus, superbe nimium sese habebat. Inter eundum enim[2] prae superbia et litteras relegebat et dictabat epistolas, multis constipato agmine praecedentibus ac subsequentibus, unde propter hominis arrogantiam Christianam religionem plerique detestabantur. Sed quid facerent nostra tempestate, qua nil vel superbiae vel pompae, nolo dicere luxuriae, addi potest? Si tot adolescentes anteambulones sericatos et coccinatos in equis praeferocibus ac phaleratis viderent, sique subsequentium presbyterorum turbam cernerent, chlamydibus optimi cuiusque[3] coloris hinc inde ab equis deauratis pendentibus? Execrarentur eos sat scio; dicerent nil eis cum Christo praeter similitudinem quandam religionis commune esse.

4   Ad Paulum redeo, quem tutius[4] reprehendere licet. Is enim inflatus[5] opinione sui ipsius ac tribunali altius quaerens, negabat Dei filium e caelo descendisse, sed a Maria coepisse originem et initium e terra habuisse. Hanc ob rem in concilio Antiocheno, omnium episcoporum qui aderant consensu, publice damnatus est, maxime vero Gregorii Caesariensis episcopi, viri sanctissimi, sententia, qui tanto concilio interfuit et postea pro fide Christi martyrii poenam subiit. In Paulum vero Malchio, Antiochenus presbyter, multa disseruit et scripsit, quia Artemonis haeresim, ut dixi, instaurare conabatur. Huic autem[6] concilio propter senium interesse Dionysius non potuit; ea tamen de re ad eum per Maximum, Alexandrinum episcopum, late perscriptum est.

5   Mortuus autem Dionysius, sepelitur in coemiterio Calixti, ubi ex institutionibus duabus mense decembri habitis presbyteros duodecim, diaconos sex, episcopos septem creasset. Sedit annis sex, mensibus duobus, diebus quattuor. Vacat[7] tum sedes dies sex.

of Antioch a man who had died, he behaved with excessive arrogance. Out of pride, while walking, he would read through and dictate letters to a throng of followers behind and in front of him. On account of this man's arrogance, many people despised the Christian religion. But what would they make of our time, when no pride or pomp, not to say luxury, is lacking? What if they were to see the many silk- and scarlet-clad youths parading on high-spirited, prettily caparisoned horses, and a crowd of priests following them with parti-colored, gold-embossed riding cloaks hanging from their horses? I know well that they would despise them; they would say that they have nothing in common with Christ apart from a kind of similarity of religion.

I return to Paul, whom I may more safely criticize. Puffed up 4 by his own opinion of himself and searching for a higher platform, he said that the son of God did not descend from heaven, but had His origin from Mary and His beginning on earth. For this reason he was publicly condemned by consent of all the bishops present at the council of Antioch; but especially by the sentence of Gregory, the bishop of Caesarea, a most holy man, who was present at this great council and later endured the punishment of martyrdom for his faith in Christ. The priest of Antioch, Malchion, spoke and wrote much against Paul for attempting to revive the heresy of Artemon, as I said. On account of old age, Dionysius was unable to attend this council, but Maximus, the bishop of Alexandria, gave him an extensive report of the matter.[3]

After ordaining twelve priests, six deacons, and seven bishops 5 in two December ordinations, Dionysius died and was buried in the cemetery of Calixtus. He was pope for six years, two months, and four days. The see was then vacant for six days.[4]

: 27 :

Felix I

1 Felix, natione Romanus, patre Constantino, Aureliani tempore
fuit, qui anno ab Urbe condita millesimo ac vicensimo septimo
imperium adeptus, vir militari disciplina clarus, Gothos apud Da-
nubium gravi proelio superat. In Asiam deinde traiiciens, Zeno-
biam, quae occiso Odenacho marito orientis tenebat imperium,
apud Thymas haud longe ab Antiochia terrore magis quam proelio vincit eamque in triumphum una cum Tetrico ducit, quo[1] apud
Catalaunos superato Gallias receperat. Aureliani tamen clementia
et humanitate Zenobia honorifice in Urbe consenuit, unde Zenobia familia Romana originem habuit, et Tetricus conservatus Lu-
canis deinde praefuit. Ad pacis vero opera conversus imperator, et
templum Apollinis et muros Urbis magnificentissimis operibus ex-
truit. Hic autem postea, mota in Christianos persecutione nonus a
Nerone, de caelo tactus, inter Constantinopolim et Heracleam in
Zenophrurio occiditur.

2 Felix autem martyrum gloriae consulens, statuit ut quotannis
sacrificia eorum nomine celebrarentur, utque nullibi quam in sacro
loco et a viris sacris initiatis sacrificium, quod missam appellant,
celebraretur, necessitatem semper excipiens. Quod si de consecratione templi ignoratum fuerit, utpote vetustate et abolitione mo-
numentorum, consecrari denuo mandat. Neque enim, ut ipse aie-
bat, iteratum dicitur, quod factum esse nescitur. Huius tempore
Manes quidam gente Persa, vita et moribus barbarus, profiteri se
Christum ausus est, ascitis in societatem duodecim discipulis, quo

: 27 :

Felix I
[269–74]

Felix, a Roman and son of Constantine, lived in the time of 1
Aurelian, who took over the empire in the year of Rome 1027.[1]
Aurelian was famous for his military discipline, and he overcame
the Goths in a pitched battle on the Danube. Then he crossed
into Asia and in Bithynia, not far from Antioch, by terror rather
than battle he vanquished Zenobia, who after her husband
Odenachus' death was ruling the Eastern empire. He led her in
triumph along with Tetricus, after whose defeat in Chalons he had
regained Gaul. Because of Aurelian's clemency and kindness,
Zenobia lived honorably until old age in the city, and this is the
origin of the Zenobian family in Rome. Tetricus was also saved
and later became the governor of Lucania. The emperor then
turned his attention to works of peace: he built a temple of Apollo
and the walls of the city with great magnificence. Later, after starting the ninth persecution against the Christians since Nero,
Aurelian was struck down by Heaven and slain in Zenophrurium,
between Constantinople and Heraclea.[2]

To promote the glory of the martyrs, Felix ordained that sacri- 2
fices should be celebrated every year in their name, and that the
sacrifice called the Mass should be celebrated only in a sacred place
and by men in holy orders, except in cases of necessity. But if a
church's consecration was in question due to its age and loss of records, he commanded it to be reconsecrated or, as he said, something cannot be said to have been repeated when it is unknown
whether it was ever done in the first place. In his time a certain
Manes, a Persian and barbarian in life and manners, dared to profess himself to be Christ and enlisted twelve disciples to make

fidem rebus in omnibus faceret. Ut autem tum impugnatur Manes ob impietatem et superbiam, ita maxime laudatur Anatolius, Laodicenus episcopus, propter religionem et doctrinam. Ausus etiam eodem tempore Saturninus est novam Antiochiam condere, exercitus opera fretus. Verum dum audacter nimium imperium quoque molitur invadere, Apameae tandem occiditur.

3   Felix autem, ubi repetitis sacris ordinibus mense decembri presbyteros novem, diaconos quinque, episcopos quinque creasset, martyr via Aurelia sepelitur III Kalendas iunii in basilica quam antea in honorem Dei condiderat secundo ab urbe miliario. Sedit autem annis quattuor, menses tres, dies quindecim. Vacat tum sedes dies quinque.

: 28 :

Eutychianus I

1   Eutychianus, natione Tuscus, patre Maximo, temporibus Aureliani fuit, cui quidem interempto Tacitus succedit, vir certe idoneus reipublicae gubernandae ob eius virtutem et integritatem. Verum in Ponto sexto mense post adeptum imperium occisus est. Florianus quoque, qui Tacito successit, tertio demum imperii sui mense apud Tarsum occiditur.

2   Eutychianus autem instituit ut in altari frugibus benediceretur, maxime vero fabae et uvae. Constituit item ne, qui martyres sepelire vellent, sine dalmatica colobiove purpureo id facere auderent, se nesciente praesertim. Sunt qui scribant huius temporibus Dorotheum eunuchum fuisse, virum certe graeca et hebraica lingua doctissimum, cuius doctrina mirifice delectatum Aurelianum fe-

himself convincing in all respects. Just as Manes is impugned for
his impiety and pride, Anatolius, the bishop of Laodicaea, is especially praised for his religion and learning. At the same time,
Saturninus endeavored to found a new Antioch, relying on his
army's assistance, but while rashly planning to invade the empire,
he was finally slain at Apamaea.[3]

As for Felix, after ordaining nine priests, five deacons, and five 3
bishops in several December ordinations, he suffered martyrdom
and was buried on the Via Aurelia on May 30 in a church that he
had earlier built for the honor of God, two miles from the city. He
was pope for four years, three months, and fifteen days. The see
was then vacant for five days.[4]

: 28 :

Eutychian I
[275–83]

Eutychian, a Tuscan and son of Maximus, lived in the time of 1
Aurelian.[1] Aurelian was slain and succeeded by Tacitus, who was
certainly suited to govern the state on account of his virtue and
integrity. In the sixth month after coming to power, however,
Tacitus was slain in Pontus. Florian, who succeeded Tacitus, was
also slain in the third month of his rule in Tarsus.[2]

Eutychian ordained that the fruits of the earth, especially beans 2
and grapes, should be blessed on the altar. He also ordained that
those who wished to bury martyrs should not dare to do so without wearing a dalmatic or a purple tunic, and especially not without his knowledge. Some write that Dorotheus the eunuch lived at
this time, a man highly learned in Greek and Hebrew, whose
learning, they say, marvelously delighted Aurelian. For in the first

runt. Nam ita primis imperii sui[1] annis Christianis favit ut Pauli Samosateni sectam ab ecclesia separaverit. Verum postea malis consiliis subornatus, in Christianos, ut dixi, persecutionem movens, scriptis iam ea de re ad praesides provinciarum litteris, divino iudicio interimitur. Ipsius autem Dorothei Scripturas sacras exponentis auditor Eusebius etiam adolescens fuit. Anatolius quoque Alexandrinus, Laodiceae Syriae episcopus, multae doctrinae vir, praeclara quaedam in mathematicis et Scriptura sacra tum composuit. Invectus est et in Manichaeorum haeresim, quae tum maxime invaluerat. Ii ad reliquos errores et duas substantias introduxerunt, bonam[2] et malam, dixereque animas ex Deo quasi ex aliquo fonte manare. Testamentum Vetus omnino respuebant; Novum vero aliqua ex parte recipiebant.

3   At Eutychianus, ubi ex sacris ordinibus[3] mense decembri habitis presbyteros quattuordecim, diaconos quinque, episcopos novem creasset, martyrio coronatur et in coemiterio Calixti via Appia sepelitur VIII Kalendas augusti. Sedit annum unum, mensem unum, diem unum. Vacat tum sedes dies octo. Sunt tamen qui scribant eum annis octo, mensibus decem, in pontificatu vixisse,[4] sed ego multo magis Damaso credo, qui primae sententiae auctor est.

: 29 :

Caius I

1   Caius, natione Dalmata, patre Caio, ex genere Diocletiani imperatoris, primum Probi tempore fuit, deinde Caio et Carino imperantibus.

years of his reign Aurelian was such a supporter of the Christians
that he separated the sect of Paul of Samosata from the Church.
But then he was corrupted by evil counsels and started a persecution against the Christians, as I have already said. After he had
sent letters to the provincial governors on this matter, Aurelian
was slain by divine judgment. When he was young, Eusebius was
a pupil of Dorotheus and heard his expositions of Holy Scripture.
At that same time, Anatolius the Alexandrian, bishop of
Laodicaea in Syria, a man of much learning, composed excellent
works on mathematics and sacred Scripture. He also inveighed
against the Manichean heresy, which flourished greatly at that
time. In addition to their other errors, the Manicheans introduced
two substances, good and evil; and they said that souls flowed
from God as if from a fountain. They entirely rejected the Old
Testament and accepted only parts of the New.[3]

As for Eutychian, after ordaining fourteen priests, five deacons, 3
and nine bishops in a December ordination, he was crowned with
martyrdom and buried in the cemetery of Calixtus on the Via
Appia on July 25. He was pope for one year, one month, and one
day. The see was then vacant for eight days. Some write that he
lived as pope for eight years and ten months; but I give greater
credit to Damasus, who reports the first view.[4]

: 29 :

Gaius I
[283–96]

Gaius, a Dalmatian and son of Gaius, was related to the emperor 1
Diocletian and lived, first in the time of Probus, and then when
Gaius and Carinus ruled.[1]

2   Probus autem, rei militaris gloria insignis, suscepta reipublicae administratione Gallias a barbaris occupatas ingenti felicitate restituit. Saturninum imperium usurpare conantem in oriente, Proculum et Bonosum Agrippinae magna celeritate oppressit. Apud Sirmium[1] tamen vir acer et iustus tumultu militari et licentia[2] occiditur, anno imperii eius sexto. Post quem Carus Narbonensis imperium suscepit ac biennio tenuit. Hic, cum filios duos, Carinum et Numerianum, ad gubernacula imperii traduxisset, bello Parthico, captis etiam Coelenis et Ctesiphonte nobilissimis urbibus, in castris fulmine ictus concidit. Numerianus vero, qui tum cum patre erat rediens, Apri soceri sui fraude necatur. Carinus autem probris omnibus contaminatus, a Diocletiano, difficili tamen bello, in Dalmatia victus, scelerum suorum poenas tandem luit.

3   Caius vero ordines in ecclesia distinxit, quibus tamquam gradibus quibusdam ad episcopatum ascenderetur. Ii erant ostiarius, lector, exorcista, acolythus, subdiaconus, diaconus, presbyter, episcopus. Idem quoque, ut quondam Fabianus, regiones diaconis divisit, qui res gestas martyrum conscriberent. Constituit etiam ne profanus quispiam sacris initiatum in iudicium vocaret, neve paganus aut haereticus accusandi Christianum hominem potestatem haberet. Huius tempore fuisse Victorinum Petabionensem episcopum constat, qui multa commentaria in sacros codices scripsit. Invectus est etiam in haereses omnes, licet non aeque graecam linguam ac latinam[3] noverit, ut Hieronymo placet, qui affirmat eius scripta grandia sensu, compositione vilissima apparuisse. Pamphilus vero presbyter, Eusebii Caesariensis episcopi necessarius, adeo divinorum voluminum cupidus fuit, ut magnam partem librorum Origenis sua manu descripserit,[4] quos quidem libros Hieronymus affirmat se vidisse in bibliotheca Caesariensi tanta aviditate ut Croesi divitias consecutum se arbitraretur. Scripsit idem Pamphi-

When Probus, distinguished for his military glory, took control   2
of the state, with amazing success he recovered the Gauls,[2] which
barbarians had overrun. With great speed, he vanquished
Saturninus, who was trying to usurp the empire in the east, and
Proculus and Bonosus in Cologne. But this brave and just man
was slain in a military riot in Sirmium, in the sixth year of his
rule. Carus of Narbonne succeeded him and ruled for two years.
After admitting his two sons, Carinus and Numerianus, to a share
in the government of the empire and capturing the most noble cities of Celaenae and Ctesiphon in the Parthian War, he was struck
by lightning and killed in camp. Numerianus, who was with his
father at the time, was slain through the deceit of his father-in-law
Aper as he returned. Tainted by every kind of misdeed, Carinus
was defeated by Diocletian in a hard-fought battle and in the end
suffered a just penalty for his crimes.[3]

Gaius created distinctions among the orders in the Church by   3
which, as if by steps, the clergy could ascend to the episcopate.
These orders are: doorman, lector, exorcist, acolyte, subdeacon,
priest, and bishop. As Fabian had done before, Gaius divided the
city's regions among deacons, who were to record the deeds of the
martyrs. He likewise ordained that no layman should bring a law-
suit against a cleric and no pagan or heretic should have the power
to accuse a Christian man. Victorinus, the bishop of Pettau, who
wrote many commentaries on holy books, evidently lived at this
time. He inveighed against all heresies, although he did not know
Greek as well as he did Latin; as Jerome liked to say, his writings
had sublime thoughts but a contemptible style. Pamphilus, a priest
and an intimate friend of Eusebius, the bishop of Caesarea, was so
eager for theological writings that he copied out in his own hand a
large part of Origen's books. Jerome claims that he was so excited
to see these books in the library of Caesarea that he thought he

lus *Apologeticum pro Origene*, quod etiam Eusebius non multo post fecit.

4   At vero Caius, orta in Christianos tempore Diocletiani tanta persecutione quanta nunquam antea, in subterraneis locis, quas cryptas vocant, diu latuit. Captus deinde a persecutoribus una cum Gabinio fratre eiusque filia Susanna, martyrio coronatur et via Appia in coemiterio Calixti sepelitur X Kalendas maii. Sunt etiam qui scribant[5] Luciam, Agatham, Agnetem non multo post martyrium passas fuisse. Sedit autem Caius annis undecim, mensibus quattuor, diebus duodecim. Quo quidem tempore presbyteros quinque et viginti, diaconos octo, episcopos quinque creavit, quater ordinibus sacris mense decembri habitis. Vacat tum sedes dies undecim.

: 30 :

Marcellinus I

1   Marcellinus, natione Romanus, patre Proiecto, Diocletiani Dalmatae, obscuro loco nati, et Maximiani temporibus fuit. Diocletianus enim anno ab Urbe condita millensimo quadragensimo uno ab exercitu imperator electus, Aprum, qui Numerianum interfecerat, ipsemet[1] occidit. Verum moto in Gallia tumultu potius quam bello, eo cum exercitu Maximianum cognomento Herculeum misit, qui agrestes facile compescuit. At vero circumstrepentibus undique bellis, cum solus Diocletianus resistere tot periculis non posset, Maximianum Augustum, Constantium vero et Maximianum[2] Galerium Caesares creat. Maximianus autem Herculeus,[3] Carausio fraude Allecti interempto, Britanniam post annos decem

had found the riches of Croesus. The same Pamphilus wrote a *Defense of Origen*, as Eusebius also did later.[4]

As for Gaius, in Diocletian's time a greater persecution against   4
the Christians arose than ever before, and Gaius lay hidden for a
long time in underground places called catacombs. At length the
persecutors captured him along with his brother Gabinius and his
daughter Susanna, and he was crowned with martyrdom and buried in the cemetery on the Via Appia on April 22. Some write that
Lucy, Agatha, and Agnes suffered martyrdom not long after. Gaius was pope for eleven years, four months, and twelve days. He
ordained twenty-five priests, eight deacons, and five bishops in
four December ordinations. The see was then vacant for eleven
days.[5]

: 30 :

Marcellinus I
[296–304]

Marcellinus, a Roman and son of Projectus, lived in the time of   1
Diocletian, a Dalmatian of obscure birth, and Maximian.[1]
Diocletian, who was elected emperor by the army in the year of
Rome 1041, killed Aper, who had slain Numerianus. When a riot
(rather than a war) broke out in Gaul, Diocletian sent Maximian,
called Herculeus, with an army, who easily suppressed the peasants. As wars were breaking out on all sides, and Diocletian could
not oppose so many dangers alone, he named Maximianus an Augustus, and Constantius and Maximianus Galerius as Caesars. After Carausius was killed through the deceit of Allectus, Maximian
Herculeus gained control of Britain in ten years. After fighting unsuccessfully at first in Gaul, in a second battle Constantius killed

recipit. At Constantius,[4] cum primo in Gallia male pugnasset, re-
novata secunda pugna, multa milia Alemannorum occidit, qui eo
venerant mercede conducti, ac Gallias pacatas reddidit. Diocletianus interim captam Alexandriam, quam Achileo resistente mensibus octo obsiderat, diripiendam militibus dedit. Praeterea vero
Maximianus Galerius, cum duobus proeliis contra Narseum bene
pugnasset, postremo[5] inter Galietium[6] et Carras superatur. Atque
tam sinistra pugna amissis copiis ad Diocletianum confugit, a quo
ita arroganter exceptus est ut per aliquot milia passuum purpura-
tus ante[7] currum eius cucurrisse dicatur. Is autem[8] hac contumelia
motus, repetito bello hostes superat ac domat.

2   Pacatis hoc modo undique rebus Diocletianus in oriente, Maximianus vero Herculeus in occidente vastari ecclesias, Christianos
affligi interficique mandant, decima post Neronem persecutione,
quae certe omnibus diuturnior et immanior est habita. Nam et
Scripturae sacrae igni exustae sunt et, si quis Christianus in ma-
gistratu fuisset, eo sublato remanebat infamis. Praeterea vero servi,
qui in Christianismo perdurabant, libertatem consequi non poterant; milites item christiani cogebantur aut immolare idolis aut
militiam pariter vitamque deponere edicto[9] principis in foro posito. Hoc vero quidam lacerare ausus, pelle nudatus, superfuso
aceto et sale tam diu cruciatur quoad vita superfuit. Hunc in fide
confirmarunt Dorotheus et Gorgonius, viri clarissimi.

3   Iisdem diebus forte fortuna in urbe Nicomediae regia domus
incendio conflagrare coepit, unde imperator, a Christianis id[10] factum falsa suspicione existimans, multos interfici plerosque vivos in
ignem coniici iubet. Eadem quoque saevitia usi sunt qui in Mili-
tene provincia, in Syria, in Africa, in Thebaide, in Aegypto cum
imperio erant. In planitie vero Palaestinae et Tyri multis saevissi-
mis bestiis expositi sunt. Nullum autem genus tormenti Christianis tum non adhibitum est. Pro ungulis enim testas fictilium vas-

many thousands of Alemanni, who had come there as mercenar-
ies, and pacified the Gauls. Meanwhile, after besieging Alexandria,
which Achilleus had defended for eight months, Diocletian captured the city and gave it to his soldiers to plunder. Moreover, after fighting two successful battles against Narses, Maximianus
Galerius was overwhelmed between Callinicus and Carrhae. He
lost many troops in that ill-fated battle and fled to Diocletian, who
received him with such disdain that they say he ran several miles
in front of the emperor's chariot dressed in his imperial purple.
Stung by this disgrace, Maximianus [Galerius] overwhelmed and
conquered the enemy in the next battle.[2]

After affairs had been settled in this way everywhere, Diocletian   2
in the East and Maximian Herculeus in the West ordered
churches to be destroyed and Christians to be tortured and killed
in the tenth persecution after Nero, which was considered longer
lasting and more savage than all the others. The Holy Scriptures
were burned and, if any Christian held a magistracy, his office was
taken away and he was left in disgrace. Slaves who persisted in
their Christian faith could not be freed. Likewise, by imperial
edict in the forum, Christian soldiers were forced either to sacrifice to idols or to give up both their military service and their
lives. Someone who dared to tear the edict down was flayed and
tortured to death with vinegar and salt applied to his wounds.
Dorotheus and Gorgonius, two very eminent men, encouraged
him in the faith.

At the same time, the royal palace in the city of Nicomedia   3
chanced to catch on fire, and since the emperor falsely believed
that the Christians had started it, he commanded many of them
to be slain and others to be burned alive. Those in power in the
province of Mitylene, in Syria, in Africa, in Thebes, and in Egypt
treated Christians with the same severity. On the plain of Palestine and Tyre, Christians were thrown to the most ferocious wild
beasts. There was no kind of torture that was not used against

culorum adhibebant; quibusdam vero harundines acutae sub
unguibus figebantur. Hoc etiam tormento vexatae mulieres sunt,
harundinibus ipsis per pudenda corporum adactis. Urbs quaedam
in Phrygia tota combusta est, quia cives idolis sacrificia exhibere
recusarunt, Adaucto Romano viro sanctissimo eos in fide reti-
nente. Ad haec postremo venere saevissimi tortores, ut oculis
effossis ac cauterio adustis saevirent. Passi etiam martyrium sunt
Anthimus Nicomediae episcopus, Lucianus presbyter Antiochenus, vir doctissimus, Pamphilus Caesariensis, Hileas Aegyptius,
qui et Thynus vocabatur. Is enim capitali poena afficitur quod et
librum de laudibus martyrum composuit et impugnare iudices
male iudicantes ausus est. Quid plura, cum Damasus referat tria
de viginti milia hominum utriusque sexus diebus triginta per di-
versas provincias martyrio coronata fuisse? Omitto eos qui in insulas relegati sunt vel ad metallum vel ad opus metalli vel ad fo-
diendas harenas excidendosque lapides damnati, quae multitudo
prope infinita est habita.[11]

4   At Marcellinus pontifex ad sacrificia gentium ductus, cum minis instarent carnifices ut thura diis exhiberet, metu perterritus
deos alienos adoravit. Habito deinde non ita multo post concilio
centum et octoginta episcoporum in Sinuessa, urbe Campaniae, eo
et Marcellinus squalidus et pulverulentus ac cilicio indutus proficiscitur petitque ut sibi pro inconstantia debita poena tribuatur.
Qui eum damnaret in tanto concilio nemo unus inventus est, cum
dicerent omnes ea ferme ratione Petrum peccasse ac flendo peccati
poenam luisse. Rediit Romam Marcellinus iratus, Diocletianum
adiit hominemque increpat, qui se impulerit diis gentium immolare. Ducitur ad martyrium Diocletiani iussu Marcellinus cum
Claudio, Cyrino, Antonino, Christi fidelibus. Inter eundum vero
Marcellum presbyterum admonet ne Diocletiani praeceptis ob-
temperet, in rebus maxime ad fidem pertinentibus, neve corpus

them. They used potsherds of clay dishes as talons against them, and shoved sharp reeds under their finger-nails. They tortured women by forcing reeds into their private parts. A certain city in Phrygia was burnt to the ground because its citizens, who were encouraged in their faith by Adauctus, a most holy Roman, refused to sacrifice to idols. In the end, these utterly savage torturers went to such extremes that in their rage they gouged out the eyes of Christians and burnt them with hot iron. Anthimus, the bishop of Nicomedia; Lucian, a most learned man and priest of Antioch; Pamphilus of Caesarea and Hileas of Egypt, who was also called Thynus, also suffered martyrdom. Hileas was executed because he composed a book in praise of the martyrs and dared to criticize the unjust judges.[3] In short, Damasus relates that 17,000 people of both sexes in different provinces were crowned with martyrdom within thirty days. I will not mention those who were exiled to the islands or condemned to the mines or the forges, to dig sand or to quarry stones, who were considered to be an almost infinite number.[4]

As for pope Marcellinus, after his tormentors dragged him 4 to the pagan sacrifices and urged him with threats to offer incense to the gods, he froze with fear and adored the pagan gods. Then, not long after this, a dirty, grimy, and penitent Marcellinus went to a council of 180 bishops, which was held in the city of Sinuessa in Campania, and begged to receive a just punishment for his cowardice. In so great a council there was yet no man who would condemn him, since all said that Peter had sinned in almost the same manner, and that his tears had already atoned for his sin. An angry Marcellinus then returned to Rome, went to Diocletian, and rebuked the man who forced him to sacrifice to the pagan gods. By Diocletian's order, Marcellinus was taken to martyrdom, along with the faithful Christians Claudius, Cyrinus, and Antoninus. While he was being taken, Marcellinus warned the priest Marcellus that he should not obey Diocletian's commands

suum sepulturae traderet, quod diceret ob negatum Salvatorem se id nequaquam mereri.[12] Horum autem simul interemptorum corpora Diocletiani iussu ad dies sex et triginta insepulta iacuerunt via publica. Unde Petri apostoli iussu, qui Marcello in somnis apparuit, via Salaria in coemeterio,[13] quod Priscillae deinceps nomen habuit,[14] sepeliuntur, VI Kalendas maias apud beati Crescentionis corpus.

5   Tandem vero aperuit oculos Deus, ut Eusebius ait, et eo[15] Diocletianum compulit ut deposito imperio privatus viveret. Idem fecit et Maximianus eius collega, acerrimus persecutionis Christianae auctor, qui post aliquot annos[16] multis variisque morbis vexatus ac post longos cruciatus insania mentis percitus furiisque scelerum agitatus, se ipsum tandem peremit. Hanc autem calamitatem quam nostri passi sunt, a Deo permissam refert Eusebius propter corruptos nimia libertate et indulgentia Christianorum mores, maxime vero ecclesiasticorum, quorum perversitatem divina iusticia frenare hac persecutione instituit, dum simulationem in vultu, dolum in corde, fallaciam in eorum verbis cerneret. Ii enim livore, superbia, inimicitiis, odiis inter se certantes, tyrannidem potius quam sacerdotium sapere videbantur, christianae pietatis omnino obliti ac divina mysteria profanantes potius quam celebrantes.

6   Sed quid futurum nostra aetate arbitramur? Qua vitia nostra eo crevere ut vix[17] apud Deum misericordiae locum nobis reliquerint? Quanta sit avaritia sacerdotum et eorum maxime qui rerum potiuntur, quanta libido undique conquisita, quanta ambitio et pompa, quanta superbia et desidia, quanta ignoratio tum sui ipsius tum doctrinae christianae, quam parva religio et simulata potius quam vera, quam corrupti mores vel in profanis etiam hominibus,

especially in matters that pertain to the faith and that he should not bury his body, since he said that, owing to his denial of the Savior, he in no way deserved it. By Diocletian's order, the bodies of these martyrs lay unburied on a public street for thirty-six days. By order of the Apostle Peter, who appeared to Marcellus in a dream, they were then buried in a cemetery, which was at that time called Priscilla's, on the Via Salaria by the body of Saint Crescentio on May 27.[5]

Finally, God opened his eyes, as Eusebius says, and compelled 5 Diocletian to resign from the empire and live a private life. His colleague Maximian [Herculeus], the violent instigator of the Christian persecution, also did the same. After some years, he was tormented with many different illnesses and after protracted torment went mad. Disturbed by the furies of his wicked deeds, he at length killed himself. Eusebius says that God permitted this disaster which the Christians suffered because Christian morals had been corrupted by excessive freedom and indulgence. By this persecution divine justice put a stop especially to the perversity of the clergy, as it saw the hypocrisy in their faces, the deceit in their hearts, and the falsity in their words. For out of malice, pride, enmity, and hatred, they fought among themselves, and seemed to smack of tyranny rather than priesthood; they entirely forgot Christian piety and desecrated rather than celebrated the divine mysteries.[6]

But what do we think will happen in our age, when our vices 6 have grown to such an extent that they hardly leave room for God's mercy towards us? It is useless to relate how great the avarice of the clergy is, especially the avarice of those who hold power, how great their lust, which is found everywhere, how great their ambition and extravagance, how great their pride and indolence, and how great their ignorance both of themselves and of Christian doctrine; and what little faith they have, which is simulated rather than real, and how corrupt their habits, which should be despised

quos saeculares vocant, detestandi, non attinet dicere, cum ipsi ita
aperte et palam peccent ac si inde laudem quaererent. Veniet, mihi
credite (utinam falsus sim vates!), veniet Thurcus, hostis christiani
nominis Diocletiano et Maximiano violentior — Italiae claustra
iam pulsat! Nos desides et somniculosi interitum communem ex-
pectamus, voluptati privatae potius quam communi utilitati
consulentes.

7   Ad Marcellinum venio, quem utinam aliquando imitati, ad sa-
nitatem redeamus. Hic enim, ut dixi, cognito errore suo quo a fide
defecerat, ad se rediens, martyrium pro fide Christi constanti
animo passus est, ubi ex sacris ordinibus bis mense decembri habitis presbyteros quattuor, diaconos duos, episcopos quinque creasset. Sedit autem annis novem, mensibus duobus, diebus sedecim.
Vacat tum sedes dies quinque et viginti.

: 31 :

Marcellus I

1   Marcellus, natione Romanus, patre Benedicto, ex regione viae
Latae, a Constantio et Galero[1] usque ad Mazentium pervenit.
Constantius enim et Galerus, abdicantibus se ab imperio Diocletiano et Maximiano, imperii gubernacula suscipientes, provincias
inter se partiti sunt. Nam Galerus Illyricum, Asiam et Orientem
sortitus est; Constantius vero, singulari moderatione usus, Gallia
tantum et Hispania contentus fuit, licet ei et Italia sorte[2] obtigerit.
Unde Galerus duos Caesares legit, Maximianum,[3] quem Orienti
praefecit, et Severum, cui Italiam commendavit. Illyricum ipse retinuit, quod ea barbaros hostes populi Romani iter facturos sentie-

even among the profane, whom they call seculars. It is useless to relate all this, since the clergy sin so openly and plainly that it is as though they sought praise for sinning. Believe me — and would that I were a false prophet! — the Turk will come, a crueler enemy of Christianity than Diocletian and Maximian. He is already knocking on the gates of Italy! Lazy and half asleep, we await universal destruction, more concerned with our own private pleasure than with public utility.

I come now to Marcellinus, and would that we could imitate 7 him and return to sanity! As I said, he recognized his own mistake of failing in faith, returned to himself and, after ordaining four priests, two deacons, and five bishops in two December ordinations, he suffered martyrdom for the Christian faith with a steadfast spirit. He was pope for nine years, two months, and sixteen days. The see was then vacant for twenty-five days.[7]

: 31 :

Marcellus I
[306–8]

Marcellus, a Roman from the Via Lata region and son of Benedict, lived from the reign of Constantius and Galerius until that of Maxentius.[1] After Diocletian and Maximian abdicated their power, Constantius and Galerius took control of the empire and divided its provinces among themselves. Galerius was allotted Illyricum, Asia, and the East, while Constantius exercised singular moderation and was content with Gaul and Spain, although Italy also fell to his lot. Galerius chose two Caesars: he gave Maximinus control of the East and entrusted Severus with Italy. He himself retained Illyricum, since he thought that the barbarian enemies of

bat. At Constantius, vir singularis mansuetudinis et clementiae, Gallis omnibus carissimus fuit, praecipue vero quod et Diocletiani vafrum ingenium et Maximiani crudelitatem non sine magno discrimine evaserant. Moritur autem Constantius Eboraci in Britannia, principatus sui anno tertio decimo, atque in divos summo omnium consensu refertur.

2   At Marcellus, divino cultui intentus, ubi Priscillam matronam Romanam impulisset coemeterium suis sumptibus via Salaria construere, titulos quinque et viginti in urbe Roma constituit, quasi dioeceses ad commoditatem baptismi et opportunitatem eorum, qui ad fidem ex gentibus quotidie veniebant, consultum iri, et eo modo sepulturis martyrum videbat. Mazentius vero, ubi Lucinam matronam Romanam instituisse ecclesiam Dei rerum suarum haeredem intellexisset, iratus, et mulierem ipsam relegavit ad tempus et Marcellum captum impellere minis conatus est ut et episcopatu se abdicaret et Christianum nomen deponeret.[4] Quem, ubi contemnere et deridere sua praecepta vidit, in cacabulum ad custodienda animalia publica, ut quidam volunt, statim inclusit, quo in loco nec orationes unquam nec ieiunia praetermisit. Parochias item, non secus ac si liber esset, epistolis gubernabat.[5] Mense autem nono captivitatis suae a clericis noctu e[6] cacabulo liberatus est, qua ex re maiore percitus ira Mazentius, sanctissimum virum in cacabulum redegit, ubi, cum foede et incommode habitaret, paedore et situ mortuus est. At vero Lucina sanctissimi viri corpus via Salaria in coemeterio Priscillae condidit XVII Kalendas februarii. Postea autem, re christiana crescente, cacabuli domus in ecclesiam erigitur beati Marcelli nomine, quae etiam aetate nostra invisitur.

3   Sunt autem qui scribant Mauritium cum una Christianorum legione apud Rhodanum flumen a persecutoribus caesum. His additur Marcus, Sergius, Cosmus, Damianus aliique complures, qui

Rome would come along that route. Constantius, a man of singular gentleness and clemency, was most dear to all the Gauls, especially as they had evaded, not without a grave crisis, both the crafty Diocletian and the cruel Maximian. Constantius died in the thirteenth year of his reign in York, England and by universal agreement was placed among the gods.[2]

Marcellus was intent on divine worship and, after he had persuaded Priscilla, a Roman matron, to build a cemetery at her expense on the Via Salaria, he created in the city of Rome twenty-five titles, which were like dioceses, for the convenience and advantage of baptism for those who were converting every day to the faith. In this way he provided for the burial of the martyrs. But when Maxentius learned that a Roman matron, Lucina, had made the Church of God heir to her fortune, he became enraged and banished the woman for a time. He also seized Marcellus and tried to force him with threats to resign his bishopric and renounce Christianity. When he saw that Marcellus was scorning and mocking his commands, Maxentius immediately imprisoned him in a stable and forced him, as some have it, to tend the public animals. He never missed his prayers or his fasting in that place, and guided his parishes with letters no differently than if he had been free. In the ninth month of his captivity, clerics freed Marcellus from the stable at night. Maxentius, however, was seized by even greater anger and sent this very holy man back to the stable, where, after living in filth and discomfort, he died of the stench and squalor. Lucina buried the body of this most holy man in the cemetery of Priscilla on the Via Salaria on January 16. Later, when Christianity was growing, the house of the stable was turned into the church of Saint Marcellus, which can be visited even today.[3]

Some write that the persecutors slaughtered Mauritius along with an entire legion of Christian soldiers by the Rhone river. In addition, Marcus, Sergius, Cosmus, Damian, and many others

ubique[7] terrarum caedebantur. Marcellus autem annis quinque se-
dens, mensibus sex, diebus uno et viginti, ex sacris ordinibus
mense decembri habitis presbyteros sex et viginti, diaconos duos,
episcopos unum et viginti creavit. Vacat tum eius morte Romana
sedes dies viginti.

: 32 :

Eusebius I

1   Eusebius, natione graecus, patre medico, pontificatum adiit Constantino et Mazentio imperantibus. Nam mortuo Constantio, sicuti dixi, Claudii ex filia nepote, Constantinus, eius et Helenae in
gratiam Herculei repudiatae filius,[1] Occidentis imperium maximo
omnium consensu adeptus est. Romae interea praetoriani excitato
tumultu Mazentium, Maximiani Herculei filium, Augustum nun-
cupant. Unde Maximianus, spe recuperandi imperii, ex solitudine
Lucaniae Romam venit, litteris Diocletianum adhortatus ut idem
ipse faceret. Contra hos motus missus a Galerio Severus cum exercitu, dum urbem Romam obsidet, fraude militum, qui cum Mazentio sentiebant, circumventus, fugiens demum Ravennae occiditur. Paululum[2] etiam abfuit quin Maximianus pater, militum
benevolentiam pollicitationibus et largitione quaerens, a filio Mazentio occideretur. Is autem in Gallias ad Constantium generum
profectus, dum circumvenire hominem studet, detecto per Faus-
tam eius filiam dolo, quae rem omnem marito aperuit, fugiens ac
Massiliae oppressus, suorum scelerum poenas tandem luit, vel se
ipsum, ut quidam volunt, desperatis rebus interfecit.

were slaughtered all over the world. Marcellus was pope for five years, six months, and twenty-one days. He ordained twenty-six priests, two deacons, and twenty-one bishops. His death then left the Roman See vacant for twenty days.[4]

: 32 :

Eusebius I
[310]

Eusebius, a Greek and son of a physician, entered the pontificate 1 during the reign of Constantine and Maxentius.[1] After the death of Constantius (who as I've said was the grandson of Claudius by his daughter), Constantine, his son by Helen (whom he divorced in Herculeus' favor),[2] took control of the Western empire by universal consent. Meanwhile a riot broke out in Rome, and the pretorian guard chose Maxentius, the son of Maximian Herculeus, as Augustus. Hoping to recover the empire, Maximian left the solitude of Lucania, went to Rome, and in a letter urged Diocletian to do the same. Galerius sent Severus with an army against these rebellions; but while he was besieging Rome, Severus was overwhelmed and finally slain in Ravenna as he was fleeing, owing to the treachery of the soldiers who favored Maxentius. Maximian, who was seeking the goodwill of the soldiers with promises and bribery, barely escaped being murdered by his son Maxentius. Maximian went to Gaul to Constantius, his son-in-law, and tried to ensnare him, but his daughter Fausta discovered the trap and revealed the matter to her husband. He fled but was seized in Marseilles, and at length paid for his wicked deeds; or, as some have it, killed himself in desperation.[3]

2   Dum autem Eusebius in pontificatu viveret, crux Domini inventa est V Nonas maii et ab Helena Constantini matre exornata ac in magna veneratione habita. Baptizatur et Iudas crucis inventor, quem postea mutato nomine Cyriacum vocarunt. Haereticos quoque idem pontifex reconciliavit, imposita tantummodo manu. Instituit praeterea ne profani, quos laicos vocant, episcopum in iudicium vocarent. Huius vero temporibus fuisse Lactantium Firmianum constat, Arnobii discipulum. Hic, cum rhetoricam Nicomediae doceret, infrequentia discipulorum motus quod id in Graeca civitate ageret, ad scribendum se contulit, qua in re tantum valuit ut post tempora Ciceronis ab eo secundus habeatur. Multa scripsit, sed illa potissimum extant quae *Contra gentiles, De opificio hominis, De ira Dei* conscripsit. In extrema senectute constitutus, Caesaris Crispi, filii Constantini, praeceptor fuit in Gallia. Eusebius quoque, Caesareae Palaestinae episcopus ac bibliothecae divinae cum Pamphilo martyre diligentissimus investigator, multa eisdem temporibus scripsit, maxime vero libros *Evangelicae praeparationis, Ecclesiasticae historiae, In Porphyrium*, Christianorum hostem acerrimum. *Apologias* item *sex pro Origene* composuit, *De vita Pamphili martyris*, a quo ob amicitiam cognomentum accepit, libros tres.

3   Eusebius autem pontifex, habita semel ratione sacrorum ordinum mense decembri, cum presbyteros tredecim, diaconos tres, episcopos quattuordecim creasset, Romae moritur ac in coemeterio Calixti via Appia sepelitur VI Nonas octobris. Sedit autem annis sex, mense uno, diebus tribus. Vacat tum sedes diem unum.

During the pontificate of Eusebius, the cross of the Lord was 2
discovered on May 3. Constantine's mother Helen refurbished it
and held it in great veneration. Judas, who found the cross, was
baptized and his name was changed to Cyriac. The pope also reconciled heretics with only the imposition of his hands. Furthermore, he ordained that the profane, whom they call the laity,
should not call bishops to trial.[4] Lactantius Firmianus, a disciple
of Arnobius, lived in Eusebius' time. While teaching rhetoric in
Nicomedia he was driven by the lack of students in this Greek city
to turn his attention to writing; and he was so able a writer that
he is considered the best writer after the time of Cicero. He wrote
much, but those works especially stand out that he wrote *Against
the Gentiles*, *On the Creation of Man*, and *On the Anger of God*. In old
age, he was appointed tutor of Caesar Crispus, Constantine's son,
in Gaul. Eusebius, the bishop of Caesarea in Palestine and, along
with Pamphilus the martyr, a most diligent seeker of divine writings, composed many works at this time, especially the books *On
the Preparation for the Gospel*, the *Ecclesiastical History*, and *Against
Porphyry*, who was a bitter enemy of Christianity. He also composed *Six Apologies for Origen*, and three books *On the Life of
Pamphilus the Martyr*, whose surname he adopted on account of
their friendship.[5]

As for pope Eusebius, after ordaining thirteen priests, three 3
deacons, and fourteen bishops in one December ordination, he
died in Rome and was buried in the cemetery of Calixtus on the
Via Appia on October 2. He was pope for six years, one month,
and three days. The see was then vacant for one day.[6]

: 33 :

Melciades I

1   Melciades, natione Afer, Mazentii, Licinii, Maximini temporibus fuit. Licinius enim ex Dacia oriundus, a Galerio[1] in partem imperii recipitur propter eius in re militari praestantiam. Ii, quod Constantinum videbant apud omnes magno esse in pretio, Christianis parcebant. Mazentius tamen milites clanculum mittebat qui obvium quemque caederent. Arte quoque magica delectatus, gravidas, maxime vero Christianas, funestis sacris adhibitas[2] scindebat infantum causa, quorum cineribus in magia utebatur, ut ostenderet tyrannidem servari etiam per nefas posse. Simili vesania et crudelitate Maximinus quoque in Oriente utebatur, qui magorum magistris et malarum artium doctoribus praemia etiam decernebat, auguriis ac[3] divinationibus fidem praestans. Saevior ceteris in Christianos, haec omnia contemnentes, est habitus. Vetera autem delubra renovari ac more veterum sacra diis exhiberi iubet.

2   In hos vero Constantinus movens, et Mazentium gravi proelio victum apud pontem Milvium ita superat ut, dum prae dolore suarum fraudum oblitus, pontem ad decipiendum hostem structum decipulis transit, cum magna parte suorum satellitum submergitur; et Licinium sororium navali ac terrestri proelio victum, apud Nicomediam dedere seipsum coegit vitamque Thessalonicae privatam ducere — ac merito quidem, cum a fide ob invidiam deficiens, Christianos Constantino faventes gravibus suppliciis persequeretur.[4]

: 33 :

Miltiades I

[311–14]

Miltiades, an African, lived in the reigns of Maxentius, Licinius,   1
and Maximin.¹ Galerius made Licinius, who was born in Dacia, a
partner in the empire because of his excellence in military matters.
Since these emperors saw that everyone greatly valued
Constantine, they spared the Christians. Nevertheless, Maxentius
secretly sent soldiers to kill any they met. Delighting in magic, he
used pregnant women, especially Christians, in his dark rites and
cut them up for their babies, whose ashes he used in magic, as
though to show that tyranny can be preserved even through wickedness. Maximin practiced a similar kind of madness and cruelty
in the East. He put so much trust in auguries and divinations that
he even gave prizes to masters of magic and professors of the evil
arts. He was considered more unfavorable toward the Christians,
who despised all these things, than other emperors. Maximin ordered the old temples to be renovated and sacrifices to be offered
to the gods in the ancient manner.²

Constantine moved against these two, and in a pitched battle   2
by the Milvian Bridge soundly defeated and vanquished
Maxentius. In his grief, the latter forgot the traps that he himself
had set, and crossed the bridge which his followers had set up to
ensnare the enemy; he drowned with most of his guards.
Constantine also defeated his sister's husband Licinius in a naval
and land battle and forced him to surrender his own person in
Nicomedia and to live life as a private citizen in Thessalonica.
Licinius got what he deserved, since out of envy he deserted the
faith and with painful tortures persecuted the Christians who favored Constantine.³

3   Maximinus vero divina ultione inflatis subito visceribus suppu-
ratisque intestinis ita distenditur, ut inter se et putridum cadaver
nil interesset, scatentibus undique vermibus et tabo serpente, tanto
paedore ut sustineri foetor non posset. Hoc volebant eius merita,
qui et nostros ad coemeteria convenire vetabat; et simulacrum
Antiochiae consecratum, subornatis sacerdotibus qui ex adytis id
enunciarent, clamasse dicebat pellendos ab urbibus Christianos; et
praemia in provinciis distribuit sacerdotibus simulacrorum qui
contra Christianos agerent. Tandem vero tyrannus, paenitentia
ductus, medico verum dicente, decreto publico vetuit Christianos
laedi eosque suis legibus uti sivit. Sed hoc nihil ei profuit, cum vi
fierent omnia. Nam gravissimis morbis diutius cruciatus, vivendi
finem tandem fecit, homo saevus et varius,[5] nunc enim in Christianos, nunc pro Christianis agebat.

4   His autem cladibus multi Christiani interfecti sunt, maxime
vero Dorothea, virgo sanctissima et pulcherrima, quae mortem potius quam stuprum tyranni pati voluit. Sophronia quoque a Mazentio saepius de stupro appellata, cum diutius vitare periculum
non posset, seipsam interfecit, Lucretiam imitata.

5   Melciadis autem institutum fuit ne die dominico neve quinta
feria ieiunaretur, quia hos dies pagani quasi sacros celebrant.
Multa quoque in oblationibus faciendis constituit, quod Manichaeorum haeresis in urbe Roma tum maxime invalescebat. His
autem peractis Maximini iussu martyrio coronatur. Idem fatum
subiere et Petrus Alexandrinus episcopus, et Lucianus Antiochenus presbyter, vir moribus et doctrina insignis, et Timotheus presbyter Romanus aliique complures episcopi et sacerdotes. Sepultus
est autem Melciades via Appia [in] Calixti in crypta[6] IIII Idus decembris. Vivens adhuc ex ordinibus sacris semel habitis, presbyteros septem, diaconos sex, episcopos duodecim creavit. Sedit annis

Divine vengeance suddenly made Maximin's intestines swell up 3 and his bowels suppurate until he exactly resembled a stinking corpse. Worms poured from every orifice and decay slithered about; so great was the filth that the stench became intolerable. His deeds earned him this punishment, as he forbade Christians to gather at the cemeteries and, having suborned some priest to announce this from the temples, said that a pagan statue in Antioch had cried out that the Christians should be expelled from the cities. Maximin also gave out rewards to pagan priests in the provinces who acted against the Christians. But at length, when the physician told him the truth, the usurper repented and by public decree ordered that Christians should not be attacked, and permitted them to live under their laws. This repentance, however, profited him in no way, since it was all made under duress. After being tortured with the most painful illnesses, this perverse and inconstant man, who at different times acted both against and for the Christians, finally died.[4]

Many Christians were slaughtered in these disasters, especially 4 the most holy and beautiful virgin Dorothea, who preferred death to being raped by a usurper. Sophronia too, after Maxentius had repeatedly tried to rape her and she could no longer avoid the danger, imitated Lucretia and killed herself.[5]

Miltiades ordained that Christians should not fast on Sundays 5 or Thursdays, since the pagans celebrated these days as though sacred. He established many rules for offering oblations, since at that time the Manichean heresy was especially strong in Rome. After he did these things, he was crowned with martyrdom by order of Maximin. Many other bishops and priests suffered the same fate, including Peter, bishop of Alexandria, Lucian, priest of Antioch, who was renowned for his habits and learning, and Timoteus, priest of Rome. Miltiades was buried on the Via Appia in the crypt of Calixtus on December 10. While he was still alive, he ordained seven priests, six deacons, and twelve bishops. He was

quattuor, mensibus septem, diebus novem. Vacat tum sedes dies septemdecim.

: 34 :

Sylvester I

1 Sylvester, natione Romanus, patre Ruffino, Constantini temporibus fuit, anno ab Urbe condita¹ millesimo nonagesimo primo, Domini vero anno trecentensimo tricensimo nono. Sub hoc tandem principe Christiani, a tyrannis antea oppressi, nonnihil respirare incipiunt. Nam corporis ac animi dotibus cum optimo quoque² principe comparari Constantinus potuit. Militaris enim gloriae appetentissimus fuit, in bello fortunatus. Pacem petentibus libenter dedit; liberalibus studiis, ubi per otium licebat, delectabatur; liberalitate et gratia omnium benevolentiam sibi comparabat. Multas leges rogavit ex aequo et bono, superfluas abscidit, severas nimium emendavit. Urbem in Byzantii ruinis de nomine suo condens, eam Romae magnitudine aedificiorum parem facere conatus, secundam Romam vocavit, ut litterae sub equestri eius statua indicabant.³

2 Is igitur tantus princeps, omnia circumspiciens, omnia considerans, ubi honestatem Christianae religionis intellexit, qua servare parsimoniam, paupertate gaudere, mansuetudinem colere, paci studere, simplicitate et constantia uti iubemur, eam ita complexus est, ut iturus ad bellum, non alio quam crucis signo uteretur. Quod sereno caelo, dum in Mazentium tyrannum copias movet, et viderat et adoraverat astantesque angelos audierat dicentes, 'Constantine, ἐν τούτῳ νικᾶ'; quod etiam fecit ac tyrannos omnes a

pope for four years, seven months, and nine days. The see was then vacant for seventeen days.[6]

: 34 :

Sylvester I
[314–35]

Sylvester, a Roman and son of Rufinus, became pope in the reign   1
of Constantine, in the year of Rome 1091 and 339 AD.[1] Christians, who had before been oppressed by usurpers, finally began to breathe a little under this emperor. Constantine was so gifted in mind and body that he could bear comparison with the best emperors. Eager for military glory and fortunate in war, he willingly granted peace to those who asked for it and, when leisure permitted, delighted in the liberal arts. By his kindness and grace, he gained universal goodwill for himself. He enacted many laws on principles of equity, repealed superfluous ones, and emended laws that were too harsh. On the ruins of Byzantium he founded a city named after himself, which he tried to make equal to Rome in the greatness of its buildings. He called it the Second Rome, as the letters under his equestrian statue indicated.[2]

This great emperor, looking about and considering everything,   2
recognized the integrity of the Christian religion, which commands everyone to live in moderation, to rejoice in poverty, to cultivate gentleness, to seek peace, and to practice simplicity and constancy. He thus embraced it to the point that, when he went to war, he used no other standard than the sign of the cross. While he was moving his troops against the usurper Maxentius, he had seen and adored this sign in the clear sky, and heard angels saying: "Constantine, conquer in this sign." He did so, thereby lifting

cervicibus populi Romani Christianorumque[4] omnium depulit, maxime vero Licinium, qui Christianos et domo et militia pulsos, aut relegatione aut carcere, ut dixi,[5] ad mortem usque macerabat aut leonibus obiiciebat aut suspensos tamquam porcos membratim lacerans[6] dissipabat.

3   Tantum itaque principem ac tam humanum Sylvester nactus, relicto Soracte monte, quo a tyrannis saevientibus relegatus fuerat vel, ut quidam volunt, secesserat,[7] Romam veniens, Constantinum, erga Christianos bene[8] animatum, promptiorem ad optime de ecclesia Dei promerendum reddidit. Nam et pontificibus diadema aureum distinctum gemmis concedebat, quod quidem Sylvester aspernatus, tamquam religioso capiti minime conveniens, phrygia mitra et candida tantummodo contentus fuit. Permotus autem Constantinus sanctitate Sylvestri, ecclesiam in urbe Roma condidit in hortis Equitii, non longe a thermis Domitianis, quae titulum Equitii usque ad tempora Damasi prae se ferebat. Cui quidem ecclesiae imperator munificus haec etiam dona praestitit: patenam argenteam librarum viginti, scyphos duos viginti librarum, calicem aureum duarum librarum, et alia vasa tum argentea tum aurea, quae enumerare longum esset. Fundum quoque[9] Valerianum dono dedit in agro Sabino positum, unde quotannis soldos octoginta capiebat; hortum intra urbem ad regionem Duorum Adamantum, unde[10] soldi quindecim capiebantur; domum in regione Orphea intra urbem, unde soldi octo et quinquaginta proveniebant.

4   Verum dum haec Romae agerentur, apud Alexandriam presbyter quidam Arius nomine, vir specie et forma magis quam virtute insignis, et laudis ac gloriae potius quam veritatis cupidus, serere discordiam in fide Christi coepit. Separare enim Filium ab aeterna et ineffabili Dei Patris substantia conabatur his verbis: 'Erat aliquando quando non erat,'[11] non intelligens Filium Patri coaeter-

from the necks of all Christians and from the people of Rome all tyrants, but especially Licinius, who had expelled the Christians from their homes and from the military, tormenting them with exile and prison until they died, as I have said, or throwing them to the lions or tearing them limb from limb like pigs that have been strung up.[3]

So once Sylvester had obtained so great and kind an emperor, 3 he left Mount Soracte, where he had been exiled by savage tyrants or, as some have it, he had taken refuge. He returned to Rome and encouraged Constantine, who was well disposed to the Christians, to earn the best of rewards through service to the Church of God. Constantine gave a golden diadem set with precious stones to the popes, but Sylvester rejected it as inappropriate for a religious head; he was content with only a white Phrygian mitre. Constantine was moved by Sylvester's sanctity and built a church in the city of Rome, in the gardens of Equitius not far from the baths of Domitian, which had the title of Equitius until the time of Damasus. The generous emperor also donated the following gifts to the church: a twenty-pound silver dish, two twenty-pound wine-cups, a two-pound golden chalice, and other silver and gold vases, which would be too long to enumerate. He also gave as a gift the estate of Valerianus in the territory of the Sabines, which brought in eighty gold pieces a year; a garden in the city near the region of the Two Lovers, which brought in fifteen gold pieces; and a house in the region Orpheus in the city, worth fifty-eight gold pieces.[4]

While these things were going on in Rome, in Alexandria a cer- 4 tain priest by the name of Arius began to sow discord in the Christian faith. He was famous more for his appearance than for his virtue, and craved praise and glory rather than truth. For he tried to separate the Son from the eternal and ineffable substance of God the Father with the words: "There was once a time when He did not exist." He did not understand that the Son was co-

num esse et eandem in Trinitate substantiam, cum dictum sit: 'Ego et Pater unum sumus.'

5   Cum autem Alexander Alexandrinae urbis episcopus frustra revocare Arium ab errore tentasset, Constantini mandato, adhibita etiam impensa munifice quidem,[12] apud Nicaeam urbem Bithyniae concilium generale indicitur, cui[13] trecenti et duodeviginti episcopi interfuere. Disputatum est in eo loco aliquandiu et quidem acriter. Nam viri aliquot in quaestionibus callidi Ario tum quidem favebant, simplicitati fidei nostrae adversantes, licet ex his quidam doctissimus philosophus, divino Spiritu motus, uno momento fidem nostram, quam antea impugnabat, ut sanctam et integram statim amplexus sit. Tandem vero re ipsa in concilio diligenter discussa, concluditur ὁμοούσιον scribi debere, id est, eiusdem cum Patre substantiae Filium confiteri. Qui vero cum Ario sentirent fuere ad decem et septem, affirmantes extrinsecus creatum esse Dei Filium et non ex ipsa Patris divinitate[14] progenitum. Cognita autem tantae controversiae veritate,[15] Constantinus decretum concilii affirmat, proposito contradicentibus exilio, unde sex tantum cum Ario exulavere; reliqui enim in sententiam bene iudicantium venere.

6   In eodem concilio damnatos ferunt et Photinianos, a Photino episcopo Gallograeciae nomen ducentes, qui Ebionitarum haeresim imitati, affirmabant Christum a Maria pio coitu fuisse conceptum. Damnati et Sabelliani, qui unam tantum personam Patri et Filio et Spiritui Sancto ascribunt. In eodem vero concilio querimoniarum libellos, ut fit, episcopi ipsi Constantino dabant, se invicem accusantes expetentesque a principe iudicium, quibus ita imperator optimus respondet, combustis eorum libellis, eos Dei tantummodo et non hominum iudicium expectare debere.

7   Praeterea autem in eodem concilio decretum est ne, qui se impatientia libidinis castrarent, in clerum amplius reciperentur; neve neophytus, antequam cautius examinaretur, clericus fieret; et ne in

eternal with the Father and the same substance in the Trinity, since it is said: "The Father and I are one."

After Alexander, the bishop of Alexandria, had tried in vain to recall Arius from error, at Constantine's command and at enormous expense, a general council was called in Nicaea, a city in Bithynia. There were 318 bishops present, and the debate was long and bitter. For some men experienced in these matters favored Arius at the time and opposed the simplicity of our faith, although one very learned philosopher among them was moved in a moment by the Holy Spirit to embrace our faith as holy and pure, which before he had been attacking. Finally, after the matter had been diligently discussed in the council, they concluded that the word *homoousion* should be written, that is, to confess that the Son was of the same substance as the Father. About seventeen bishops agreed with Arius and affirmed that the Son of God was created from outside and not begotten from the divinity of the Father. When the truth of this great controversy became known, Constantine confirmed the decree of the council and proposed exile as punishment for those who disagreed. Only six went into exile with Arius; the rest returned to the orthodox view.[5]

They say that the Photinians were also condemned in the same council.[6] They take their name from Photinus, the bishop of Galatia, and in imitation of the Ebionite heresy assert that Mary conceived Christ in pious copulation. The Sabellians were also condemned, who believed that the Father, Son, and Holy Spirit were only one person. In the same council, as is customary, the bishops laid before Constantine formal complaints against each other and sought the emperor's judgment. But the good emperor burnt their complaints and responded to them that they ought to await the judgment of God only and not that of men.

Furthermore, in the same council it was decreed that no one should be admitted to holy orders who had castrated himself as unable to endure lust; that no neophyte should become a cleric be-

militiam Dei ascitus cum extraneis mulieribus habitet—cum
matre vero, sorore, amita id tantummodo licere; ne episcopus in
ordinem asciceretur, nisi ab omnibus vel saltem a tribus provinciae episcopis; et ne quem alius episcopus expulerit, vel clericum vel laicum, alius suscipiat. Decernitur etiam, ac quidem
sancte, ne cuiquam fieret iniuria, ut singulis annis concilium in
provincia habeatur. Quare hoc sanctum institutum aboleverint
nostrae aetatis pontifices non video, nisi quod[16] censuras bene vi-
ventium ac sentientium reformidant. Constitutum quoque est ut
qui absque tormentis in persecutionibus lapsi fuerint, annos
quinque inter catechumenos vitam ducant. Postremo vero decernitur ne quis de minore ecclesia ad maiorem transeat ambitionis et
avaritiae causa, quod certe non observatur, cum siccis faucibus,
tamquam lupi famelici, precibus, pollicitationibus, muneribus, largitione uberiores episcopatus, omissis primis, omnes quaerant et
efflagitent.

8   Sylvestri autem constitutiones hae sunt habitae: ut chrisma ab
episcopo tantum consecraretur, ut episcopi baptizatum signarent
propter haereticam suasionem, ut baptizatum chrismate liniat
presbyter occasione mortis. Addit praeterea laicus clericum in iudicium ne vocet. Diaconus in ecclesia celebrandi causa dalmatica
induatur et palla linostima laeva eius tegatur. Clericus causas in
curia ne agat, nec ante iudicem secularem causam dicat. Presbyter
celebraturus neque serico neque panno tincto utatur, sed lineo et
quidem albo. Sic in albis celebrandum esse dicebat, quemadmodum in linea syndone et alba Christi corpus sepultum fuit. Gradus
quoque in ordinibus ecclesiasticis constituit, ut unusquisque uno
tantum ordine contentus sit et unius solum uxoris vir.

9   Constantinus autem, augendae Christianae religionis cupidus,
basilicam Constantinianam, quam Lateranensem vocant, aedifica-

fore undergoing a strict examination; and that, once enlisted into the service of God, he should not live with women other than his mother, sister, and aunt; that no one should be admitted to the episcopacy except with the approval of all, or at least three provincial bishops; and that no bishop should receive either a cleric or a layman whom another had expelled. It was also decreed in a sacred spirit that a provincial council should be held every year to address any wrongs. I do not see why the popes of our age have abolished this sacred institution, unless because they fear the censure of the pious and orthodox. It was also decreed that those who lapsed in the persecutions before being tortured should live among catechumens for five years. Finally, it was decreed that no one should leave a smaller church for a larger one out of ambition or greed. This decree is certainly not observed today, since, like hungry wolves with thirsty mouths, by prayers, promises, gifts, and bribes they all seek and demand fatter bishoprics, having abandoned their first ones.[7]

The following decisions were considered Sylvester's: that 8 chrism oil should only be consecrated by a bishop, that bishops should mark those baptized at the urging of heretics, and that a priest should anoint a baptized person with chrism oil on the occasion of his death. He added that no layman should call a cleric into court; that a deacon should wear a dalmatic and a linen cloak on his left arm for the celebration of Mass in a church; and that a cleric should not plead cases in the curia nor defend himself before a secular judge. In celebrating Mass, a priest should not wear silk or dyed cloth, but white linen. For he said that Mass should be celebrated in white, just as the body of Christ was buried in a white linen shroud. He determined the levels of ecclesiastical orders, and said that everyone should be content with only one order and with only one wife.[8]

Constantine desired to promote the Christian religion. He built 9 the Constantinian basilica, which they call the Lateran, and

vit donisque plurimis eandem exornavit. Nam et fastigium argenteum templo obtulit, habens in fronte Salvatorem sedentem in sella quinque pedum, centum et triginta librarum, et duodecim apostolos in quinis pedibus librarum nonaginta cum coronis argenti purissimi. Salvatorem quoque addidit respicientem in apsida, sedentem in throno quinque pedum, cuius pondus centum quadraginta librarum erat. Angelos quattuor ex argento ponderis centum et quinque librarum, coronas quattuor ex auro purissimo cum delphinis viginti librarum, altaria septem ex auro purissimo ducentarum librarum. In usum vero luminum massae Gargilianae proventum ex agro Suessano constituit soldos quadringenti.[17] Additur et massa Urbana, quae in agro Antiati est. Sacrumque praeterea fontem instituit apud eandem basilicam ex lapide porphyretico, cuius tota pars illa, quae aquam continet, ex argento erat. In medio autem fontis columna porphyretica posita erat, in qua aurea phiala quinquaginta librarum balsamo plena, in celebritate Paschae usum nocturni luminis praestabat. In labro fontis stabat agnus auri purissimi, unde aqua fundebatur. Non longe ab agno erat Salvatoris statua argenti purissimi centum et septuaginta librarum. Ad alteram partem stabat Ioannis Baptistae statua argentea centum librarum, hunc titulum prae se ferens: 'Ecce agnus Dei, ecce qui tollit peccata mundi.' Septem vero cervi aquam fundebant; quorum singuli octoginta librarum erant. Proventus autem sacri fontis ex massa Statiliana in agro Corano, ex fundo Bassi, ex domibus et hortis, aliquot in Urbe positis, ex quibusdam fundis in Africa, Numidia, Graecia sitis.

10   Idem etiam Constantinus rogatu beati Sylvestri Petro apostolorum principi basilicam in Vaticano aedificat, non longe a templo Apollinis, quo in loco eiusdem apostoli corpus splendide ac mirifice collocavit; ex aere enim et cupro undique clausum erat. Supra beatissimi apostoli sepulchrum crux centum et quinquaginta librarum extabat ex auro purissimo. Aderant circumquaque candelabra quattuor argento conclusa cum sigillis argenteis, unde apos-

adorned it with many gifts. He presented the church with a silver pediment, which had in front a five-foot enthroned Savior weighing 135 pounds and twelve apostles, each five feet tall, weighing ninety pounds with crowns of the purest silver. In the apse he added a five-foot enthroned Savior, whose weight was 140 pounds; four silver angels weighing 105 pounds, four twenty-pound crowns of the purest gold with dolphins, and seven two-hundred-pound altars of the purest gold. To pay for candles, he assigned the revenue of the Gargiliana estate in the Suessa territory, which was four hundred gold pieces. The Urbana estate was also added, which is in the territory of Anzio. Furthermore, he set up a holy font of porphyry, of which the water basin was made entirely of silver. In the middle of the font was placed a porphyry column, on which there was a fifty-pound golden basin full of balsam to provide light at night during Easter celebrations. On the rim of the font stood a lamb of the purest gold, from which water was poured. Not far from the lamb was a statue in the purest silver of the Savior weighing 170 pounds. On the other part stood a silver statue of John the Baptist weighing one hundred pounds and bearing the inscription: "Behold the lamb of God, who takes away the sins of the world." Seven deer poured water, each weighing eighty pounds. Provisions for the sacred font came from the Statiliana estate in the Cora territory, from the farm of Bassus, from homes and gardens, some in the City, and from certain farms in Africa, Numidia, and Greece.[9]

At the request of the blessed Sylvester, Constantine built a ba- 10
silica for Peter, the Prince of the Apostles, on the Vatican, not far from the temple of Apollo, in which he placed the apostle's body marvelously enclosed in bronze and copper. A cross of the purest gold weighing 150 pounds hung over the most blessed apostle's tomb. Four silver-encrusted candelabra surrounded it with silver

tolorum actus cernebantur. His addidit calices aureos tres librarum duodecim, calices argenteos viginti, quorum singulis decem librarum erant, metretas argenteas quattuor ducenti librarum, patenam auream cum thure et columba ornatam gemmis hyacinthinis
et margaritis triginta librarum. Ipsum autem altare erat clausum
argento et auro distinctumque pluribus gemmis. Hos vero proventus huic basilicae addidit: in Antiochia domum Datiani, soldos
centum et quinquaginta praestantem; cellam in Aphrodisia soldos
quingenti quindecim praebentem. Hortum Maronis, thermas
complures, popinas, pistrina condonavit, unde multum colligeba-
tur ad usum sacerdotum. Idem quoque Constantinus instante Sylvestro basilicam Pauli via Ostiensi extruxit; corpus vero apostoli
ita condidit, ut de Petro diximus. Vasa etiam aurea, argentea, aenea totidem donavit quot[18] divo Petro, maxime autem crucem auream centum et quinquaginta librarum supra loculum beati Pauli
collocavit. Venere proventus ad eandem basilicam ex Tarso Ciliciae; ex possessione Tyri venit oleum, venere aromata et cassiae;
venit balsamum ex locis haec eadem ferentibus; venit crocum, sal,
piper, cinnama.

11   Aedificatur etiam imperatoris iussu basilica in atrio Sessoriano
sub titulo Sanctae Crucis in Hierusalem, ubi sanctae Crucis partem aliquam reposuit, inventam ab Helena matre, femina incom-
parabilis fidei et religionis. Haec enim magnitudine animi[19] mota
et visis nocturnis, Hierosolymam petiit ut lignum crucis perquire-
ret. Difficile id quidem erat, quia ab antiquis persecutoribus eo
loci simulacrum Veneris collocatum fuerat, ut Christiani Venerem
Salvatoris loco adorarent. At mulier religione percita, ubi locum
ipsum ruderibus purgasset, tres confuso ordine cruces reperit. In
una inscriptio illa legebatur tribus linguis: Iesus Nazarenus Rex
Iudaeorum. Astabat autem Macarius, illius urbis tum episcopus,
qui unam ex his manibus cum religione retinens, veram esse dicebat, at tertia, mulieri mortuae admota, eidem vitam restituit.
Hanc ob rem Constantinus motus, edicto vetuit ne quispiam dein-

seals showing the Acts of the Apostles. In addition, there were three golden chalices weighing twelve pounds, twenty silver chalices (each weighing ten pounds), four silver measures weighing two hundred pounds, and a golden incense paten adorned with sapphires and pearls weighing thirty pounds. The altar itself was enclosed with silver and gold and adorned with many gems. To this basilica he added the following provisions: the house of Datianus in Antioch with revenues of 150 gold pieces and a sanctuary in Aphrodisia with revenues of 515 gold pieces. He donated Maro's garden, many baths, restaurants and bakeries for the use of priests. At Sylvester's behest, Constantine built the basilica of Paul on the Via Ostiense and buried that apostle's body just as he had Peter's. He donated as many golden, silver, and bronze vases as he did for Saint Peter; and put a golden crucifix weighing 150 pounds over Saint Paul's tomb. Supplies for the basilica came from Tarsus in Cilicia; the oil, perfumes, and cassia came from an estate in Tyre; balsam came from places that produced it; as well as saffron, salt, pepper, and cinnamon.[10]

On the emperor's orders, a basilica was also built in the 11
Sessorian Palace under the title of the Holy Cross of Jerusalem. He placed in it a part of the holy cross, which his mother Helen, a woman of incomparable faith and religion, had found. Moved by her great heart and nocturnal visions, Helen went to Jerusalem to search for the wood of the cross. The search was difficult, since ancient persecutors had set up a statue of Venus in that place, so that Christians might worship Venus in place of the Savior. But the woman was moved by piety, and after she had cleared the place of rubbish, she found three crosses in a confused state. On one an inscription read in three languages: Jesus of Nazareth, King of the Jews. The bishop of that city at the time, Macarius, stood by and piously held the first of these to be the true cross; but when the third one was placed next to a dead woman, it restored her to life. Constantine was moved by this and by edict forbade anyone to be

ceps eo supplicio uteretur.[20] Helena vero, aedificato eo in loco templo ubi crucem reppererat, abiens, clavos, quibus Christi corpus
cruci affixum fuerat, secum ad filium portat. Horum ille unum[21]
in frenos equi transtulit quibus in proelio uteretur, alio pro cono
galeae utebatur, tertium in mare Hadriaticum, ut ait Ambrosius,
ad compescendas saevientis maris procellas deiecit.[22] Illa autem
crucis pars, quam eadem mulier secum in thecis argenteis detule-
rat, gemmis et auro distincta in basilica Sessoriana collocatur.
Huic haec munera adduntur: argentea candelabra quattuor, argentei scyphi quattuor, calices aurei decem, patena argentea auro clusa
librarum quinquaginta, altare argenteum ducenti quinquaginta librarum. Agros quoque circa palatium positos, ecclesiae dono dedit. Ex Faliscis autem et Nepesino agro fundos quosdam donavit.

12   Sunt qui scribant et basilicam Sanctae Agnetis Constantini
iussu aedificatam esse rogatu Constantiae eius filiae et baptisterium ecclesiae additum, ubi et filia et soror Constantini eiusdem
nominis baptizatae sunt. Huius basilicae haec fuere munera: patena aurea librarum viginti, calix aureus librarum decem, calices
argentei quinque, fundus ex agro Fidenatium, fundus ex vico Pisonis. Idem quoque imperator basilicam Sancti Laurentii extra muros aedificat in agro Veranio super harenarium cryptae gradusque
extruxit, quibus ascensus ac descensus his daretur qui ad visen-
dum beati Laurentii corpus accederent. Templi ornamentum erat
apsis argento et porphyreticis lapidibus ornata. In aditu cryptae lu-
cerna erat ex auro purissimo librarum viginti. Ante corpus martyris erant lucernae decem argenteae librarum quindecim. Fundus
autem Cyriacetis feminae, quem fiscus persecutionum tempore oc-
cupaverat, huic basilicae assignatur; fundus item Veranius, unde
soldi sexaginta veniebant.

13   Via etiam Lavicana idem imperator inter duas lauros basilicam
beatis martyribus Marcellino presbytero et Petro exorcistae aedificat. Non longe vero mausoleum erexit in honorem matris, quam

punished henceforth by crucifixion. After building a church in the place where she had found the Cross, Helen left and brought her son the nails with which Christ's body was affixed to the Cross. He made one into a bridle for the horse he used in battle; another he placed on the top of his helmet; and the third one, Ambrose says, he threw into the Adriatic to calm raging sea storms.[11] The part of the Cross which Helen had carried with her in silver cases was decorated with gems and gold and placed in the Sessorian basilica. The following gifts were added to this: four silver candelabra, four silver goblets, ten golden chalices, a silver paten embossed with gold weighing fifty pounds, and a silver altar weighing 250 pounds. He also donated the area around the palace to the church and certain estates from Falerii and Nepete.[12]

Some write that the basilica of Saint Agnes was built by command of Constantine at his daughter Constantia's request, and that he added a baptistry to the church, where his daughter and sister were baptized. His gifts to the basilica were as follows: a golden paten weighing twenty pounds, a golden chalice weighing ten pounds, five silver chalices, an estate near Fidenae, and an estate near Vicus Pisonis. The same emperor built the basilica of Saint Lawrence outside the walls in the Ager Veranus over the sandpit of his crypt, and built steps so that pilgrims could walk up and down to visit the body of blessed Lawrence. The decoration of the church was a vault of silver and porphyry stones. In the entrance to the crypt was a lamp of the purest gold weighing twenty pounds, and in front of the martyr's body were ten silver lamps weighing fifteen pounds. The estate of a woman named Cyriaces, which the treasury had seized during the persecutions, was allotted to the basilica, as was an estate in Veranus, with a revenue of sixty gold pieces.

The emperor built a basilica on the Via Labicana between the Two Laurels for the blessed martyrs, the priest Marcellinus and Peter the exorcist. Not far from here, he erected a mausoleum to

sepulchro[23] porphyretico inclusit. Huic templo martyrum et matris gratia haec dona data sunt: patena ex auro purissimo librarum quinque et triginta, candelabra argentea quattuor auro clusa in pedibus duodecim, calices aurei tres cum gemmis prasinis et hyacinthinis, amae aureae duae, ara ex argento purissimo librarum ducenti, scyphus ex auro purissimo librarum viginti, fundus Laurentinus cum balneo iuxta formam prodeuntis aquae posito, fundus Augustae Helenae, unde soldos trecentos et viginti sacerdotes quotannis habebant. Sunt qui scribant, sine auctore tamen, Sardiniam cum fundis suis et Mesanam et Matiniam[24] cum monte Argentario ac fundis omnibus huic ecclesiae dono datam.

14   Ad has basilicas in urbe Roma aedificatas, alias quoque foris exstruit. Nam et Ostiae, non longe a portu, eius mandato templum aedificatur in honorem beatorum apostolorum Petri et Pauli ac Ioannis Baptistae, quibus etiam haec dona eius munificentia oblata sunt: patena argentea librarum triginta, calices argentei decem, patena argentea chrismalis librarum decem, pelvis ex argento ad usum baptismi librarum viginti. His muneribus additi et Graccorum[25] fundi Ardeatini agri, fundus Quirini in agro Ostiensi. In Albano quoque Ioanni Baptistae templum aedificat, cui haec dona obtulit: patenam argenteam librarum triginta, scyphum argenteum deauratum librarum duodecim, amas argenteas librarum viginti; fundum Laurentinum cum adiacentibus praediis, fundum cum lacu Albano, fundum Tiberii Caesaris. Capuae etiam basilicam Apostolorum condidit quam cives Constantinianam appellarunt. Cui et haec dona oblata: patenae argenteae quadraginta librarum, candelabra graeca quattuor cum pedibus decem. His additur fundus ex agro Caietano et fundus Paternus ex agro Suessano. Aliam postremo basilicam Neapoli aedificavit, ut ait Damasus; in cuius honorem eam erexerit, non satis constat. Proinde reticere donaria

honor his mother, whom he enclosed in a porphyry tomb. For the sake of the martyrs and his mother, he donated the following gifts to the church: a paten of the purest gold weighing thirty-five pounds, four silver candelabra chased with gold twelve feet in size, three gold chalices with emeralds and sapphires, two gold ewers, an altar of the purest silver weighing two hundred pounds, a goblet of the purest gold weighing twenty pounds; the farm Laurentum with a bath next to an aqueduct; an estate of the empress Helen, with yearly revenues of 320 gold pieces for the priests. There are those who write (but with no authority) that he donated to this church Sardinia with its estates, and the islands Meseno and Mattidia with Monte Argentario and all its estates.[13]

In addition to these basilicas built in the city of Rome he con-   14
structed others outside. In Ostia not far from the harbor a church was built at his command in honor of the blessed Apostles Peter and Paul and John the Baptist. His munificence supplied the following gifts: a silver paten weighing thirty pounds, ten silver chalices, a silver chrism-paten weighing ten pounds, a silver baptismal basin weighing twenty pounds. The estates of the Gracchi in the territory of Ardea and the estate of Quirinus in the territory of Ostia were added to these gifts. The emperor Constantine built a church for John the Baptist in Albanum and presented the following gifts: a silver paten weighing thirty pounds, a silver-gilt goblet weighing twelve pounds, silver ewers weighing twenty pounds; a Laurentian estate with adjacent lands, an estate with the Alban Lake, and Tiberius Caesar's estate. He also founded the Basilica of the Apostles in Capua, which the citizens called Constantinian. He offered the following gifts: silver patens weighing forty pounds, four Greek candelabra with ten feet, an estate from the territory of Gaeta and the Paternum estate in the territory of Suessa. Finally, according to Damasus he built another basilica in Naples, but it is not known in whose honor he erected it. (I have accordingly decided to remain silent about the offerings

templo dedicata institui, ne videar cum aliis errare. Sunt etiam qui scribant Sylvestrum titulum suum in tertia regione urbis apud thermas Domitianas instituisse; Equitium quidam vocant. Huic titulo multa dona Constantinus obtulit, ut patenam argenteam librarum viginti, cerostrata aenea sedecim; fundum Barbatianum ex agro Ferentinati, fundum Sulpicianum ex agro Corano.

15   Ne autem novae Romae sacerdotes imperatoriae munificentiae expertes essent, duas item basilicas Constantinopoli aedificat, quarum altera Hirene, altera Apostolorum vocatur, eversis prius paganorum templis aut in usum Christianorum translatis, sublatisque e medio tripodibus delphicis, unde infinita mala oriebantur. Haec sunt Constantini dona, quae antea narravimus, quibus hoc etiam addidit.[26] Certum enim vectigal a civitatibus pendi solitum ecclesiis provincialibus cleroque distribuit. Donationem vero ipsam decreti sui auctoritate validam in perpetuum esse voluit. Ut autem virginibus et qui in coelibatu viverent testari liceret aliquidque sacerdotibus ex testamento relinquere—qua ex re ego arbitror ecclesiae patrimonium auctum esse—legem sustulit antea latam ad propagandam sobolem, qua illi vetabantur haereditatem adire qui vigesimoquinto aetatis anno uxorem non duxissent. Hinc ius illud trium liberorum inventum a principibus est, quo in amicos prole carentes plerunque utebantur. Haec Socrates et Sozomenes in *Tripartita* sua accurate scribunt.[27]

16   Fuere autem et Sylvestri temporibus multi praeclari viri, quorum opera et labore gentes et nationes pleraeque ad fidem nostram venere, maxime vero Iuliani, Frumentii et Edisii praedicationibus, quos philosophi quidam Alexandrini eo perduxerant. Iberorum quoque gens, quae sub axe Pontico iacet, fidem Christi intelligunt a captiva muliere et credunt, Baccurio rege omnes ad id cohortante. Valuit etiam multum illis temporibus ad movendos[28] homines Antonii heremitae sanctissimi auctoritas, cui litteris et nuntiis Helena se ac filios saepius commendavit. Eius cibus solus panis

dedicated to the church, lest I be seen to err with the others.)
Some say that Sylvester established his *titulus* in the third region of
the city near Domitian's baths; certain people call it Equitius.
Constantine offered many gifts to this *titulus*: a silver paten weighing twenty pounds, sixteen bronze candlesticks, the Barbatianus
estate from the territory of Ferentinum, and the Sulpicianus estate
from the territory of Cora.[14]

So that the priests of the new Rome might share in his imperial   15
munificence, he likewise built two basilicas in Constantinople, one
of which was called Irene, the other of the Apostles. Before this,
the pagan temples were destroyed or converted for Christian use,
and the Delphic tripods were removed altogether, from which
infinite evils arose. Besides Constantine's gifts listed above was the
following: he distributed to the provincial churches and clergy a
certain tribute, which the cities usually paid him. He made the donation valid in perpetuity by the authority of his decree. So that
virgins and celibates might be permitted to make wills and to leave
something by testament to priests — it was owing to this, I believe,
that the Church's patrimony grew — he removed a law passed earlier for propagating offspring, which forbade those who had not
married by the age of twenty-five to claim an inheritance. The emperors invented this "right of three children," which they generally
assigned to friends with no offspring. Socrates and Sozomen in
their *Tripartite History* accurately describe these laws.

In Sylvester's time, there were many outstanding men whose in-   16
dustry and labor brought many peoples and countries to our faith,
and most of all the preaching of Julian, Frumentius, and Edisius,
whom certain Alexandrian philosophers had brought to that
point. The people called the Hiberes, who live near the Black Sea,
learned about the faith of Christ from a captive woman, and, with
the encouragement of their king Bacurius, they believed. At this
time people were much moved by the authority of the most holy
hermit Anthony; Helen often commended herself and her chil-

erat, aqua potus, nec unquam, nisi in occasu solis, comedebat; homo aegyptius omnino contemplationi deditus.[29] Huius quidem[30] vitam Athanasius Alexandrinae urbis episcopus insigni volumine perscripsit.

17   Sylvester autem, ubi ex sacris ordinibus septies mense decembri habitis presbyteros duos et quadraginta, diaconos sex et triginta, episcopos quinque et sexaginta creasset, moritur ac sepelitur in coemiterio Priscillae via Salaria tertio ab urbe miliario pridie Kalendas ianuarii. Sedit autem annos tres et viginti, menses decem, dies undecim. Vacat tum sedes dies quindecim.

: 35 :

Marcus I

1   Marcus, natione Romanus, patre Prisco, magni Constantini temporibus fuit, de quo varia scribunt historici. Sunt enim qui affirmant Constantinum ultimis imperii sui annis, instigante sorore, Arium ab exilio revocasse, quod invidia damnatum hominem mulier diceret, in eiusque dogma declinasse. Hos ego deceptos similitudine nominis puto et patri illud ascribere quod filii scelere factum est. Neque enim simile veri est principem illum sapientissimum, quod semper improbaverit, ea potissimum aetate qua sapere datur, illud idem collaudasse. Scribunt praeterea Constantinum ab Eusebio Nicomediae episcopo, Ariani dogmatis imitatore, baptizatum esse. Quod quidem falsum esse et religio principis ostendit et baptisterium huius rei causa Romae ab eo magnificentissimis operis aedificatum. A Sylvestro enim una cum Crispo filio[1] baptizatur, pulsis ab Urbe tyrannis,[2] fidemque edocetur. Aiunt qui aliter[3] sen-

dren to him by letter and messenger. Bread was his only food, and water his only drink, and he only ate at sunset. He was an Egyptian man wholly devoted to contemplation. Athanasius, the bishop of Alexandria, wrote about Anthony's life in a famous book.[15]

As for Sylvester, after ordaining forty-two priests, thirty-six 17 deacons, and sixty-five bishops in seven sacred December ordinations, he died, and was buried on December 31 in the cemetery of Priscilla at the third mile from the city on the Via Salaria. He was pope for twenty-three years, ten months, and eleven days. The see was then vacant for fifteen days.[16]

: 35 :

Mark I

[336]

Mark, a Roman and son of Priscus, lived in the time of 1 Constantine the Great.[1] Historians have given different accounts of Constantine. Some maintain that in the last years of his reign Constantine recalled Arius from exile and lapsed into his doctrine at the urging of his sister, since she used to say that the man had been condemned out of envy. I think that these historians were deceived by a similarity of names, and ascribed to the father the wicked deed of the son. For it is not probable that this wisest of emperors would approve of something that he had always condemned, especially at a time of life when one is given wisdom.[2] Furthermore, they write that Constantine was baptized by Eusebius, the bishop of Nicomedia and a follower of the Arian heresy. That this is false is demonstrated by the emperor's piety and the baptistry of magnificent construction which he built in Rome for that purpose. After he had expelled the usurpers from

tiunt Constantinum tantam rem distulisse, quoad ei ad Iordanem pervenire contingeret, in quo ad imitationem Salvatoris baptizari cupiebat. Verum dum in Parthos proficiscitur, Mesopotamiam incursionibus vastantes, primo et tricensimo imperii sui anno, aetatis vero sexto et sexagensimo apud Nicomediam villa[4] publica diem extremum obiisse, nec ad Iordanem baptismi causa pervenire potuisse atque illic tum demum extremo vitae tempore baptizatum fuisse.[5]

2   Misceant isti, ut volunt, rem hanc,[6] et nos, quod omnes ferme sentiunt,[7] credamus: Constantinum qui in signo crucis toties hostes vicerat, qui tot templa in honorem Dei aedificaverat, qui sacris conciliis interfuerat, qui toties cum sanctis patribus in mysteriis oraverat,[8] baptismatis caractere, ubi sapere coepit, muniri etiam contra hostem humani generis voluisse. Non latet me certe quid Socrates et Sozomenes in *Tripartita* sua velint quidque alii plerique; veritatem sequor,[9] optimi principis religioni et pietati convenientem. Quod vero in lepram inciderit, ut vulgo dicitur, baptismoque mundatus sit, conficta prius de sanguine infantum nescio qua fabula, nullo modo credo, Socratem hac in re secutus, qui affirmat Constantinum ipsum, ubi quintum et sexagesimum aetatis annum attigisset, aegritudine captum, ex urbe Constantinopoli ad aquas calidas egressum valetudinis causa, nulla de lepra mentione habita. Praeterea vero hac de re a nullo scriptorum fit mentio, non dico ab his qui ethnici sunt habiti, sed ne a nostris quidem. Non reticuisset hoc Orosius, non Eutropius, non illi qui Constantini res gestas quam diligentissime scripsere.[10] Ante vero tanti principis mortem stellam crinitam inusitatae magnitudinis, quam Graeci cometem appellant, fulsisse aliquandiu constat.

Rome, Constantine along with his son Crispus was baptized and thoroughly instructed in the faith by Sylvester.[3] Those who think differently say that Constantine deferred this important matter until he could get to the river Jordan, in which he desired to be baptized in imitation of the Savior. But while marching out against the Parthians, whose raids were devastating Mesopotamia, in the thirty-first year of his reign, at the age of 66, he met his end at the public villa of Nicodemia. He was unable to get to the river Jordan for his baptism, and so was baptized there on his deathbed.

But let them confuse the matter as they wish, and let us believe what almost everyone thinks, that Constantine, who so often conquered enemies in the sign of the Cross, who built so many churches for God's honor, who participated in holy councils, and who so often prayed with the holy fathers at the mysteries, would also, when he began to grow in wisdom, have wanted to fortify himself against the enemy of humanity with the imprint of baptism. I am certainly not unaware of what Socrates and Sozomen in the *Tripartita Historia* and many others believe, but I follow the truth, which is fitting to the religious devotion and piety of the best of emperors.[4] In no way do I believe the commonly-told story that he had contracted leprosy and was cured by baptism, or the fictitious story about the blood of infants. I follow Socrates in this matter, who maintains that when Constantine reached the age of sixty-five he fell ill and for health reasons left the city of Constantinople for the baths; there is no mention of leprosy. Besides, no mention is made of this by any writer; not even by our own [Christian] writers, to say nothing of the pagans. Orosius would not have been silent about this, nor Eutropius, nor those who wrote down as diligently as possible the deeds of Constantine.[5] It is well known that a crested star of unusual size, which the Greeks call a comet, blazed for some time before the death of this great emperor.[6]

3   Marcus autem Romanus pontifex ad curam Christianae religionis conversus, instituit ut episcopus Ostiensis, a quo Romanus consecratur, pallio uteretur. Voluit praeterea diebus solemnibus, statim post evangelium, symbolum a clero et populo magna voce decantari et eo modo quo fuerat in Nicaeno concilio declaratum. Duas item ecclesias Romae condidit, unam via Ardeatina, in qua sepultus est, alteram in urbe Roma ad Palatinas, quas quidem Constantinus his muneribus exornavit et auxit: fundo Rosarum cum omni agro campestri, patena argentea librarum viginti, scypho argenteo decem librarum, corona argentea librarum decem, fundo Antoniano, qui est via Claudia, fundo ad Bacchanas via Appia, fundo Marmoreo via Ardeatina. Huius autem et Constantini temporibus fuit Iuvencus Hispanus, presbyter genere nobilis, qui tetravangelia, hexametris versibus fere ad verbum transferens, quattuor libris composuit. Scripsit et quaedam eo genere metri ad sacramentorum ordinem pertinentia.

4   Marcus autem, posteaquam ex sacris ordinibus bis mense decembri habitis presbyteros quinque et viginti, diaconos sex, episcopos octo et viginti creasset, moritur ac sepelitur in coemeterio Balbinae via Ardeatina III Nonas octobris. Sedit autem annis duobus, mensibus octo, diebus viginti. Vacat tum sedes dies viginti.

The Roman pontiff Mark, however, turned his attention to the 3
care of the Christian religion, and decreed that the bishop of
Ostia, who consecrates the bishop of Rome, should wear the
pallium. Furthermore, he decided that on holy days, immediately
after the Gospel, the clergy and the people should sing aloud the
Creed in the manner prescribed by the Council of Nicaea. He
likewise built two churches in Rome, one on the Via Ardeatina, in
which he is buried, the other in the city of Rome by the Palatine.
Constantine embellished these churches with gifts and enlarged
them with the following: the estate of the Rosae along with all its
fields, a silver paten weighing twenty pounds, a silver goblet
weighing ten pounds, a silver crown weighing ten pounds; the
Antonian estate, which is on the Via Claudia; the estate at
Bacchanae on the Via Appia; and the Marmorean estate on the
Via Ardeatina. In Pope Mark's and Constantine's time lived
Juvencus, a Spanish priest of noble birth, who translated the four
Gospels almost verbatim into hexameter verse in four books. He
also wrote in the same meter certain things pertaining to the order
of the Sacraments.

As for Mark, after ordaining twenty-five priests, six deacons, 4
and twenty-eight bishops in two sacred December ordinations, he
died and was buried in the cemetery of Balbina on the Via
Ardeatina on October 5. He was pope for two years, eight
months, and twenty days. The see was then vacant for twenty
days.[7]

: 36 :

Iulius I

1   Iulius, natione Romanus, patre Rustico, temporibus Constantii fuit, qui cum Constantino et Constante fratribus imperium adeptus, annis quattuor et viginti imperavit. Habitus est etiam inter successores magni Constantini Dalmatius Caesar, fratris filius, adolescens sane praeclarae indolis, qui haud ita multo post tumultu militari opprimitur, sinente potius Constante quam iubente.

2   Interea vero Ariana haeresis invaluit, favente Constantio, qui nostros cogebat Arium recipere. Secundo itaque Constantii anno apud Laodiceam urbem Syriae vel, ut alii volunt, apud Tyrum concilium indicitur. Eo convenere catholici et Ariani; disputatur quotidie *homoousion* ne, an secus, Christum cum Patre vocarent. Instabat Athanasius Alexandrinus episcopus rationibus et argumentis, affirmans Filium Patri *homoousion* esse. Id, cum refellere Arius non posset, ad convicia versus, magicas artes Athanasio viro sanctissimo obiicit, prolato in loculis Arsenii brachio. Damnatur itaque violenter iubente Constantio Athanasius, qui quidem fugiens, sex continuis annis in lacu cisternae carentis aqua ita delituit, ut solem nunquam viderit. Indicante deinde ancilla quadam, cum in eo esset ut caperetur, Dei monitu ad Constantis partes confugit, qui fratrem Constantium minis certe[1] coegit Athanasium recipere. Arius interim episcoporum et populi frequentia stipatus, dum levandi ventris causa[2] ad publicum locum declinat, egerere

: 36 :

Julius I
[337–52]

Julius, a Roman and son of Rusticus, lived in the time of 1
Constantius.¹ Along with his brothers Constantine and Constans,
Constantius took control of the empire and ruled for twenty-four
years. Constantine the Great's nephew Dalmatius Caesar, a youth
of outstanding character, was considered one of his successors.
But not much later he was crushed in a military revolt, with
Constantius' permission if not at his command.²

Meanwhile the Arian heresy grew strong with the support of 2
Constantius, who forced good Christians to accept Arius. In the
second year of Constantius' reign, a council was convened at
Laodicea, a city in Syria, or, as some have it, in Tyre. Catholics
and Arians attended and debated daily whether or not to call
Christ consubstantial with the Father. Athanasius, the bishop of
Alexandria, took a stand with arguments and reasons, and asserted that the Son was consubstantial with the Father. When
Arius could not refute him, he turned to invectives and accused
Athanasius, a most holy man, of practicing the magical arts. The
arm of a man named Arsenius in a satchel was brought forth
as evidence. At Constantius' command, Athanasius was forcibly
condemned. He fled and hid in an empty cistern for six continu-
ous years, so that he never saw the sun. When a certain servant
girl betrayed him and he was about to be seized, by God's warning
he took refuge with the party of the emperor Constans, who
forced his brother Constantius with threats to receive Athanasius.
Meanwhile, Arius was being thronged by a crowd of bishops and
people until he turned into a public place to relieve his bowels.

conatus,[3] intestina omnia in cuniculum latrinae demisit, mortem certe passus vita turpissima condignam.

3   Iulius autem pontifex multis incommodis vexatus in tanta rerum perturbatione, tandem post menses decem Romam ab exilio rediit, audita praesertim Constantini morte, qui bellum fratri Constanti inferens, dum apud Aquileiam inconsulte dimicat, occiditur. Non destitit tamen Iulius orientales episcopos reprehendere, maxime vero Arianos, qui iniussu Romani pontificis Antiochiae concilium indixerant, cum id sine eius auctoritate fieri non posset, quod Romana ecclesia ceteris praeesset. Confutabant id orientales, non sine ironia, quod dicerent a se ad occidentem Christianae religionis principes commigrasse, hanc ob rem suam ecclesiam tamquam perennem fontem, unde tanta gratia manaverat, ceteris praeferendam.[4]

4   Constat autem Iulium ipsum, omissis his contentionibus,[5] duas aedificasse basilicas, unam[6] iuxta Forum Romanum, aliam in Transtiberina regione. Tria item coemeteria exstruxit: unum via Flaminea, aliud via Aurelia, tertium via Portuensi. Constituit praeterea ne sacerdos alibi quam apud iudicem ecclesiasticum causam diceret. Voluit item ut omnia ad ecclesiam pertinentia per notarios aut per primicirium notariorum conscriberentur — hos hodie, ut arbitror, protonotarios vocamus, quorum officium est res gestas praecipue conscribere. Verum nostra aetate adeo plerique, nolo dicere omnes, litterarum ignari sunt, ut vix sciant nomen suum latine exprimere, nedum aliorum res gestas perscribere. De moribus nolo dicere, cum e lenonum numero et parasitorum quidam in hunc ordinem relati sint.

5   Constantini autem et Constantii tempore in pretio fuit Marcellus Anticyranus episcopus, qui multa scripsit, maxime vero contra Arianos. Feruntur tamen contra hunc Asterii et Apollinarii libri,

When he tried to discharge his bowels, he released all of his intestines into the hole of the latrine. Thus Arius suffered a death worthy of his most wretched life.[3]

Amid such great upheaval, Pope Julius was distressed by many troubles, and after ten months he finally returned to Rome from exile, especially after he heard about Constantine's death. Constantine was slain while waging war on his brother Constans and unwisely fighting near Aquileia. Julius did not stop criticizing the eastern bishops, especially the Arians, who called a council in Antioch without the Roman pontiff's orders, since a council cannot take place without his authority, the Roman Church holding precedence over the other churches. The easterners turn this around, not without irony, saying that the leaders of the Christian religion migrated from themselves to the West, and that on this account their church, like a perennial fountain whence had flowed such great grace, should be placed before the rest.

Putting these contentions aside, it is known that Julius built two basilicas, one next to the Roman Forum, the other in Trastevere. He likewise constructed three cemeteries, the first on the Via Flaminia, the second on the Via Aurelia, and the third on the Via Portuensis. Furthermore, he decreed that no priest should plead a case except before an ecclesiastical judge. He likewise decided that all Church matters should be recorded by notaries or by the *primicerius notariorum* — I believe that today we call these protonotaries, whose duty it is to record deeds.[4] But in our time most, not to say all, are so ignorant of letters that they barely know how to write their own name in Latin, let alone record the deeds of others. I do not wish to discuss morals, since certain men have been brought into this order from the ranks of pimps and parasites.

Marcellus, the bishop of Ancyra, was held in esteem during the time of Constantine and Constantius. He wrote much, especially against the Arians. Asterius and Apollinarius wrote books against

eum Sabellianae haeresis arguentes; eiusdem quoque erroris eum
Hilarius arguere conatur, quem certe Marcellus refellens, se tamen
nequaquam cum Iulio et Athanasio sentire ostendit. Contra hunc
praeterea scripsit et Basilius Anquiranus episcopus librum unum
De virginitate. Nam Basilius Macedoniae partis una cum Eustasio
Sebasteno princeps fuit. Theodorus quoque, Heracleae Thracia-
rum episcopus, elegantis copiosaeque elocutionis vir, multa tum
scripsit, maxime vero commentarios in Mattheum, in Ioannem, in
Psalterium, in Apostolum.

6   Iulius vero, cum ex sacris ordinibus ter mense decembri in Urbe
habitis presbyteros duo de viginti, diaconos tres, episcopos novem
creasset, moritur ac sepelitur via Aurelia in coemeterio Calopodii,
ab urbe Roma miliario tertio, pridie Idus augusti. Sedit annos
quindecim, menses duos, dies sex. Vacat tum sedes dies quinque
et viginti.

: 37 :

Liberius I

1   Liberius, natione Romanus, patre Augusto, Constantii et Constantis temporibus fuit. Constantinus enim, ut ante dixi, dum
Constantem fratrem bello incautius persequitur, ab eius militibus
opprimitur. Constans autem varia fortuna contra Persas usus, cum
nocte intempesta seditione militum suscipere proelium cogeretur,
tandem vincitur. Verum postea, cum seditiosis militibus suscipere
poenas instituisset, Magnentii dolo ac fraude in oppido Helena interficitur, anno imperii sui decimo septimo, aetatis vero tricensimo. Mortuo autem Constante, rursum in Athanasium consur-

him and accused him of the Sabellian heresy. Hilarius also tried to accuse him of the same error. Marcellus certainly refuted this, but demonstrated that he in no way agreed with Julius and Athanasius. Basil, the bishop of Ancyra, also wrote one book *On Virginity* against him. For Basil along with Eustasius of Sebastia was a leader of the Macedonian party. Theodorus, bishop of Heraclea in Thrace and a man of elegant and copious eloquence, wrote much at that time, especially commentaries on Mathew, John, the Psalms, and Paul.

As for Julius, after ordaining eighteen priests, three deacons, 6 and nine bishops in three sacred December ordinations in Rome, he died and was buried on the Via Aurelia in the cemetery of Calepodius on the third mile from the city on August 12. He was pope for fifteen years, two months, and six days. The see was then vacant for twenty-five days.[5]

: 37 :

Liberius I
[352–66]

Liberius, a Roman and son of Augustus, lived in the time of 1 Constantius and Constans.[1] Constantine [the younger], as I said before, was crushed by his soldiers while recklessly fighting his brother Constans. Constans' campaign against the Persians was various in its fortune, and after a revolt of his soldiers in the dead of the night he was forced to join battle and at length was defeated. Later, after he had decided to punish the seditious soldiers, Constans was slain through the deception and fraud of Magnentius in the town of Helena in the seventeenth year of his reign and the thirtieth of his age. Now that Constans was dead,

gunt veteres illi Arianae haeresis suscitatores. Nam concilio apud Mediolanium habito, omnes qui Athanasio favebant in exilium pelluntur. Praeterea vero, cum in synodo Ariminensi orientales sacerdotes, callidi homines et acuti, occidentales simplices et imperitos argumentis ac fallaciis convincerent, praetermittere eam disputationem pro tempore satius visum est. Christum enim cum Patre *homoousion* esse negabant. Hoc autem, quia primum Liberius pontifex aperte impugnabat, quodque etiam damnare Athanasium iubente imperatore nolebat,[1] in exilium ab Arianis pellitur atque ita triennio ab Urbe abfuit.

2   At vero sacerdotes, congregata synodo, in Liberii locum Felicem presbyterum, virum optimum, pontificem crearunt, qui statim octo et quadraginta episcoporum conventu duos presbyteros, Ursatium et Valentem, ab ecclesia separavit, quod cum Constantio Augusto in fide sentirent. Hanc ob rem rogatu et precibus eorundem Constantius Liberium ab exilio revocat, qui imperatoris beneficio motus, cum haereticis in rebus omnibus, ut quidam volunt,[2] sentiens, illud tamen cum catholicis tenebat haereticos ad fidem redeuntes non esse rebaptizandos. Ferunt Liberium apud coemeterium Sanctae Agnetis aliquandiu habitasse cum Constantia Constantii sorore, quo eius rogatu et auxilio Urbem tutius ingrederetur, sed mulier catholica dolum inesse sentiens, id se facturam omnino recusavit. Tandem vero Constantius, instigantibus Ursatio et Valente, pulso Felice, Liberium introduxit. Unde persecutio ita vehemens exorta est ut in ecclesiis ipsis presbyteri et clerici passim necarentur. Sunt tamen qui scribant mulieres Romanas in circensi spectaculo reditum Liberii ab imperatore precibus impetrasse.[3] Pontifex[4] autem, tametsi cum Arianis sentiebat, ecclesias Dei quam diligenter exornavit, maxime autem sepulchrum beatae Agnetis et basilicam quam de nomine suo fecit apud macellum Lydiae.[5]

the old followers of the Arian heresy rose up against Athanasius again. For a council was held in Milan, and all of Athanasius' supporters were forced into exile. Furthermore, since at the synod of Rimini the clever and subtle Eastern priests used arguments and sophistries to refute the simple and inexperienced Westerners, it seemed better to postpone debate for a time. The Easterners were denying that Christ was consubstantial with God the Father.[2] Since Pope Liberius at first openly argued against this and did not want to condemn Athanasius, he was forced into exile at the emperor's command by the Arians, and was absent from the city for three years.

The clergy then assembled in synod and elected the priest Felix, 2 a very good man, to be pope in place of Liberius. In a congress of forty-eight bishops, Felix immediately excommunicated two priests, Ursatius and Valens, for agreeing with Constantius Augustus in faith. As a result, their pleading and prayers moved Constantius to recall Liberius from exile. Liberius was moved by the emperor's kindness and, although he agreed with the heretics in all things (as some maintain), he nevertheless held with the Catholics that heretics who returned to the faith should not be rebaptized. They say that Liberius lived in the cemetery of Saint Agnes for some time with Constantia, Constantius' sister, in order to enter the city more safely with her influential support and pleading; but this Catholic woman sensed there was deceit, and refused to do anything. Finally, at the urging of Ursatius and Valens, Felix was deposed, and Constantius recalled Liberius. From this such a violent persecution arose that many priests and clerics were killed in their own churches.[3] Some write that Roman women secured Liberius' return from the emperor by their prayers during a circus race. Although he agreed with the Arians, the pope diligently embellished God's churches, especially the tomb of Saint Agnes and the basilica that he named after himself in the Livian market.[4]

3   Fuit autem hac misera tempestate Eusebius Enisenus episcopus, qui multa contra Iudaeos, gentes et Novatianos docte admodum et eleganter scripsit. Eriphylus quoque, Cypri Letrensis sive Leucontae episcopus, in Cantica Canticorum copiose et accurate commentarios composuit. Praeterea vero[6] Donatus Afer, a quo Donatiani nomen sumpsere, multa in catholicos scribens, totam paene Africam et Iudaeam sua persuasione decepit. Affirmabat enim Patre minorem esse Filium et Spiritum Sanctum minorem Filio catholicosque rebaptizandos esse. Extabant autem Hieronymi tempore eius multa scripta ad haeresim pertinentia et *De Spiritu Sancto* liber, Arianae doctrinae conveniens. Et ne quicquam Arianae perfidiae tum deesset, Asterius, eius factionis philosophus, imperante[7] Constantio multa scripsit ad Romanos, in Evangelia, in Psalmos, quae ab hominibus suae haeresis[8] studiosissime leguntur.

4   Lucifer praeterea Caralitanus episcopus cum Pancratio et Hilario Romanis clericis[9] ad Constantium a Liberio missus, cum nollet sub nomine Athanasii Nicenam damnare fidem, relegatus, contra Constantium imperatorem scripsit librumque ei legendum misit; moritur tamen sub Valentiniano principe. Ferunt autem Fortunatianum Aquileiensem episcopum Liberium fidei causa in exilium pergentem, ut in haeresim et discordiam laberetur, sollicitasse. Serapion quoque, qui ob elegantiam ingenii Scholastici cognomen meruit, edidit tum adversum Manichaeum librum egregium, nec unquam Constantii minis a confessione veritatis destitit. Ad hominem enim profectus, quo eum pacationem[10] magno Athanasio redderet, minis tanti principis e gradu constantiae nunquam decidit. Ideo autem Athanasius magnus est habitus, quod paganis et haereticis constanti animo semper restitit.[11]

Eusebius, the bishop of Emissa, lived in this miserable time. 3
He wrote very learnedly and elegantly against the Jews, heathens,
and Novatians. Eriphylus, bishop of Letra or Leuconta in Cyprus,
also composed copious and accurate commentaries on the Song of
Solomon. Furthermore, the African Donatus (from whom the
Donatists take their name) wrote much against the Catholics, and
deceived almost all of Africa and Judaea with his persuasive powers. He asserted that the Son was less than the Father, and the
Holy Spirit was less than the Son, and that Catholics should be
rebaptized. Many of his heretical writings were extant in the time
of Jerome, including his book *On the Holy Spirit*, which agreed with
the Arian doctrine. So that Arian perfidy might not lack for
anything, a philosopher of that faction named Asterius, at
Constantius' behest, wrote many works to the Romans about the
Gospels and the Psalms which were most zealously read by the
followers of that heresy.

Liberius sent the bishop of Cagliari, Lucifer, along with the Ro- 4
man clerics Pancratius and Hilarius, to Constantius as an embassy; but he himself was banished, since he did not want to
condemn the Nicene Creed in the name of Athanasius. Lucifer
then wrote a book against the emperor and sent it to him to read.
He lived nevertheless until the time of emperor Valentinian. They
say that when Liberius was heading off to exile for his faith,
Fortunatus, the bishop of Aquileia, urged him to fall into heresy
and discord.[5] At that time Serapion, who earned the surname
Scholasticus for his elegant genius, also produced a distinguished
book against the Manichee, and never left the true faith despite
Constantius' threats. In fact, Serapion went to the emperor to
make him more amenable to Athanasius the Great, and never re-
treated from his constancy under the threats of this powerful emperor.[6] Thus is Athanasius held to be "the Great," because he
steadfastly opposed pagans and heretics.

5   Liberius vero,[12] ubi ex sacris ordinibus bis in urbe Roma habitis presbyteros duodeviginti, diaconos quinque, episcopos unum de viginti creasset, moritur ac sepelitur via Salaria in coemeterio Priscillae IX Kalendas maii. Sedit autem annos sex, menses tres, dies quattuor. Vacat sedes dies sex.

: 38 :

Felix II

1   Felix Secundus, natione Romanus, patre Anastasio, Constantii temporibus fuit, qui solus post interfectum a Magnentio Constantem imperio potitus est. Mox Iulianum patruelem suum, quippe qui ex Constantio patris Constantini fratre natus erat.[1] Caesarem creatum in Gallias seditione quorundam tyrannorum tumultuantes misit, qui brevi et Gallorum et Germanorum motus virtute sua compescuit, unde militum omnium consensu Augustus etiam[2] appellatur.[3] Quo audito Constantius, rebus Parthicis occupatus, ad bellum civile conversus, apoplexia[4] in itinere obiit inter Ciliciam Cappadociamque in Mopsocreni oppido, anno imperii quarto et vigensimo,[5] aetatis quinto et quadragesimo. Hoc autem morbo dixere medici hominem interiisse ob dolorem animi et gravem cogitationem, in quam rebellante Iuliano inciderat.[6] Ob eius autem moderationem (Christianorum causam semper excipio, in quam unice impius fuit) et comitatem inter divos more veterum referri meruit.

2   Nam post susceptum imperium Romam cum triumpho via Flaminea ingressus, aureo carpento cives obviam factos mira benignitate inspexit et veneratus est, dictitans illud Cyneae Pyrrhi legati

As for Liberius, after ordaining eighteen priests, five deacons, 5
and nineteen bishops in two sacred ordinations held in Rome, he
died and was buried on the Via Salaria in the cemetery of Priscilla
on April 23. He was pope for six years, three months, and four
days. The see was then vacant for six days.[7]

: 38 :

Felix II
[355–65]

Felix the Second, a Roman and son of Anastasius, lived in the 1
time of Constantius.[1] The latter gained sole control of the empire
after Constans was killed by Magnentius. Soon afterwards he
made Julian, his cousin on his father's side, Caesar and sent him
against the Gauls, who were in rebellion owing to the sedition of
some tyrants. In a short time Julian suppressed the revolts of the
Germans and the Gauls by his valor, so that his soldiers unanimously proclaimed him Augustus as well and made him emperor.
Constantius was occupied in Parthia and dealing with a civil war
when he heard of this. He died of apoplexy on the road between
Cilicia and Cappadocia in the town of Mopsocrene, in the twenty-
fourth year of his reign and the forty-fifth year of his life. The
doctors said that he died of this illness thanks to the mental an-
guish and grief that afflicted him when Julian rebelled. Because of
his moderation (except towards Christianity, against which he was
uniquely impious) and kindness, Constantius deserved to be reck-
oned among the gods according to the old custom.[2]

After coming to power, Constantius entered Rome in triumph 2
by the Via Flaminia, and with wonderful kindness gazed upon
and honored the citizens who had come out to meet his golden

verum esse, tot se videre reges in urbe Roma quot cives.[7] In una tamen re populum Romanum ad risum potius quam ad indignationem concitavit, quod portas urbis ingrediens, celsas et fastigiatas arcusque triumphales praealtos et latos homo parvae staturae caput incurvaret more anserum,[8] laesionem veritus. Is praeterea Campum Martium cum admiratione inspiciens, sepulchrum Augusti Caesaris, tot simulacris marmoreis et aeneis ornatum, Forum Romanum, Iovis Tarpeii delubra, thermas, porticus in provinciae modum auctas, amphitheatrum Tyburtino lapide exstructum tantae altitudinis, ut eo vix inspicere humanus oculus posset, Pantheon mira altitudine spatiosis molibus fornicatum, templum Pacis, Pompeii theatrum, Circum Maximum, Septisolium, tot arcus triumphales, tot aquaeductus, tot statuas per urbem ad ornatum positas, obstupuit ac tandem dixit naturam vires omnes in unam urbem effudisse. Stabat Traiani equus aeneus in atrio, cuius instar alterum sibi fieri Constantinopoli Constantius petebat ab Hormisda architecto, quem secum duxerat. Cui Hormisda: stabulum quoque tale condas oportet, si voles equum late succedere. Idem quoque Hormisda a Constantio interrogatus quid de urbe Roma sentiret, id tantum sibi placere respondit, quod didicisset ibi quoque homines mori, ut philosophum decebat locutus.

3   Felix autem, quem diximus in Liberii locum a catholicis subrogatum esse (licet id factum ab haereticis Eusebius et Hieronymus affirment, quod certe miror). Statim ubi pontificatum iniit, Constantium, magni Constantini filium, haereticum et secundo rebaptizatum promulgat ab Eusebio Nicomediensi episcopo in Aquilone villa, non longe a Nicomedia. Hinc autem deprehendi error potest, quo ducuntur nonnulli qui hanc haeresim magno Constantino ascribunt. Quod profecto, ut ex historia vides, in tantum

chariot. He repeated that Cineas, Pyrrhus' ambassador, spoke truly when he said: "I see as many kings in Rome as there are citizens."[3] Nevertheless, the emperor provoked the Romans to laughter rather than anger in one matter. When he entered the high and sloping gates of the city and the lofty wide triumphal arches, this man of small stature bent his head down like a goose for fear of hitting it. Constantius also viewed with wonder and astonishment the Campus Martius, the tomb of Augustus embellished with so many marble and bronze statues, the Roman Forum, the temple of Jupiter Capitolinus, the baths, the porticoes as big as a province, the amphitheatre built out of Tiburtine stone of such great height that the human eye could barely see it, the Pantheon with its spacious and wonderfully high vault, the temple of Peace, Pompey's theater, the Circus Maximus, the Septizodium, so many triumphal arches, so many aquaducts, and so many statues placed throughout the city for its ornamentation. After seeing all this, he finally said that nature had poured forth all her powers into this one city. Trajan's bronze horse stood in the atrium, and Constantius asked the architect Hormisda, whom he had brought with him, to make an exact copy of it for him in Constantinople. Hormisda replied, "You need to build a stable of like size if you want the horse to fit inside easily." Constantius asked Hormisda what he thought of Rome, and he answered that only one thing pleased him, that he had learned that there too men died — speaking as befits a philosopher.[4]

As we said, the Catholics elected Felix in place of Liberius (although Eusebius and Jerome say that heretics did it, which certainly makes me wonder). As soon as Felix began his pontificate, he proclaimed Constantius, the son of Constantine the Great, to be a heretic who had been rebaptized by Eusebius, bishop of Nicomedia, in a villa called Aquilo not far from Nicomedia. In this we may detect the error that led some to ascribe this heresy to Constantine the Great — a charge which, as you see from history, 3

principem tamque religionis Christianae amantissimum nec debuit cadere, nec potuit. Dum autem altercatio esset, et quidem magna, ut diximus, inter Liberium et Felicem, Ariana haeresis bifariam dividitur. Nam Eunomius (unde Eunomiani), vir corpore et animo leprosus, nec secus interius quam exterius morbo regio correptus, affirmabat in rebus omnibus et Filium dissimilem Patri et Sanctum Spiritum cum Patre et Filio nil habere commune. Macedonius autem, quem nostri ante errorem Constantinopolitanum episcopum fecerant, ab Arianis expellitur, quia Filium Patri similem fatebatur, licet Spiritum Sanctum non secus atque illi blasphemaret.

4   Aiunt quidem Felicem concilium octo et quadraginta episcoporum habuisse, in quo decernitur ut episcopi omnes aut ad concilium generale veniant aut litteris rationem reddant quare id facere nequeant, quod quidem institutum Carthaginiensi in concilio postea renovatum est. Huius autem temporibus fuit Achatius, quem, quia[9] luscus erat, *monophthalmon* vocarunt. Hic vero Caesariensis ecclesiae in Palaestina episcopus multa in Ecclesiasticen conscripsit tantaeque auctoritatis ob eloquentiam et versutiam[10] apud Constantium fuit, quemadmodum Hieronymus ait. Quod ego certe miror ut Romae in Liberii locum Felicem Arianum episcopum constitueret, quem profecto catholicum fuisse constat, ut scripsimus, et Arianos semper damnasse.

5   Felix[11] autem postremo, cum nulla in re orthodoxae fidei deesset, ab adversariis captus, una cum militia secum bene sentientibus interficitur sepeliturque in basilica quam ipse aedificavit[12] via Aurelia, secundo ab urbe Roma miliario, XII Kalendas decembris. Sedit autem tantummodo annum unum, menses quattuor, dies duos propter seditionem a Liberio motam, quem, Damasum secutus, licet immerito, inter pontifices numeravi.

neither should nor could fall upon so great an emperor and lover of the Christian faith. During this great altercation between Liberius and Felix, as we said, the Arian heresy split into two parts. For Eunomius (leader of the Eunomians) was a leprous man in body and mind, and was seized with jaundice both within and without. He asserted that the Son was different from the Father in all things, and that the Holy Spirit had nothing in common with either the Father or the Son. Macedonius, whom our Catholics made bishop of Constantinople before his heresy, was expelled by the Arians for affirming that the Son was similar to the Father, although he was no less blasphemous than they were on the subject of the Holy Spirit.[5]

They say that Felix held a council of forty-eight bishops, in which it was decided that all bishops had to attend general councils or supply in writing the reason why they were unable to attend; this decree was later renewed in the Council of Carthage. In his time lived Achatius, whom they called Monophthalmus since he had one eye. As bishop of the church of Caesarea in Palestine, he wrote much on Ecclesiastes, and on account of his eloquence and cleverness he enjoyed great authority with Constantius, as Jerome says. But for my part I wonder about [Jerome's report] that he appointed Felix, an Arian bishop, to replace Liberius in Rome, for it is surely evident that Felix was Catholic, as I have written, and that he always condemned the Arians. 4

In short, since Felix held fast to his orthodox faith, he was seized by his enemies and killed along with many orthodox believers. He was buried on November 20 in the basilica which he himself built on the Via Aurelia at the second mile from the city. Felix was pope for only one year, four months, and two days, on account of the sedition that Liberius raised. (Following Damasus, I have numbered Liberius among the pontiffs, though he doesn't deserve it.)[6] 5

⁚ 39 ⁚

Damasus I

1 Damasus, natione Hispanus, patre Antonio, Iuliani temporibus fuit, viri certe egregii si domi, si foris eius ingenium respicis. Nam et Eubolo sophista et Libanio philosopho praeceptoribus usus,[1] liberalibus disciplinis ita erat imbutus tum graece tum latine ut cuivis optimo principi comparari posset. Multae erat memoriae, ingentis facundiae, in amicos liberalis, provincialibus iustissimus, gloriae cupidus. Verum haec omnia ad extremum evertit, dum Christianos persequitur. Callidior tamen ceteris persecutor, non vi neque tormentis primo, sed praemiis, honoribus, blanditiis,[2] persuasionibus, maiorem fere populi partem, quam si atrocior fuisset, elicuit. Vetuit autem ne Christiani auctorum gentilium studia adirent, neve scholae, nisi his qui deos deasque venerarentur, paterent. Uni tamen Proheresio, viro doctissimo, concessum est ut Christianos publice doceret, quam gratiam ipse indignatus contempsit. Militare cingulum dari nisi gentilibus vetuit. Statuit praeterea procurationes provinciarum iurisque dictionem Christianis non debere permitti, quippe quibus lex ipsa Christiana proprio uti gladio vetat.

2 Athanasium tamen aperte oppugnat atque in exilium mittit, a magis, ab auguribus instigatus (quorum artibus maxime delectabatur), quod dicerent Athanasium obstare quo minus eorum artes in pretio essent. Cum Daphnius quoque in suburbano Antiochiae

: 39 :

Damasus I
[366–84]

Damasus, a Spaniard and son of Antonius, lived in the time of   1
Julian.[1] Julian was certainly a distinguished man if you consider
his abilities at home or abroad. He had Eubolus the sophist and
Libanius the philosopher as teachers, and was so imbued with the
liberal arts, both Greek and Latin, that he could be compared to
the best of emperors. He had a capacious memory and great eloquence. He was generous towards his friends, utterly just to
provincials, and desirous of glory. But he utterly destroyed all
these qualities when he persecuted the Christians. He was a craft-
ier persecutor than others had been. He coaxed them at first not
with violence or tortures, but with prizes, honors, flattery, and
persuasion. He lured a greater number of people than if he had
been more savage. Julian forbade Christians to study pagan authors, and the schools were open only to those who worshipped
the gods and goddesses. Only one man, the very learned
Proaeresius, was permitted to teach the Christians openly, but he
himself was indignant at this favor and disregarded it. Julian forbade all but pagans to gird a soldier's belt. Furthermore, he decreed that the administration and jurisdiction of provinces should
not be permitted to Christians, since Christian law itself forbade
the use of a sword.[2]

Emperor Julian openly opposed Athanasius and sent him into   2
exile at the instigation of his sorcerers and soothsayers (he especially delighted in their arts), since they blamed Athanasius for the
low esteem in which their arts were held. Once when he was
offering a sacrifice to Apollo at Daphne in the suburbs of Antioch

iuxta fontem Castalium litaret Apollini et nulla ex his quae quae-
rebantur responsa susciperet, causasque silentii percontaretur a
sacerdotibus, daemones aiunt sepulcrum Babyllae martyris prope
astare et ideo responsa non reddi. Tum Iulianus 'Galilaeis' imperat—hoc enim nomine Christianos appellabat—ut sepulcrum
martyris inde auferant. Qui, dum sepulcrum mira exultatione tra-
herent, dicentes 'Confundantur omnes qui adorant sculptilia et
qui gloriantur in simulacris suis,' ita iram Iuliani principis concita-
runt ut multos praeter institutum suum interfici iusserit. Miror
ego id a Iuliano factum, cum diaboli artes iam vanas esse cognos-
ceret. Semel enim magum quendam in speluncam secutus, cum
voces daemonum perhorresceret, signo crucis usus est, quo fugati
sunt daemones. Cum vero Iulianus diceret signo crucis aliquid vi-
rium inesse, respondit magus daemones etiam genus illud supplicii
formidare. Hanc ob rem Iulianus pertinacior quam antea factus
est, adeo vanitati magicae deditus erat, licet prius Christianam religionem simulato animo amplexus fuisset, ut Constantii odium
vitaret, legissetque publice divinos codices ac basilicam nomine
martyrum aedificasset.[3]

3   Praeterea vero idem imperator,[4] quo nostris stomachum faceret,
Iudaeis templum Hierosolymitanum restituit, cum dicerent se
alibi sacrificare non posse. Qui certe tanta arrogantia elati sunt ut
maiore impensa quam antea restituere templum conarentur. Verum non ita multo[5] post, terraemotu templum corruens et multos
Iudaeos simul oppressit, et illud approbatum est: lapidem supra lapidem poni non debere. Sequenti autem die incendio divinitus im-
misso et ferramenta ipsa consumpta sunt; et eo miraculo multi Iudaei perterriti, ad fidem Christi venere.

next to the Castalian fountain, Julian received no responses to his questions. He asked his priests the reason for the silence, and the demons said that the tomb of the martyr Babylas was too close and that this was the reason why no responses were given. Julian then commanded the "Galileans" (he called Christians by this name) to remove the tomb of their martyr from that place. While removing the tomb with wonderful and great rejoicing the Christians recited the Psalm: "Confounded be all they that serve graven images, that boast themselves of idols. Let all those who adore graven images and boast in their own likenesses be confounded."[3] This stirred such rage in Emperor Julian that he ordered the execution of many more than he had originally planned. I wonder that Julian did this, since he already recognized the vanity of the Devil's arts. Once he followed a certain sorcerer into a cave, and, after taking fright at demons' voices, used the sign of the cross, by which the demons were put to flight. When Julian said that there was power in the sign of the Cross, the sorcerer replied that demons fear even that kind of punishment. As a result, Julian became more stubborn than before, and utterly devoted to the vanity of magic, although in order to avoid Constantius' disfavor he had earlier falsely embraced the Christian religion, publicly read the Scriptures, and built a basilica in the name of the martyrs.[4]

In order to spite the Christians, the same emperor restored the temple of the Jews in Jerusalem, since they said that they could not sacrifice anywhere else. The Jews were filled with such great arrogance that they tried to restore the temple at a greater expense than before. Not much later, however, the temple collapsed in an earthquake and crushed many Jews; this proved the saying that stone should not be placed upon stone.[5] Fire was divinely sent down the following day, and the builders' tools were destroyed. Many Jews were terrified by this miracle and embraced the Christian faith.[6]

4   In Persas vero proficiscens Iulianus, quos intellexerat res novas
moliri, in reditu suo malam quidem rem Christianis minatur.
Cum autem superatis hostibus incomposito agmine[6] victor rediret,
apud Ctesiphontem confossus periit. A suis an[7] ab hostibus id factum sit, incertum est, quanquam sunt qui scribant sagitta ex incerto missa transfixum fuisse, eundemque exclamasse manu ad
coelum extensa: 'Vicisti Galileae, vicisti' — nam Christum 'Gali-
laeum' appellabat et fabri filium, unde illud adolescentis in Liba-
nium sophistam, interrogantem quid ageret fabri filius, 'Iuliano,'
inquit, 'locellum componit,' nam paulo post eius cadaver locello
avectus est.[8] Sunt etiam qui scribant hunc antea clericum fuisse ac
postea a fide nostra defecisse, unde hominem Apostatam vocant.
Periit autem post annum et octo imperii sui menses, anno vero aetatis secundo et tricensimo.

5   Huic deinde succedit Iovinianus, qui ab exercitu imperator electus, non prius profiteri imperatoris nomen voluit quam omnes
conclamarunt[9] se Christianos esse. Quibus collaudatis et imperium suscepit et exercitum e manibus barbarorum liberavit, Nisibi
ac magna Mesopotamiae parte Sapori regi Persarum relicta. Hic
autem octavo imperii sui mense cruditate stomachi sive tetro
odore prunarum moritur.

6   Damasus autem electus ad pontificatum obeundum, Ursicinum
diaconum competitorem habuit in basilica quae Sicinini appellatur, ubi multi utrinque cecidere in ipso templo, cum res non suf-
fragiis tantum, sed vi et armis tractaretur. Verum non ita multo
post, sacerdotum ac populi consensu Damasus[10] episcopus con-
firmatur, et Ursicinus[11] ad Neapolitanam ecclesiam traducitur. Damasus autem adulterii accusatus, publico concilio causam dixit;
ubi et innocens absolvitur et Concordius atque Calixtus diaconi,

When Julian set out against the Persians, having learned that   4
they were planning a revolt, he threatened the Christians with
misfortune upon his return. After he had vanquished the enemy,
and was returning as victor with his troops in disarray, he was
wounded and died at Ctesiphon. It is uncertain whether enemies
or his own men did it, although some write that he was shot with
an arrow from an unknown place, and that he stretched his hand
to the sky and called out: "You have won, O Galilean, you have
won!" He used to call Christ the Galilean and the carpenter's son,
which led to that famous response of a youth who had been asked
by the philosopher Libanius what the carpenter's son was doing.
He said: "He is building a coffin for Julian." Soon after this reply,
the emperor's cadaver was carried away in a coffin. Some write
that Julian had been a cleric and later left our faith, which is why
they call him the Apostate. He died after a reign of one year and
eight months, and in the thirty-second year of his life.[7]

Julian's successor was Jovinian, who was chosen emperor by the   5
army. But he did not accept the title of emperor until they all proclaimed themselves Christians. Jovinian commended their actions,
took control of the empire, and freed his army from the hands of
the barbarians by leaving Nisibis and most of Mesopotamia to
Shapur, king of the Persians. In the eighth month of his reign he
died from indigestion or the foul fumes of charcoal.[8]

Although Damasus was chosen for the pontificate, he had a ri-   6
val candidate called Ursicinus, who was deacon in the Basilica
Sicinini.[9] Many on both sides were killed in that very church,
since the matter was debated not only by votes but by force of
arms. Not much later, however, a consensus of clergy and the
people confirmed Damasus as bishop [of Rome], and Ursicinus
was transferred to the church of Naples. When Damasus was then
accused of adultery, he defended himself in a public council, where
he was proven innocent and his false accusers, the deacons
Concordius and Calixtus, were condemned and excommunicated.

falsi accusatores, damnati ac reiecti ab ecclesia sunt. Cautumque lege est ut deinceps poenam talionis subeant qui aliquem falso accusaverint.

7   Pacata tandem ecclesia, Damasus ocio litterario delectatus, vitas pontificum omnium qui ante se fuere conscripsit easque ad Hieronymum misit. Non destitit tamen et templa et cultum divinum augere. Duas enim basilicas aedificavit, unam iuxta Theatrum, alteram via Ardeatina ad catacumbas. Dedicavit et platoniam ubi corpora Petri et Pauli aliquando iacuerant. Versibus quoque elegantibus sanctorum corpora eo loci sepulta exornavit ad memoriam posteritatis. Praeterea vero basilicam quam ipse in honorem divi Laurentii non longe a theatro Pompeiano[12] condiderat, maximis muneribus ornavit: patena argentea[13] librarum viginti, ama argentea librarum quindecim, scypho argenteo anaglypho librarum decem, calicibus argenteis quinque, coronis argenteis quinque. Domos quoque circa basilicam[14] positas dono dedit, fundum etiam Papyrianum agri Ferentinatis, fundum Antonianum, balnea non longe a templo posita. Ut psalmi quoque alternis vicibus in ecclesia canerentur in fineque eorum verba haec ponerentur, 'Gloria Patri et Filio et Spiritui Sancto,' instituit. Primus etiam Hieronymi scriptis auctoritatem dedit, cum prius Septuaginta interpretum scripta tantummodo in pretio essent. Nam et Biblia Hieronymi legi coepta est et psalmi eiusdem fideliter ex hebraico traducti, cum antea apud Gallos potissimum incomposite legerentur. Mandavit item ut in principio celebrationis, quam Missam vocant, confessio diceretur, ut hodie fit.

8   Idem vero Damasus, ubi ex sacris ordinibus quinquies habitis presbyteros unum et triginta, diaconos undecim, episcopos duos et sexaginta creasset, moritur ac sepelitur via Ardeatina cum matre et sorore[15] in basilica a se condita III Idus decembris. Sedit annos unum de viginti, menses tres, dies undecim. Vacat tum sedes diem unum et viginti.

A law was passed that thereafter those who falsely accused someone would suffer a penalty like the one they had sought of the accused.

Once Church affairs were settled, Damasus delighted in literary 7
pastimes. He wrote the lives of all the popes who preceded him
and sent them to Jerome.[10] Nor did he fail to increase the number
of churches and to promote divine worship. He built two basilicas:
one next to Pompey's theater, the other at the catacombs on the
Via Ardeatina. He dedicated a tablet where the bodies of Peter
and Paul once lay. For posterity, he adorned the bodies of the
saints buried in that place with verses. He embellished with the
greatest gifts the basilica that he had built for St. Lawrence not far
from the theater of Pompey. The gifts were the following: a silver
paten weighing twenty pounds, a silver ewer weighing fifteen
pounds, a silver goblet decorated in relief weighing ten pounds,
five silver chalices, and five silver crowns. He also donated the
houses around the basilica, the Papirana estate near Ferentinum,
the Antonian estate, and the baths not far from the church.
Damasus decreed that the Psalms should be sung antiphonally
and followed by these words: "Glory be to the Father, to the Son,
and to the Holy Spirit." He was the first to give authority to
Jerome's translation of the Bible, since before only the Septuagint
was respected. People began to read Jerome's Bible and the Psalms,
which he faithfully translated from the Hebrew, whereas before
this they were read in a confused manner, especially in Gaul.
Damasus likewise decreed that confession should be heard at the
beginning of the celebration called the Mass, as we do today.[11]

After ordaining thirty-one priests, eleven deacons, and sixty- 8
two bishops in five sacred ordinations, Damasus died and was
buried on December 11 on the Via Ardeatina with his mother and
sister in the basilica that he built. He was pope for nineteen years,
three months, and eleven days. The see then vacant for
twenty-one days.[12]

: 40 :

Siricius I

1 Siricius, natione Romanus, patre Tyburtio, Valentiniani temporibus fuit, qui a Iuliano multa incommoda ob fidem Christi passus
pulsusque militia, cum scutatorum princeps esset. Mortuo autem[1]
Ioviniano,[2] militum omnium consensu imperator electus, Valentem fratrem in partem imperii accipiens, eidem Orientem assignat.
Postea vero imperii sui anno tertio Gratianum filium, necdum
bene puberem, socrus et uxoris hortatu Augustum creat. Proco-
pium[3] quidem[4] apud Constantinopolim res novas molientem cum
satellitibus suis mira celeritate opprimit. Sed Valens, ab Eudoxio
Ariani dogmatis episcopo baptizatus, in saevissimam haeresim de-
clinans, nostros persequitur et in exilium pellit, mortuo praesertim
Athanasio, quo vivente res Christiana sex et quadraginta annis[5]
mirifice sustentata est. Instabat Lucius haereticus hostilem in modum nostros persequens, neque illis quidem parcens qui in eremo
erant; eos enim immissis militibus aut trucidabat aut in exilium
mittebat.

2 Magnae auctoritatis tunc erant Antonii discipuli, Macharii[6]
duo in Syria, quorum alter in superiore, alter in inferiore habitabat
eremo. Isidorus quoque tum in pretio erat, Panucius, Pambos,
Moses, Beniamin, Paulus Apheliotes, Paulus Phocensis, Ioseph
qui mons Antonii dicebatur. Hos, cum exilio vexaret Lucius, mulier fanatica proclamat viros Dei in insulam Aegypti nequaquam
mittendos esse. Mannia quoque, Saracenorum gentis regina, cum
frequentibus proeliis Romanorum opes attrivisset, Palaestini et
Arabici limitis oppida vastans, orata pacem, non aliter repromittit

: 40 :

Siricius I
[384–99]

Siricius, a Roman and son of Tiburtius, lived in the time of 1
Valentinian.[1] Valentinian endured many hardships from Julian on
account of his Christian faith and was expelled from the military,
although he was head of the heavily-armed troops. When Jovinian
died, Valentinian was unanimously elected emperor by the soldiers. He shared the empire with his brother Valens and assigned
him the East. Later, in the third year of his reign, he appointed his
son Gratian as Caesar, who was still a boy, at the urging of his
mother-in-law and wife. With marvelous speed, he suppressed
Procopius along with his followers, who were planning a revolt in
Constantinople. Valens was baptized by the Arian bishop
Eudoxius and lapsed into that most savage heresy. He persecuted
the orthodox Christians and forced them into exile, especially after
Athanasius died, who had wonderfully sustained Christianity for
forty-six years. The heretic Lucius violently set upon the orthodox
and persecuted them, sparing not even the hermits. He sent out
soldiers who slaughtered them or drove them into exile.[2]

At that time two disciples of Anthony, the two Macarii in 2
Syria, had great authority; one lived in the upper desert and the
other in the lower desert. Also esteemed at this time were Isidore,
Panucius, Pambos, Moses, Benjamin, Paul Apheliotes, Paul of
Phoenicia, and Joseph who was called the "mountain of Anthony."
When Lucius was threatening them with exile, a certain inspired
woman proclaimed that these men of God should in no way be
sent into exile on an Egyptian island. When Mannia, queen of the
Saracens, was wearing down the Romans in frequent battles and
devastating the towns of the Palestinian and Arabian border, they

nisi Mosen, Christianum virum sanctissimum, genti suae episcopum designarent. Id agere Lucius conabatur, verum Moses incla-
mat: 'Arguunt te, o Luci, per metalla damnati Christiani, in insulas relegati et carcere inclusi; quare manus tuas ad me
consecrandum nunquam iniicies.' Revocatis itaque episcopis qui se
consecrarent, datur reginae praesul ac pax Romanis redditur. Saeviebat in Christianos Valens et Lucius, licet Themistii philosophi
litterae[7] Valentem aliquantulo mitiorem reddiderint.[8] Saeviebat et
Thanaricus[9] Gothorum rex, qui plurimos barbarorum martyrio
affecit.

3   Interim vero Valentinianus Saxones, gentem in Oceani littori-
bus positam, locis inviis, et Burgundiones virtute ac rei militaris
scientia oppressit. At vero dum Sarmatae sese per Pannonias effu-
dissent, bellumque in eos parat, subita sanguinis effusione apud
Brigionem oppidum moritur. Tum Gothi sedibus suis pulsi, per
omnes se Thracias effundunt, quibus dum Valens ire obviam cum
exercitu parat, revocatis prius, sed sero, ab exilio episcopis et monachis, quos etiam militare coegerat, proelio victus, igni exuritur.
Haec quidem clades Romani imperii ac totius Italiae exitium fuit.

4   Siricius autem, dum haec agerentur, censuit monachos, quorum
vita probata esset, posse sacris initiari a primis ordinibus usque ad
episcopatum. Censuit item ordines per intervalla dandos.[10] Manichaeos praeterea, qui in urbe erant, vetuit communicare cum fidelibus. Paenitentes autem et redeuntes ad gremium orthodoxae fidei
recipiendos esse censuit, si monasterium ingrederentur atque ibi
ieiuniis et orationibus se toto suae vitae tempore macerarent. Viaticum siquidem tum demum ab ecclesia recipiebant, ubi de optima
eorum vita constaret. Consecrari autem presbyterum ab episcopo

begged her for peace, but she promised it only if they would assign Moses the Christian, a most holy man, as bishop to her people. Lucius tried to do this, but Moses protested: "You stand accused, Lucius, by the Christians who have been condemned to the mines, banished to the islands, and imprisoned. You will never use your hands to consecrate me." Bishops were therefore recalled from exile to consecrate him; a bishop was given to the queen, and peace returned to the Romans.[3] Valens and Lucius continued to rage against the Christians, although the letters of Themistius the philosopher placated Valens somewhat. Athanaricus, king of the Goths, also ran amok and martyred numerous barbarians.

Meanwhile, Valentinian by his skill and military knowledge conquered the Saxons, a people living on the pathless shore of Ocean, and the Burgundians. While he was preparing war against the Sarmatians who had spread throughout the Hungaries, Valentinian died of a sudden effusion of blood in the town of Brigetio. Then the Goths, who had been expelled from their land, overran Thrace. Valens prepared to go out against them with his army, but first (but too late) recalled from exile the bishops and monks, whom he forced to enlist. He was defeated in battle and was burned in a fire. This disaster led to the ruin of the Roman empire and all Italy.[4]

While these things were taking place, Siricius decided that monks of proven morals could be admitted into the clergy from the first orders up to the episcopacy. He likewise decided that orders should be assigned at intervals. He forbade the Manicheans in the city to receive communion with the faithful. He decided that any who repented and returned to the orthodox faith should be received back into the Church provided they entered a monastery and passed their entire lives fasting and praying. If then their lives were shown to be pure, they would at length receive the viaticum from the Church. He decided that only a bishop should consecrate a priest. He decreed that anyone marrying a widow or a

tantum[11] censuit. Instituit item ut quicunque aut viduam aut secundam uxorem duxisset, ab officio ecclesiastico pelleretur.[12] Haereticos quoque per manus impositionem recipiendos censuit.

5   Huius temporibus Hilarius fuit, urbis Pictaviorum Aquitaniae episcopus, qui et contra Arianos duodecim libros scripsit et alterum contra Valentem et Ursatium, atque non ita multo post Pictaviis moritur. Victorinus autem, natione Afer, Romae tum primum rhetoricam docuit; postea vero in extrema senectute fidei nostrae se tradens, contra Arium libros more dialectico scripsit. Multa quoque composuit ad commendationem fidei nostrae Gregorius Lacticus Hilverti episcopus. Photinus autem Gallograecus, Marcelli Anticyrani episcopi discipulus, Hebionis haeresim instaurare tum conatus est. Hebion enim Christum, pio coitu Mariae natum, virum iustum putavit. Is quidem a Valentiniano imperatore pulsus, plura scripsit volumina ac praecipua contra gentes. At Didymus Alexandrinus, a teneris annis oculis captus et ob id etiam primarum litterarum ignarus, ita geometriam et dialecticam, quae magno usu indigent, iam grandis natu cum primis elementis didicit, ut praeclara quaedam opera in mathematicis scripserit, in Psalmos quoque et in Evangelium Matthaei ac Ioannis et contra Arianos multa edidit. Optatus quoque Afer, episcopus Milvetanus, libros sex contra Donatianos composuit. Severus autem Caecilius Hispanus, agnationem ab illo Severo ducens ad quem Lactantii duo extant epistolarum libri, volumen[13] composuit quod *Catastrophen* vocavit.

6   Siricius vero, compositis ecclesiae rebus ac creatis sex et viginti presbyteris, diaconis sedecim, episcopis duobus et triginta, ex sacris ordinibus quinquies habitis, moritur ac sepelitur in coemeterio Priscillae via Salaria VIII Kalendas martii. Sedit enim annos quindecim, menses undecim, dies quinque et viginti. Vacat tum sedes dies viginti.

second wife should be removed from ecclesiastical office. He decided that heretics should be received back by the laying on of hands.[5]

In his time lived Hilarius, the bishop of Poitiers in Aquitaine, who wrote twelve books against the Arians and another against Valens and Ursatius, and who died not much later in Poitiers. Victorinus the African at that time first taught rhetoric in Rome. He converted to Christianity in extreme old age, and wrote books against Arius in the dialectical manner. Gregory Lacticus, bishop of Elvira, also composed many books in praise of our faith. And at that time Photinus, a Galacian and follower of Marcellus, bishop of Ancyra, tried to revive the heresy of Ebion, who believed that Christ was a just man conceived in righteous intercourse by Mary. Exiled by emperor Valentinian, he wrote many volumes, especially against the heathens. Didymus of Alexandria, who was blind from an early age and therefore illiterate, in old age learned grammar as well as geometry and logic, which require much practice. He did this so well that he wrote outstanding works in mathematics and produced many on the Psalms, the Gospels of Matthew and John, and against the Arians. Optatus, the African bishop of Milevis, also composed six books against the Donatists. The Spaniard Severus Caecilius, who traced his lineage from the famous Severus — to whom Lactantius addressed two extant books of letters — composed a volume which he called *Catastrophe*.[6]

As for Siricius, after having settled Church affairs and ordained twenty-six priests, sixteen deacons, and thirty-two bishops in five sacred ordinations, he died and was buried in the cemetery of Priscilla on the Via Salaria on February 22. He was pope for fifteen years, eleven months, and twenty-five days. The see was then vacant for twenty days.[7]

: 41 :

Anastasius I

1 Anastasius, natione Romanus, patre Maximo, imperante Gratiano urbis Romae episcopus creatur. Nam Gratianus adolescens religione clarus, militia strenuus, apud Argentariam, oppidum Galliae, uno proelio ad triginta milia Alamannorum, fines Romanorum vastantes, cum minimo suorum incommodo interfecit. In Italiam deinde rediens, pulsa Ariana haeresi, totam provinciam ad veram Christi fidem redegit. At vero, cum instantibus Gothis rem publicam in magno discrimine videret, Theodosium, ex Hispania oriundum, virum clarissimum, socium ac imperii comitem sibi delegit, qui superatis Alanis, Hunnis et Gothis orientale imperium restituit, icto cum Athalarico rege Gothorum foedere; quo quidem mortuo ac Constantinopoli egregie sepulto, omnes eius milites Theodosium, virum optimum, secuti sunt. Interim vero Maximus, in Britannia tyrannidem occupans ac in Galliam traiiciens, apud Lugdunum Gratianum interfecit; quare Valentinianus, iunior[1] frater, metu perterritus ad Theodosium in Orientem confugit.

2 Sunt autem qui scribant hos quidem fratres in tantam calamitatem incidisse matris Iustinae crimine, quae Arianam haeresim fovens, Christianos persequebatur, maxime vero Ambrosium, quem etiam invitum populus Mediolanensis tum episcopum delegerat. Mortuo enim Auxentio, haereticorum episcopo, statim seditio Mediolani exorta est. Cum hanc itaque reprimere Ambrosius conaretur, qui tum consularis eiusdem provinciae fasces regebat, ecclesiamque ingressus, multa de concordia partium disseruisset, ab

: 41 :

Anastasius I

[399–401]

Anastasius, a Roman and son of Maximus, became the bishop of   1
Rome when Gratian was emperor.[1] The young Gratian was
known for his religious piety and skilled at war. At Argentaria, a
town in Gaul, he killed in a single battle with very few losses of
his own around 30,000 Alemanni, who were marauding in the
Roman borderlands. Then he returned to Italy, banished the
Arian heresy, and brought the entire province to the true Christian faith. When he saw the state in grave peril due to the approach of the Goths, he appointed Theodosius, a highly distinguished man from Spain, as his associate and partner in the
empire. Theodosius conquered the Alans, the Huns, and the
Goths. He restored the Eastern empire after striking a truce with
Athanaricus, king of the Goths. When the latter had died and
was buried in Constantinople with distinction, all his soldiers then
followed Theodosius, best of men. Meanwhile, Maximus seized
power unlawfully in Britain and crossed over into Gaul, where in
Lyons he killed Gratian, whose younger brother Valentinian was
struck with terror and fled to Theodosius in the East.[2]

Some write that the great misfortune suffered by these brothers   2
was caused by the offense of their mother Justina, who favored the
Arian heresy and persecuted the Christians, especially Ambrose,
whom the Milanese people had at that time chosen against his will
to be their bishop. For on the death of the heretics' bishop
Auxentius, a revolt immediately broke out in Milan. And when
Ambrose, the consul of the province at that time, tried to suppress
the revolt, entering the church and speaking at length about con-
cord among the parties, from everyone the cry went up that the

omnibus succlamatum est non alteri quam Ambrosio episcopatum committi debere. Quod etiam factum est; ex catechumino enim Christianus factus et sacris initiatus, Mediolanensis episcopus creatur. Cuius doctrina et sanctitas quanta fuerit, eius vita ac opera doctissime et elegantissime scripta ostendunt.

3   Tunc autem Anastasius, rei divinae cavens, constituit ne sacerdotes ullo modo sederent, sed curvi et venerabundi starent cum sacrum Evangelium aut caneretur aut legeretur in ecclesia Dei, neve peregrini, maxime autem transmaritimi, in clerum reciperentur, nisi quinque episcoporum prae se ferrent chirographa. Hoc autem factum esse aiunt propter Manichaeos, qui tum in Africa magno in pretio erant et ad corrumpendam fidem de suis quoquo versum mittebant. Constituit item ne debiles et manci neve aliquo membro carentes in numerum clericorum reciperentur. Basilicam quoque, quae Crescentina vocatur, in regione secunda via Mamertina dedicavit.

4   Huius et Damasi et Siricii tempora illustrarunt non modo optimi imperatores, Iovinianus, Valentinianus, Gratianus, Theodosius, verum etiam sanctissimi atque excellentes in quavis facultate doctores tum Graeci tum Latini. Gregorium nobis Christianis cum Basilio Cappadocia genuit, ut ait Eusebius, ambo fuere nobiles, ambo Athenis eruditi. Basilius enim Caesareae Cappadociae, quae prius Maza vocabatur, episcopus *Contra Eunomium* egregios libros edidit. Scripsit et volumen de Spiritu Sancto et monachorum instituta. Duos habuit fratres, Gregorium et Petrum, viros doctissimos. Gregorii extabant Eusebii temporibus aliqua volumina. At Gregorius Nazianzenus, qui Basilium ad monasterium perduxit, Hieronymi praeceptor, multa scripsit, maxime vero in laudem Cypriani, Athanasii, Maximi philosophi. Scripsit et *Contra Eunomium* libros duos, *Contra Iulianum imperatorem* librum unum. Laudavit et nuptias et virginitatem hexametro versu. Levavit et Constantinopolitanos ab haeresi rationibus et suo elegantissimo

bishopric should be given to no other than to Ambrose. That is what happened: from a catechumen, he was made into a Christian and a cleric, and appointed bishop of Milan. His life and most learned and elegant writings attest to his great learning and sanctity.[3]

Attending to Church matters, Anastasius decreed that, when 3 the holy Gospel is either being sung or read in church, priests should not be seated but should stand bowing in reverence. He also decreed that no pilgrims, especially from overseas, should be received as clergy unless they present the signatures of five bishops. They say that this was done because of the Manicheans, who were at that time greatly esteemed in Africa and were sending out some of their own to corrupt the faith. Anastasius likewise ordained that the infirm and crippled and those missing limbs should not be accepted into the clergy. He also dedicated a basilica called the Crescentina in the second region of the city on the Via Mamertina.[4]

In the time of Anastasius, Damasus, and Siricius, there flour- 4 ished not only the best emperors — Jovinian, Valentinian, Gratian, and Theodosius — but also the most holy and excellent Greek and Latin doctors in every field. As Eusebius writes, Cappadocia gave us Christians Gregory and Basil, both of whom were noblemen educated in Athens. Basil, the bishop of Caesarea in Cappadocia (formerly called Maza), published remarkable books *Against Eunomius*, and wrote a volume about the Holy Spirit and the orders of the monks. He had two brothers, Gregory and Peter, who were very learned men. Some volumes of Gregory were extant in the time of Eusebius. Gregory of Nazianzus, who led Basil to the monastery and taught Jerome, wrote many things, especially in praise of Cyprian, Athanasius, and Maximus, the philosopher. He also wrote two books *Against Eunomius* and one *Against the Emperor Julian*. He praised marriage and virginity in hexameter verse. By his arguments and most elegant manner of speaking (in which he

dicendi genere, in quo Polennonum,[2] virum eloquentissimum, secutus est. Is postremum, dum senex admodum esset, successorem sibi deligens, ruri vitam monachi duxit. Basilius autem sub Gratiano, hic vero sub Theodosio moritur. Epiphanius quoque, Cypri Salaminae episcopus, haereses omnes elegantissimis voluminibus impugnavit. Composuit tum etiam multa sermone Syro Ephren, Edessenae ecclesiae diaconus, qua ex re ad tantam venit dignitatem ut post lectionem Scripturae Sacrae publice in quibusdam ecclesiis eius scripta legerentur.

5   Anastasius autem, ubi ex sacris ordinationibus bis in Urbe mense decembri habitis presbyteros octo, diaconos quinque, episcopos decem creasset, moritur et sepelitur in coemeterio ad Ursum Pileatum V Kalendas maii. Annos vero tres, dies decem sedit. Vacat tum sedes dies unum et viginti.

: 42 :

Innocentius I

1   Innocentius, natione Albanus, patre Innocentio, particeps Theodosii temporum fuit, qui singulari celeritate et consilio usus, Maximum tyrannum, Gratiani interfectorem, apud Aquileiam occidit. Hanc calamitatem Maximo ipsi Martinus, vir sanctissimus, antea praedixerat, dum Britanniam militaribus copiis spoliat, in Italiam contra ius fasque venturus. Tunc enim a circio Scothi, ab aquilone Picti insulam vacuam militibus ingressi, longe ac late omnia vastarunt. Theodosius autem, divino auxilio fretus, et Andragatium Maximi comitem et Victorem eiusdem tyranni filium, Arbogastem

followed Polemon, a most eloquent man), Gregory freed the citizens of Constantinople of their heresy. When he was very old, he chose his successor, and led the life of a monk in the country. Basil died under Gratian, and Gregory under Theodosius. Also at this time Epiphanius, bishop of Salamis in Cyprus, battled all heresies in most elegant volumes. Ephraem, deacon of the church of Edessa, also composed many works in Syriac. On account of this, he achieved such great honor that in certain churches his writings were publicly read out loud after the reading of Holy Scripture.[5]

As for Anastasius, after ordaining eight priests, five deacons, and ten bishops in two sacred December ordinations in Rome, Anastasius died and was buried in the cemetery Ad Ursum Pileatum on April 27. He was pope for three years and ten days. The see was then vacant for twenty-one days.[6]

: 42 :

Innocent I
[401–17]

Innocent, born in Albano and son of Innocent, lived in the time of Theodosius.[1] With singular speed and strategy, Theodosius slew Maximus, the usurper and killer of Gratian, near Aquileia. The most holy Martin had predicted this disaster to Maximus himself while he was robbing Britain of its soldiers and planning to invade Italy against human and divine law. For Britain, empty of soldiers, was invaded from the northwest by the Scots and from the north by the Picts, who laid waste to it far and wide. Relying on divine help, Theodosius with amazing speed defeated Maximus' lieutenant Andragatius and his son Victor as well as the usurpers

et Eugenium tyrannos mira celeritate usus opprimit, unde merito Claudiani[1] poetae carmina in laudem Theodosii extant:

O nimium dilecte Deo, tibi militat aether,
Et coniurati veniunt ad classica venti.

2   Accedit Theodosio ad disciplinam militarem laus ingenii, qua plurimum valuit, et religionis. Nam cum[2] Mediolani ingredi ecclesiam vellet mysteria visurus, prohibitus ob quoddam facinus, ut fieri solet, ab ingressu ecclesiae nisi paeniteret, ita aequo animo id tulit, ut ultro ipsi Ambrosio gratias egerit atque paenituerit. Huius uxor Facilla fuit, ex qua Arcadium et Honorium suscepit. Iratus semel Theodosius quod Thessalonicenses in theatro militem occidissent vel, ut alii volunt, iudicem suum,[3] aegre retentus a sacerdotibus Italicis est, quo minus omnes[4] Thessalonicenses occideret. Qui postea ad se rediens, re cognita et lacrimis paenitentiam prope patrati sceleris egit et legem tulit ut sententiae principum super animadversione prolatae in tertium diem differrentur, quo misericordiae vel paenitentiae locus daretur. Ferunt principem ipsum, si quando ira percitus fuisset, hac deinceps cunctatione usum, ut notas omnes litterarum expresse recenseret, quo interim irae daretur locus. Affirmant quidam[5] principem ipsum familiaritate cuiusdam Ioannis monachi anachoritae in Thebaide usum, cuius consilio tum[6] bellum tum[7] pacem gerebat. Theodosius autem, quinquagesimum aetatis agens annum, Mediolani moritur.

3   Innocentius vero, tanta imperii tranquillitate et benignitate principis usus, multa ad religionem Christianam pertinentia meditatus est. Constituit enim ut sabbato ieiunium celebraretur, et quod tali die Christus in sepulchro iacuisset et quod eius discipuli ieiunassent. De Iudaeis quoque et paganis deque monachis regulas quasdam tulit. Cataphrygas autem haereticos, quorum auctores fuere Montanus, Prisca et Maximilla, ut ante dixi, ab Urbe expu-

Arbogastes and Eugene. The verses of the poet Claudian in praise
of Theodosius deservedly survive :

> O man especially beloved of God, heaven fights for you,
> and the winds conspire to come to your bugle-call.[2]

In addition to his military skill, Theodosius earned praise for   2
his great intelligence and his piety. When he wanted to enter a
church in Milan to view the divine rites, Ambrose forebade his entering without repenting of a certain misdeed, as is the custom.
Theodosius bore it so well that of his own accord he thanked
Ambrose and repented. His wife was Facilla, who bore him
Arcadius and Honorius. Once Theodosius was enraged at the
Thessalonians for killing a soldier in the theater or, as others believe, his own judge, and he was barely held back by Italian priests
from executing all the Thessalonians. Later he returned to himself, understood the matter, and with tears did penance for the
crime that he had almost committed. And he passed a law that the
decisions of rulers should be deferred for three days of review in
order to leave room for mercy or repentance. They say that the
ruler himself, whenever moved to anger, used to give himself
pause by reciting out loud all the letters of the alphabet, so that in
the meantime his anger might subside. Certain writers also affirm
that Theodosius enjoyed the friendship of a certain John, an anchorite monk in Egypt near Thebes, whose advice he followed in
war and peace. Theodosius died in Milan at the age of fifty.[3]

Having enjoyed great peace in the empire and the ruler's kind-   3
ness, Innocent devised many measures concerning the Christian
religion. He decreed that a fast should be observed on the Sabbath, because on that day Christ lay in the tomb and because
his disciples fasted. He also passed rules concerning Jews and pagans and concerning monks. With Theodosius' consent, Innocent
expelled the Cataphrygian heretics from Rome or forced them into
monasteries, as some maintain. (As I said earlier, Montanus,

lit, Theodosio annuente, vel in monasteria, ut alii volunt, relegavit. Praeterea vero Pelagium monachum et Celestinum haeresos damnavit, et quod liberum arbitrium divinae gratiae anteferrent et quod dicerent ad implenda divina iussa voluntatem per se sufficientem esse. Contra hos quoque multa scripsit Augustinus. Pelagius autem in Britanniam proficiscens, totam insulam errore suo infecit, adiuvante Iuliano, tanti mali comite et socio.[8]

4   Basilicam vero Gervasii et Protasii dedicavit, Vestinae mulieris impensa structam et ornatam, divenditis eius bonis ex testamento relictis iusto pretio. Templi dona haec fuere: patenae argenteae duae sexaginta librarum, coronae duodecim, cerostrata argentea quattuor. Ad ornatum baptisterii cervum obtulit quinque et viginti librarum fundentem aquam, vas chrismatis ex argento librarum quinque, scyphos duos argenteos anaglyphos viginti librarum. Dos autem templi erat domus ad basilicam Blinam,[9] balneum ad templum Mamuri, domus item in clivo Salutis balneatae, fundus in agro Clusino, alter fundus in agro Fundano. His addita domus Emeriti in clivo Mamertino, domus altera in vico Longo, balneum quoque in eodem vico. Curam vero et administrationem huius basilicae et sanctae Agnetis Leopardo ac Paulino presbyteris commisit.

5   Huius temporibus fuit Apollinaris,[10] Laodiceae Syriae episcopus, vir sane in disputando vehemens et ita acutus ut ausus sit dicere corpus, non animam,[11] a Domino in dispensatione susceptum. Postea vero, cum rationibus urgeretur, ait eum quidem habuisse animam, non tamen ex ea parte qua rationabilis est, sed ex ea solum qua corpus vivum reddit; ad supplementum vero rationabilis partis ipsum verbum Dei fuisse perhibeat. Quae quidem sententia et a Damaso antea et Petro Alexandrino episcopo explosa est. Hinc Apollinaristae originem habuere. Martianus autem, Barcilonae urbis episcopus, castitate et eloquentia insignis,

Prisca and Maximilla were the founders of that heresy.) Moreover, he condemned the heretics Pelagius, the monk, and Celestine for placing free will above divine grace and for saying that the will was sufficient on its own to fulfill the divine commandments. Augustine also wrote much against them. Pelagius went to Britain, where with the assistance of Julian, his companion and colleague in evil-doing, he infected the whole island with his heresy.[4]

Innocent consecrated the basilica of Gervasius and Protasius,   4 which was built and decorated at the expense of a woman named Vestina, who left her property in her will and sold it at a just price for the church. The gifts of the church were the following: two silver patens weighing sixty pounds, twelve crowns, and four silver candlesticks. To adorn the baptistry, he gave a stag pouring water weighing twenty-five pounds, a silver vessel with the oil for chrism weighing five pounds, and two silver embossed goblets weighing twenty pounds. A gift for the church was also a house near the Basilica Liviana, a bath by the temple of Mamurus, a house with a bath in the Clivus Salutis, an estate in the territory of Clusium, and an estate in the territory of Fundi. To these was added the house of Emeritus on the Clivus Mamertinus, another house in the Vicus Longus quarter, and a bath in the same Vicus. He entrusted the care and administration of this basilica and of Saint Agnes to the priests Leopardus and Paulinus.[5]

In his time lived Apollinaris, bishop of Laodicea in Syria. He   5 was powerful in debate and so keen-witted that he dared to say that the Lord took a body but not a soul at the Incarnation. Later, however, when pressed in argument, he admitted that He had a soul—not the rational part, only the part that gives the body life. He asserted that the Word itself of God supplied the rational part of the soul. Both Damasus and Peter, the bishop of Alexandria, condemned this idea, the source of the Apollinarian heresy. Martian, bishop of Barcelona, renowned for his chastity and eloquence, agreed wholly with the faith, and opposed the Novatian

bene cum fide sensit et Novatianos scriptis suis impugnavit. Cyrillus vero Hierosolymitanus[12] episcopus, saepe pulsus ecclesia et receptus, ad extremum sub Theodosio principe annis octo episcopatum tenuit multaque scripsit. Esicius item[13] apud Thespesium rhetorem cum Gregorio Nazianzeno episcopo adolescens Caesareae eruditus, plurimo labore Origenis et Pamphili corruptam bibliothecam membranis instaurare conatus est. Scripsit et ipse multa. Eodem quoque tempore Hieronymus presbyter, in Bethleem habitans, ingenio ac facundia sua Christi fidem mirum in modum auxit, quod etiam eius scripta declarant. Improbatur item[14] eo tempore in synodo Burdegalensi Prisciliani dogma, sumptum ex Gnosticorum et Manichaeorum haeresi, de qua superius diximus.

6   Innocentius vero, ubi per sacros ordines quater in Urbe habitos presbyteros triginta, diaconos duodecim, episcopos quattuor et quinquaginta creasset, moritur ac sepelitur in coemeterio ad Ursum Pileatum V Kalendas augusti. Sedit annis quindecim, mensibus duobus, diebus quinque et viginti. Vacat tum sedes dies duo et viginti.

∶ 43 ∶

Zozimus I

1   Zozimus, natione Graecus, patre Abrahamo, mortuo Theodosio, Arcadii et Honorii, qui patri in imperio successere, temporibus fuit. Ii quidem[1] gubernacula imperii suscipientes, paribus auspiciis illud rexere, divisis tantummodo administrationibus. Arcadius enim Orientem, Honorius vero Occidentem gubernabat, licet Theodosius filiis adhuc adolescentibus tres duces reliquerit qui

heresy with his writings. Cyril, bishop of Jerusalem, who had been often deposed and reinstated, finally held his bishopric for eight years under emperor Theodosius and wrote many works. Esicius, who as a youth along with Gregory of Nazianzus had been educated under Thespesius the rhetor in Caesarea, took great pains to restore on parchment the decaying library of Origen and Pamphilus. He also wrote much himself.[6] At the same time, the priest Jerome, living in Bethlehem, wonderfully increased the Christian faith by his genius and eloquence, as his writings also attest. In the contemporary synod of Bordeaux, Priscillian's teaching was condemned, for it derived from the Gnostic and Manichean heresies, about which we spoke above.[7]

As for Innocent, after ordaining thirty priests, twelve deacons,   6
and fifty-four bishops in four sacred ordinations in Rome, he died and was buried in the cemetery Ad Ursum Pileatum on July 28. He was pope for fifteen years, two months, and twenty-five days. The see was then vacant for twenty-two days.[8]

:   43   :

Zosimus I
[417–18]

Zosimus, a Greek and son of Abraham, lived in the time of   1
Arcadius and Honorius.[1] Arcadius and Honorius succeeded their father Theodosius in the empire. They took up the reins of power and ruled with equal authority, divided only in their administrative structures. Arcadius governed the East and Honorius the West. Yet in fact, while his sons were still young, Theodosius left

Romanum gubernarent imperium, Ruffinum qui[2] Orientem, Stiliconem qui Occidentem, Gildonem qui Africam regerent. Qui deinceps[3] cupiditate imperandi moti, spretis parvulis regnum occupare conati sunt. Gildoni res novas in Africa molienti Mascelger, frater eius, crudelitatem veritus, cum exercitu obviam factus, hominem fundit fugatque, qui vel dolore animi[4] vel veneno non ita multo post moritur. Idem quoque Mascelger, tanta victoria elatus, cum nec Deo nec hominibus parceret, a militibus occiditur. Ruffinus vero ab Arcadio opprimitur dum orientale imperium conatur invadere. Ingressus tum Italiam Radagasius, Gothorum rex immanissimus, ferro ac flamma omnia vastabat.

2   Verum Romani comparato exercitu barbarum in Faesulanis montibus opprimunt duce Stilicone. Huic vero successit Alaricus, quem Stilico, regni cupidus, cum superare posset, et fovit et iuvit. Verum postremo, cum Alaricus in Galliam proficiscens, concedente eo loci sedes ad incolendum Honorio, apud Pollentiam consedisset, Saulum, gente et religione Hebraeum, a Stilicone cum militibus immissum, quo foedus turbaretur, hostem sensit. Facile enim fuit, barbaros nil tale suspicantes et diem Paschae observantes, incautos[5] perturbare. Verum sequenti die sumptis armis et Saulum cum exercitu ad internecionem caedit et omissa Gallia in Stiliconem et Romanos movet. Quibus superatis urbem Romam post longam et gravem obsidionem capiunt anno eiusdem conditae millesimo ac centesimo et sexagesimo quarto, salutis vero Christianae anno duodecimo et quadringentesimo. Hac tamen moderatione Alaricus usus est et clementia ut suis mandaverit a caede et sanguine, quoad fieri poterat, abstinere utve confugientibus ad basilicas Petri ac Pauli parceretur. Rex vero tertia die ab urbe discedens (minus calamitatis quam putaretur perpessa; parum enim incendii senserat), in Lucanos et Bruttios proficiscitur, ubi apud Consentiam vi captam et direptam, moritur.

3   Cui statim omnium Gothorum consensu Athaulphus ob affinitatem et genus succedit, quem quidem ad urbem Romam cum

three generals to command the Roman Empire. Rufinus ruled the East, Stilicho the West, and Gildo Africa. Driven by lust to rule, they scorned the boys and tried to take control of the empire. When Gildo planned a rebellion in Africa, his brother Mascezel, fearing his cruelty, marched with his army against him, defeating and routing him. Gildo died shortly after, either through grief or poison. Puffed up with his victory, Mascezel spared neither God nor men and was slain by his soldiers. Rufinus tried to invade the Eastern empire and was killed by Arcadius. Then Radagasius, the most savage king of the Goths, entered Italy and laid everything waste with fire and sword.

Under the command of Stilicho, however, the Roman army 2 overwhelmed the barbarian in the hills of Fiesole. In his lust for power Stilicho supported and assisted Radagasius' successor Alaric when he could have conquered him. But at length when Alaric had gone into Gaul and settled in Pollentia (the place Honorius had granted him as a habitation), he discovered that Stilicho had sent Saul, a Jew by race and religion, with soldiers to break the truce. It would have been easy to throw the careless barbarians into disarray, as they suspected no such thing and were celebrating Easter. But the following day Alaric raised his soldiers, massacred Saul along with all of his army, left Gaul, and moved against Stilicho and the Romans. After overcoming them, they captured Rome after a long and difficult siege in the year 1164 since its founding and the year 412 of the Christian era. Yet Alaric was so moderate and merciful that he commanded his soldiers to avoid killing and bloodshed as far as possible, and he spared anyone who took refuge in the basilicas of Peter and Paul. On the third day the king left the city, which had suffered less damage than expected, since it suffered little from fires. Alaric went against the Lucani and the Bruttii and died after capturing and sacking Cosenza.[2]

With all the Goths in agreement, Alaric was succeeded by 3 Athaulf owing to his kinship and descent. When he returned to

exercitu redeuntem Galla Placidia, superioris Theodosii filia, eius
uxor, ita placavit ut a caedibus et rapinis temperatum et suis ma-
gistratibus urbs dimissa sit. In animo certe ei prius fuerat urbem
Romam delere ac novam condere eamque Gothiam appellare et
imperatoribus nomen de se relinquere, ut non Augusti deinceps,
sed Athaulphi vocarentur. Mentem hominis Placidia non modo a
tanto facinore avertit, verum etiam foedus inter Athaulphum, Honorium et Theodosium iuniorem composuit, Arcadii iam mortui
filium.

4   Zozimus autem in tanta rerum perturbatione rem divinam
numquam omisit. Constituit enim ut diaconi, dum celebraretur,
laevas tectas haberent linostimis. Concessit item ut in parochiis ce-
rei sancto sabbato benedici possent. Bibere[6] autem in publico clericis vetuit; in cellis fidelium id fieri posse non negavit. Vetuit etiam
ne servi in clerum reciperentur, quod huiuscemodi viros liberos et
integros esse oporteret. Asciscuntur nunc non modo servi et vulgo
concepti ac nati, verum etiam flagitiosi omnes ex flagitioso quoque
geniti, quorum sceleribus ecclesia Dei magnum aliquod incommo-
dum tandem capiet. Ferunt tum Zozimum misisse ad Carthagi-
niense concilium Faustinum episcopum duosque urbis Romae
presbyteros, ut ostenderet nil usquam publice agi debere sine
consensu ecclesiae Romanae.[7]

5   Huius autem pontificatu fuit Lucius, Arianae partis episcopus,
qui *Variarum hypotheseon* libellos scripsit. Diodorus quoque Tarsen-
sis episcopus, dum Antiochiae presbyter esset, multa tum scripsit,
Eusebii sententias, non autem eloquentiam, imitatus propter igno-
rationem saecularium litterarum. Scripsit et Tiberianus apologeticum ob suspicionem haereseos, quia cum Priscilliano accusabatur.
Evagrius praeterea, acris et ferventis ingenii, *Vitam beati Antonii* de
graeco Athanasii in sermonem nostrum transtulit. Scripsit et
Ambrosius Alexandrinus, auditor Didymi, in Apollinarem volu-

Rome with his army, his wife Galla Placidia (daughter of the elder Theodosius) placated him so that he restrained his soldiers from slaughter and plunder and left the city to its magistrates. Before this he had planned to destroy Rome and found a new city, calling it Gothia, and to name every future emperor after himself, so that hencefoth they would be called not Augusti but Athaulfi. Placidia not only turned his thoughts from so great a crime, but set up a league among Athaulf, Honorius, and the younger Theodosius (son of the late Arcadius).[3]

Amid these great disturbances, however, Zosimus never ne- 4 glected the Church. He decreed that, when Mass is said, deacons should cover their left arms with a *pallium* that is half wool and half linen. He likewise allowed candles to be blessed in parishes on Holy Saturday. He forbade clerics to drink in public houses, but allowed them to do so in the rooms of the faithful. He also forbade servants to become clerics, since such men had to be freeborn and upright. Nowadays, not only servants and bastards are admitted to the priesthood, but also all the disgraceful men born of disgraceful parents, from whose wicked deeds the Church of God in the end will experience some great misfortune. At this time Zosimus reportedly sent to the Council of Carthage the bishop Faustinus and two priests of the city of Rome, so that he might show that nothing should be publicly decided without the consensus of the Roman Church.[4]

During his pontificate lived Lucius, an Arian bishop who wrote 5 short works of *Miscellaneous Propositions*. Diodorus, the bishop of Tarsus, wrote much at that time while he was priest of Antioch. He imitated Eusebius' views but not his eloquence, owing to his ignorance of secular letters. Tiberianus also wrote a defense against the charge of heresy of which he and Priscillian were accused. Evagrius, a man of sharp and fervent intellect, translated Athanasius' *Life of the Blessed Antony* from Greek into our language. Ambrose of Alexandria, a student of Didymus, wrote an out-

men praeclarum. Fuere tum etiam in pretio Ioannes Constantinopolitanus et Theophilus Alexandrinus, illustres episcopi. Hunc
ego arbitror Ioannem Chrysostomum fuisse, qui ob elegantiam dicendi hoc cognomentum merito adeptus est quique Theodorum et
Maximum condiscipulos suos ad fidem Christi traduxit, relictis
praeceptoribus Libanio et Andragathio philosopho. Interrogatus
Libanius, iam morti propinquus, quem potissimum in schola successorem relinquere vellet, 'Non alium quam Chrysostomum,'
dixit, 'nisi hominem Christiani ad se traduxissent.'[8]

6   Perlata tum etiam sunt ad Zozimum synodalia decreta, quibus
confirmatis Pelagiana haeresis ubique damnatur. Sunt qui scribant
et Petronium Bononiensem episcopum, virum sanctissimum, et
Posidonium, Africae provinciae episcopum, magnam sanctitatis
opinionem de se tum[9] concitasse. Scripsit et multa contra haereses
Primasius ad Fortunatum episcopum. Sunt qui scribant Probam,
Adelphi proconsulis uxorem, centonas Virgilii in laudem Christi
tum composuisse. Hanc certe laudem quidam Eudochiae ascribunt, Theodosii iunioris uxori. Augustinus vero, beati Ambrosii in
fide discipulus, homo certe omnium qui tum fuere doctissimus,
Hippone in Africa episcopus, fidem nostram scriptis et disputatio-
nibus tum maxime tuebatur.

7   At Zozimus, creatis in urbe Roma presbyteris decem, diaconis
tribus, episcopis octo, moritur ac sepelitur via Tiburtina apud corpus beati Laurentii martyris VII Kalendas ianuarii. Sedit annum
unum, menses tres, dies duodecim. Vacat tum sedes dies undecim.

standing volume against Apollinaris.[5] At that time two famous bishops were also held in esteem: John, bishop of Constantinople, and Theophilus, bishop of Alexandria. I believe the former was John Chrysostom, who deservedly received his surname on account of the elegance of his style. He converted his fellow disciples Theodore and Maximus to Christianity, and they abandoned their teachers, Libanius and the philosopher Andragatius. Nearing death, Libanius was asked whom he wanted most to succeed him in his school. "No one else but Chrysostom," he said, "if the Christians had not converted him."[6]

At that time Zosimus received and approved the decrees of the 6 Council of Carthage, by which the Pelagian heresy was condemned everywhere. Some write that Petronius, a most holy man and the bishop of Bologna, and Posidonius, bishop of the African province, had gained a great reputation for sanctity at this time. Primasius also wrote much against heresies to bishop Fortunatus. Some write that Proba, wife of the proconsul Adelphus, composed Virgilian centos in praise of Christ. Others confidently ascribe this praise to Eudochia, the wife of Theodosius the younger. But the most learned man of all who lived at that time was Augustine. A disciple in the faith of St. Ambrose and bishop of Hippo in Africa, he greatly defended our faith in discourse and writing.[7]

As for Zosimus, after ordaining ten priests, three deacons, and 7 eight bishops, he died and was buried on the Via Tiburtina next to the body of St. Lawrence the martyr on December 26. He was pope for one year, three months, and twelve days. The see was then vacant for eleven days.[8]

∶ 44 ∶

Bonifacius I

1   Bonifacius, natione Romanus, patre Iucundo presbytero, Honorii
temporibus fuit. Orta quidem¹ tum in clero seditio est. Nam dum
Bonifacius in basilica Iulii urbis Romae episcopus creatur, Eulalius, in Constantiniana electus,² huic statim obiicitur. Quod ubi
Honorius, qui tum Mediolani erat, intellexisset, instante Placidia
cum filio Valentiniano, ambo ab Urbe pelluntur. Revocatur tamen
septimo mense post Bonifacius et solus urbis praesul constituitur.

2   Interea vero mortuo Athaulpho Gothorum rex Vallias decernitur, qui Dei iudicio perterritus, Placidiam apud se, tamen honeste,
habitam Honorio fratri reddidit, pacemque cum eo datis dilectissi-
mis³ obsidibus iniit.⁴ Idem fecere Alani, Vandali et Svevi. Placidiam vero Honorius Constantio, quem Caesarem declaraverat, in
matrimonium collocat, unde Constantius Valentinianum filium
suscepit; quae postea a fratre pulsa, ad Orientem cum filiis Honorio et Valentiniano proficiscitur.

3   Bonifacius autem pontifex tum constituit ne mulier ulla aut
monacha sacratam pallam attrectaret aut thura contingeret, neve
servus aut obnoxius vel obaeratus in clerum reciperetur. Condidit
praeterea oratorium in coemeterio sanctae Felicitatis martyris
eiusque sepulchrum ornavit marmoribus et argento. Nam et patenam argenteam dono dedit librarum viginti et scyphum argenteum
librarum decem et coronas argenteas tres, calices minores duos.

4   Huius quoque pontificatum insignem reddidere multi praeclari
viri, maxime vero Hieronymus presbyter, patre Eusebio, natus op-

: 44 :

Boniface I
[418–22]

Boniface, a Roman and son of the priest Jocundus, lived in the 1
time of Honorius. Dissension arose among the clergy at that time,
for Boniface was created bishop of Rome in the Julian basilica, but
Eulalius was elected in the Constantinian and immediately opposed him.[1] When Honorius learned of this in Milan, both were
expelled from the city at the instance of Placidia and her son
Valentinian. Six months later Boniface was recalled and made sole
bishop of the city.[2]

Meanwhile, Athaulf died, and Wallia was declared king of the 2
Goths. He was terrified of God's judgement and returned
Placidia, whom he had honorably kept, to her brother Honorius.
Wallia made peace with Honorius, and valuable hostages were ex-
changed. The Alans, Vandals, and Suevians did the same.
Honorius gave Placidia in marriage to Constantius, whom he
made Caesar. From this marriage, Constantius had a son named
Valentinian. Later, Placidia was banished by her brother and fled
to the East with her sons Honorius and Valentinian.[3]

Pope Boniface ordained that no woman, not even a nun, should 3
touch a consecrated altar cloth or handle incense; and that no
slave, no person under obligation, nor any debtor should be admitted to the clergy. He built an oratory in the cemetery of the martyr
St. Felicity and adorned her tomb with marble and silver. He gave
as gifts the following: a silver paten weighing twenty pounds, a silver goblet weighing ten pounds, three silver crowns, and two
smaller chalices.[4]

Many famous men gave distinction to Boniface's pontificate, es- 4
pecially the priest Jerome. He was the son of Eusebius, born in a

pido Stridonis, quod a Gothis eversum, Dalmatiae quondam Pannoniaeque in finibus fuit. Quantum iste iuverit ecclesiam Dei vita et scriptis non attinet dicere, cum et vita eius sanctissima omnibus praeluceat et scripta eius ita in pretio et in honore sint ut nemo magis legatur, ab eruditis praesertim. Moritur autem Hieronymus in Bethleem, aetatis suae anno nonagensimo, pridie Kalendas octobris. Laudatur et Gelasius, Caesareae Palaestinae post Eunomium episcopus, vir accurati elegantisque ingenii. Scripsit et historiam Dexter Patiani filius ad Hieronymum. Laudavit et Spiritum Sanctum Amphilotius eleganti stilo. Laudat et Sophronium Hieronymus, quod *De eversione Serapis* librum copiose ac docte scripserit.

5   Aiunt et Lucianum presbyterum Deo innuente[5] tum quidem reliquias Stephani protomartyris et Gamalielis, Pauli praeceptoris, invenisse deque ea re sermone Graeco ad omnes ecclesias scripsisse, quam scriptionem postea Abundius presbyter Hispanus Latinam fecit ad Orosium presbyterum. Sunt etiam qui[6] huic aetati addunt Ioannem Cassianum et Maximinum, viros doctissimos. De Eutropio autem, Augustini discipulo, non ita ambigitur, qui historiae Romanae epitomen fecit ab Urbe condita usque ad tempora sua, satis eleganti stilo et oratione. Scripsit ad duas sorores Christo dedicatas de pudicitia et amore religionis. Laudatur et Iuvenalis, qui tum Constantinopolitanus episcopus erat. Fuit etiam in pretio Haeros, vir sanctus ac beati Martini discipulus, Arelatensis episcopus iniuria[7] pulsus.

6   Bonifacius autem, ubi ex sacris ordinibus semel habitis presbyteros tredecim, diaconos tres, episcopos sex et triginta creasset, moritur ac via Salaria sepelitur apud corpus sanctae Felicitatis martyris VIII Kalendas novembris. Sedit annis tribus, mensibus octo, diebus septem. Mortuo Bonifacio, clerici quidam Eulalium statim ad urbem revocant, qui vel indignatione vel contemptu rerum humanarum revocationem spernens, anno post Bonifacium moritur. Vacat tum sedes dies novem.

town called Strido, formerly on the border of Dalmatia and Hungary, but destroyed by the Goths. It is not my concern to discuss how greatly he helped the Church by his life and writings, although his most holy life outshines everyone, and his writings are so honored and esteemed that no one is read more, especially by the learned. Jerome died in Bethlehem at the age of ninety on September 30. Also praised is Gelasius, who succeeded Eunomius as bishop of Caesarea in Palestine, a man of sharp and elegant intellect. Dexter, the son of Patian, wrote a history for Jerome. Amphilotius praised the Holy Spirit in elegant style. Jerome praised Sophronius for his learned and copiously written book *On the Overthrow of Serapis*.[5]

They say that at this time Lucian, a priest, with God's approval 5 discovered the remains of the protomartyr Stephen and those of Gamaliel, Paul's teacher, and that he wrote about it in Greek to all the churches. The Spanish priest Abundius later translated his account into Latin for the priest Orosius. Some also say that the most learned John Cassian and Maximin lived in this age. There is no doubt, however, concerning Eutropius, Augustine's disciple, who made an epitome of Roman history from its founding to his own time in a fairly elegant style. He also wrote about chastity and religious love to his two sisters, who were consecrated to Christ. Juvenal, who was bishop of Constantinople at that time, is also praised, as is Heros, a holy man and disciple of blessed Martin, the wrongfully deposed bishop of Arles.[6]

As for Boniface, after ordaining thirteen priests, three deacons, 6 and thirty-six bishops in one sacred ordination, he died and was buried on the Via Salaria near the body of the martyr St. Felicity on October 25. He was pope for three years, eight months, and seven days. When Boniface died, certain clerics immediately recalled Eulalius to the city. Either out of anger or contempt for the world, Eulalius spurned their recall, and died one year after Boniface. The see was then vacant for nine days.[7]

∴ 45 ∴

Celestinus I

1   Celestinus, natione Campanus, Theodosii iunioris temporibus fuit. Hic enim, mortuo Honorio principe clarissimo, Valentinianum, Placidiae amitae suae filium, Caesarem creatum ad regendum occidentale imperium mittit. Qui statim totius Italiae consensu imperator creatus, gubernacula imperii apud Ravennam suscipiens, hostes Romani nominis, maxime vero Ioannem tyrannum, mira felicitate in Italia compescuit. Interea vero Vandalorum, Alemannorum et Gothorum effera gens, ab Hispania in Africam Genserico rege traiiciens, provinciam ferro ac flamma depopulata, fidem quoque catholicam Ariana impietate foedavit, pulsis etiam in exilium quibusdam episcopis bene sentientibus; in qua perturbatione[1] beatus Augustinus Hipponensis episcopus[2] tertio obsidionis mense V Kalendas septembris moritur, septimo et septuagesimo aetatis anno.

2   Vandali autem capta Carthagine in Siciliam traiicientes, insulam depopulantur et vastant. Idem fecere Pictavi et Scoti, insulam Britanniam occupantes. Accitus autem a Britannis in auxilium Aëtius patricius, vir bellicis artibus insignis, non modo laborantibus auxilium non fert, verum etiam regnandi cupidus Hunnos ad invadendam Italiam sollicitat. Unde Britanni ab Aëtio destituti, ab Anglis auxilium[3] petiere, quos hostes deinceps,[4] non auxiliares sensere. Ab his enim oppressi et patriam simul et nomen amisere. Interim vero, Theodosio Constantinopoli[5] mortuo, septimo et vigesimo imperii sui ac patrui Honorii anno, Bleda et Attila fratres, Hunnorum reges, Illyricum ingressi, omnia incendunt et vastant.

∶ 45 ∶

Celestine I

[422–32]

Celestine, a Campanian, lived in the time of Theodosius the youn- 1
ger.¹ When the most noble emperor Honorius died, Theodosius
appointed Valentinian, the son of his aunt Placidia, as Caesar and
sent him to rule the empire in the East. Immediately after becom-
ing emperor by the consent of all Italy, Theodosius took up the
reins of power at Ravenna and with wonderful success halted the
enemies of Rome in Italy, especially the tyrant John. Meanwhile,
the savage Vandals, Alemanni, and Goths crossed into Africa from
Spain under their king Genseric. They ravaged that province with
fire and sword, and polluted the Catholic faith with the Arian heresy. They also exiled certain orthodox bishops. During this trou-
ble, the blessed Augustine, bishop of Hippo, died in the third
month of siege, on August 28, at the age of seventy-seven.²

After capturing Carthage, the Vandals crossed over into Sicily 2
and ravaged and devastated that island. The Picts and the Scots
did the same, and took over the island of Britain. The Britons
summoned for help Flavius Aëtius, a Roman patrician and distinguished commander, who not only did not help them, but in his
desire to rule urged the Huns to invade Italy. Abandoned by
Aëtius, the Britons then sought help from the Angles, whom they
soon realized to be enemies, not helpers, since they were attacked
by them and at the same time lost their country and their name.
Meanwhile, while Theodosius was dying in Constantinople in the
twenty-seventh year of his own reign and that of his uncle
Honorius, two kings of the Huns, the brothers Bleda and Attila,
invaded Illyricum and burnt and devastated everything.³

3   At Celestinus divino cultui intentus, constituit ut psalmi David
ante sacrificium antiphonatim ab omnibus canerentur, quod ante
fieri non consueverat; perlecta enim epistola et evangelio, finis sacrificio imponebatur. Refert Martinus Cassinas 'Iudica me, Deus,
et discerne causam meam,' quod in principio sacrificii dicitur, eius
inventum fuisse. Graduale quoque huic ascribitur. Multa praeterea
constituit de omni ecclesia quae tum in archivis legebantur. Dedicavit et basilicam Iuliam, cui etiam haec dona obtulit: patenam argenteam[6] librarum quinque et viginti, scyphos duos argenteos viginti librarum, aquamanulos argenteos viginti librarum, candelabra
argentea duo sextaginta librarum, cantharos, cerostrata aenea
quattuor et viginti[7] magni ponderis.

4   Nestorius autem Constantinopolitanus episcopus novum tum
errorem inducere conatus est. Praedicabat enim Christum ex Maria hominem tantum et non Deum natum eique[8] divinitatem col-
latam esse pro meritis, cui impietati et Cyrillus Alexandrinus episcopus et Celestinus pontifex mirum in modum adversati sunt.
Nam habita apud Ephesum synodo ducentorum episcoporum, impius Nestorius cum haeresi nominis sui cumque Pelagianis omnibus, qui dogma illud prope cognatum iuvabant, omnium consensu
tredecim canonibus eorum stultitiam impugnantibus damnantur.
Praeterea Germanum Antisiodorensem episcopum in Britanniam
mittit, qui deturbatis haereticis insulares ad catholicam fidem redi-
geret. Misit ad Scotos, Christi fidem optantes, Palladium, quem
ipse episcopum creaverat. Huius certe atque suorum opera magna
pars occidentis ad veram Christi fidem conversa est.

5   Ferunt hoc tempore diabolum, personam Moysi indutum, multos Iudaeos decepisse, dum eos ex Creta in terram promissionis ad
similitudinem historiae veteris sicco pede per mare deducere pollicetur. Multi enim ex his, falsum Moysem secuti, in undis periere.
Aiunt autem illos solos evasisse qui tum Christum verum esse
Deum credidere.

Intent on divine worship, Pope Celestine ordained that the   3
Psalms of David should be sung by all antiphonally before the Eucharist. This was not usually done before, for once the Epistle and
the Gospels were read, the Eucharist was concluded. Martin of
Cassino says that it was his [Celestine's] innovation to begin the
Mass by reciting [Psalm 43]: "Judge me, o God, and defend my
cause." The Gradual is also ascribed to him. He ordained many
other things concerning the whole Church, which used to be read
in the archives. He dedicated the Julian basilica and offered the
following gifts for it: a twenty-five pound silver paten, two twenty-
pound silver goblets, twenty-pound silver handbasins, two sixty-
pound silver candelabra, tankards, and twenty-four pound bronze
candlesticks.[4]

At this time Nestorius, the bishop of Constantinople, tried to   4
introduce a new heresy. He preached that Christ was only born as
a man from Mary and not as God, and that divinity was conferred on him for his merits. Cyril, the bishop of Alexandria, and
Pope Celestine strenuously opposed Nestor's impiety. At a synod
of two hundred bishops held in Ephesus, Nestorius was unanimously condemned along with his heresy and all the Pelagians,
who supported his heresy as being akin to their own. Thirteen
canons were leveled against their folly. Moreover, Celestine sent
Germanus, the bishop of Auxerre, to England in order to bring
the inhabitants back to orthodoxy from heresy. He made Palladius
a bishop and sent him to the Scots, who were eager to embrace
Christianity. Indeed, a large part of the West was converted to
Christianity because of the work of Celestine and his men.[5]

They say that at this time the devil took the human form of   5
Moses and deceived many Jews by promising to lead them out of
Crete to the promised land, walking over the sea with dry feet in
imitation of the old miracle. Many of them followed this false Moses and drowned in the waves. They say that only those escaped
who believed that Christ was the true God.

6   At Celestinus, ubi ex sacris ordinibus ter in Urbe mense decembri habitis presbyteros duos et triginta, diaconos duodecim, episcopos duos et sexaginta creasset, moritur ac sepelitur in coemeterio Priscillae via Salaria VIII Idus aprilis. Consederat annis octo, mensibus decem, diebus tribus de viginti. Vacat tum sedes dies unum et viginti.

: 46 :

Sixtus III

1   Sixtus Tertius, natione Romanus, patre Sixto, Valentiniani tempora attigit, qui occidentalis imperii gubernator pacem cum Genserico Vandalorum rege iniit ac certis finibus[1] Africam, sibi ac Genserico divisam, Vandalis incolendam dedit. Subornatus deinde Gensericus ab Arianis, eorum impietatem extollens, variis terroribus episcopos nostros persequitur. Interim vero, dum Valentinianus Constantinopolim proficiscitur et Theodosii filiam in uxorem ducit, Vandali Genserico duce Carthaginem iterum capiunt ac diripiunt anno quingentesimo et octogensimo quarto postea quam Romanorum esse coeperat.

2   Dum haec autem in Africa gererentur, Attila cum Bleda fratre, Hunnorum reges, non contenti occupasse Pannonias, Macedoniam, Mysiam, Achaiam et utrasque Thracias ferro ac flamma devastat Bledamque fratrem obtruncat, quo solus regno potiretur. Inde vero animos sumens ad occupandum occidentale imperium, copias undique celeriter colligit atque iter statim carpit. Quod ubi Aëtius intellexisset, legatos de pace statim Tolosam ad Theodoricum regem mittit, cum quo foedera ita sunt inita, ut communi impensa et paribus copiis bellum contra Attilam gereretur. Romano-

As for Celestine, after ordaining thirty-two priests, twelve dea- 6
cons, and sixty-two bishops in three sacred December ordinations
in Rome, he died and was buried in the cemetery of Priscilla on
the Via Salaria on April 6. He was pope for eight years, ten
months, and seventeen days. The see was then vacant for twenty-
one days.[6]

: 46 :

Sixtus III

[432–40]

Sixtus III, a Roman and son of Sixtus, lived in the time of 1
Valentinian.[1] As governor of the Western Empire, Valentinian
made peace with the Vandal king Genseric. By fixing boundaries,
he divided Africa with Genseric and gave the Vandals part of it to
inhabit. Having been corrupted by the Arians, Genseric praised
their heresy and persecuted our bishops with various acts of terror. Meanwhile, while Valentinian was on his way to Constantinople to marry the daughter of Theodosius, the Vandals under
Genseric took Carthage and sacked it for the second time in the
584 years since it had become a Roman province.[2]

While this was going on in Africa, the kings of the Huns, 2
Attila and his brother Bleda, were not content to have occupied
both Hungaries, but with sword and fire laid waste to Macedonia,
Mysia, Achaia, and both Thraces. Then, in order to gain sole
power, Attila killed his brother Bleda. Plotting to take over the
Western Empire, Attila quickly gathered reinforcements from
everywhere and immediately set out. When Aëtius learned of this,
he at once sent ambassadors of peace to King Theodoric at
Toulouse, with whom they made a pact to wage war against Attila

rum ac Theodorici auxiliares copiae fuere Alani, Burgundiones, Franci, Saxones atque omnes fere occidentales populi. Tandem vero, superveniente Attila in campis Catelaunicis, magno ardore animorum proelium utrinque committitur. Pugnatum erat aliquandiu atque acriter, cum vox superveniens incerto auctore certamini finem imposuit. Ad centum et octoginta milia hominum in eo proelio utrinque cecidisse constat, neutra inclinante acie aut cedente. Ferunt tamen Theodoricum, Thurismondi regis patrem, eo proelio cecidisse.

3 At Sixtus pontificatum iniens, a Basso quodam reus in iudicium accersitur. Hic autem, congregata septem et quinquaginta episcoporum synodo, ita causam dixit ut ab omnibus uno consensu absolveretur. Damnatur Bassus calumniator iniquus annuente Valentiniano et Placidia eius matre in exiliumque mittitur, ita tamen ut ultimo die viaticum ei ob pietatem ecclesiae non negaretur. Eius autem praedia non fisco sed ecclesiae ascribuntur. Aiunt Bassum post exilium non multum vixisse; tertio enim mense diem extremum obiit, cuius corpus Sixtus episcopus linteaminibus involutum et aromatibus conspersum propriis manibus ad Sanctum Petrum sepelivit in loculis parentum.

4 Aedificavit autem Sixtus basilicam beatae Mariae Virginis, quae ab antiquis Liberii cognominabatur iuxta macellum Libyae.[2] Accepit deinde nomen ad Praesepe; postremo vero Sancta Maria Maior vocata est. Sixtum autem huius templi auctorem fuisse titulus ipse[3] in frontispicio primi fornicis declarat his verbis: 'Xyxtus episcopus plebi Dei.' Per X enim in principio et Y scribitur graeca orthographia,[4] licet nostra aetas,[5] consuetudini serviens, Sixtum scribat per S et iota. Huic quoque[6] templo idem pontifex haec dona obtulit: altare argenteum purissimum tricentarum librarum, patenas argenteas tres centum et viginti librarum, scyphos argenteos quinque, calices decem, coronas argenteas octo et viginti, candelabra argentea tria, thymiamatarium librarum quindecim, fundum Scauri in agro Caietano, fundum Celeris, cervum argenteum

with shared expenses and equal forces. The auxiliary troops of the Romans and Theodoric were the Alani, the Burgundians, the Franks, the Saxons, and almost all the western peoples. Attila finally came upon them in the fields near Chalons and a high-spirited battle was joined on both sides. They fought long and bitterly until an anonymous cry put an end to the battle. It is well known that about 180,000 men on both sides died in that battle, neither side giving way or yielding. They say that Theodoric, father of king Thurismond, fell in that battle.[3]

At the beginning of his pontificate, Sixtus was summoned to court by a certain Bassus. But Sixtus defended himself in a synod of fifty-seven bishops so well that they all unanimously absolved him. Bassus, his unjust slanderer, was condemned with the consent of Valentinian and his mother Placidia and sent into exile, but Last Communion was not denied him on account of his piety to the church. His estate was given, not to the imperial treasury, but to the Church. They say that Bassus did not live long after his exile, but died within three months. Bishop Sixtus wrapped and embalmed his corpse with his own hands, and buried him among the tombs of his family in Saint Peter's.

Sixtus built the basilica of the blessed Virgin Mary, which the ancients called the Basilica of Liberius, close to the Livian market. Later it had the name of Mary at the Manger, and was finally called Santa Maria Maggiore. An inscription on the front of the first arch declares that Sixtus was the founder of this church, "Xystus Bishop to the People of God" — in Greek orthography X and Y are written at the beginning of the name, while our age writes Sixtus with an S and an I, in keeping with tradition. The same pontiff offered the following gifts to the church: an altar of the purest silver weighing three hundred pounds, three silver patens weighing 120 pounds, five silver goblets, ten chalices, twenty-eight silver crowns, three silver candelabra, a censer weighing fifteen pounds, the estate of Scaurus in Gaeta, the estate of

fundentem aquam in fontem baptisterii. Ornavit et ambonem ecclesiae porphyreticis lapidibus, quem nos suggestum appellamus, ubi Evangelium et Epistola canitur.[7]

5   Praeterea vero rogatu Sixti Valentinianus templa quaedam sanctorum mirifice excoluit. Nam et supra confessionem beati Petri auream Salvatoris imaginem gemmis aureis distinctam collocavit et fastigium argenteum basilicae Constantinianae, a barbaris sublatum, restituit. Ornavit et confessionem beati Petri ex argento.

6   Aiunt praeterea huius temporibus Petrum episcopum, natione Illyricum, aedificasse templum divae Sabinae in monte Aventino, non longe a monasterio Sancti Bonifacii, in quo divus Alexius iacet. Quod ego factum Celestini primi tempore crediderim, ut etiam carmina heroica indicant, quae adhuc leguntur his fere verbis:

Culmen apostolicum cum Caelestinus haberet,
primus et in toto fulgeret episcopus orbe,
haec, quae miraris, fundavit presbyter Urbis
Illyrica de gente Petrus, vir nomine tanto
dignus, ab exortu Christi nutritus in aula.
Pauperibus locuplex, sibi pauper, qui bona vitae
praesentis fugiens, meruit sperare futura.[8]

Sunt etiam qui scribant huius temporibus fuisse Eusebium Cremonensem et Philippum, Hieronymi discipulos, qui pleraque eleganti oratione scripsere. Laudatur et Eucherius Lugdunensis episcopus doctrina et dicendi copia. Non improbatur postremo Hilarius Arelatensis episcopus, vir sanctitate et doctrina ea tempestate insignis.

7   Sixtus autem, cum omnia quae habuerat aut in aedificiis et ornamentis ecclesiarum aut pauperibus erogasset, creatis presbyteris octo et viginti, diaconis viginti,[9] episcopis duobus et quinquaginta, moritur ac sepelitur in crypta viae Tiburtinae[10] apud corpus beati

Celer, and a silver stag pouring water for the baptismal font. He decorated with porphyry the church's pulpit, which we call the speaker's platform, where the Gospels and Letters are intoned.

At Sixtus' request, Valentinian also wonderfully adorned cer- 5
tain churches of the saints. Over the *confessio* or crypt of Saint Peter he placed a golden image of the Savior adorned with gold gems. He restored the silver gable of the Constantinian basilica, which the barbarians had destroyed. He also embellished the crypt of Saint Peter with silver.[4]

In Sixtus' time, they say, bishop Peter, an Illyrian by birth, built 6
the church of Santa Sabina on the Aventine hill not far from the monastery of Saint Boniface, where the holy Alexius is buried.[5] But I think this was done in the time of Celestine the First, as the following inscription in epic verse, which can still be read, indicates:

When Celestine held the apostolic summit and as first bishop shone over the entire city, a Roman priest from Illyria,
Peter, a man worthy of so great a name and nurtured from
his birth in the court of Christ, founded the things you are
admiring. Rich to the poor, poor to himself, he fled the
goods of this present life and deservedly hoped for good
things to come.

Some write that Jerome's disciples Eusebius of Cremona and Phillip, who were very elegant writers, lived in Sixtus' time. Eucherius, the bishop of Lyons, is also praised for his learning and eloquence. Hilary, the bishop of Arles, a man famed for his sanctity and learning at that time, is also not lacking in praise.[6]

As for Sixtus, after spending all that he had on building and 7
decorating churches and on the poor, and ordaining twenty-eight priests, twenty deacons, and fifty-two bishops, he died and was buried in a crypt on the Via Tiburtina near the body of St. Law-

Laurentii. Sedit autem annis octo, diebus uno de viginti. Vacat tum sedes dies duos et viginti.

: 47 :

Leo I

1   Leo, natione Thuscus, patre Quintiano, eo tempore fuit quo Attila a pugna Catelaunica rediens, in Pannonias, comparatis magnis copiis, Italiam hostili manu ingressus ac primo Aquileiam, in limitibus provinciae positam, triennio obsedit. Verum cum iam desperatis rebus in eo esset ut stativa moveret, vidissetque ciconias ex urbe in agros pullos suos[1] deferentes, auspicio motus, adhibitis machinis miseram civitatem acriter oppugnatam tandem capit, diripit et incendit, nec ulli generi hominum parcit, 'flagellum Dei' se vocitans. Inde Hunni, veluti ruptis claustris per totam Venetiam sese effundentes, urbes omnes occupant, Mediolanum ac Ticinum diripiunt. Iturus deinde Romam infestis signis, cum eo loci consedisset ubi Mincius Padum influit, amnem traiecturus, vir sanctissimus Leo pontifex, calamitatem Italiae et urbis Romae miseratus, adhortante etiam Valentiniano, ei fit obviam persuadetque Alarici exemplo, qui statim Dei iudicio post captam urbem mortuus est, ne ultra progrediatur. Monitis pontificis optimi obtemperans Attila, quod, dum simul loquerentur, cernere duos viros supra caput suum, strictos tenentes gladios ac mortem minitantes nisi pareret, visus est; ii Petrus et Paulus apostoli putati sunt. Inde mo-

rence. He was pope for eight years and nineteen days. The see was
then vacant for twenty-two days.[7]

: 47 :

Leo I

[440–61]

Leo, a Tuscan and son of Quintianus,[1] lived at the time when At-   1
tila, after returning from the battle of Chalons and obtaining reinforcements in Hungary, invaded Italy with a hostile army. Attila
first laid siege to the provincial border town of Aquileia for three
years. Having already given up hope, he was about to abandon his
camp when he saw storks carrying their young from the city to the
countryside. Moved by this omen, he advanced his siege engines
and at length captured, sacked, and burned the miserable and
fiercely contested city. He did not spare any human being, calling
himself the "scourge of God." After this, as if the gates had burst
open, the Huns poured through the Veneto, occupied all the cities, and destroyed Milan and the Ticino. Then on his march to
Rome, when he had set up camp at the place where the Mincio
flows into the Po and was about to cross the river, he was met by
Pope Leo, a most holy man, who with Valentinian's encouragement had taken pity on the disaster of Italy and Rome. Citing the
example of Alaric, who by God's judgement had died immediately
after taking the city, Pope Leo persuaded Attila to proceed no further. Attila obeyed the good pope's warnings, for as they were talk-
ing, he seemed to observe two men close above his head holding
swords and threatening death, if he did not obey. They were
thought to be the Apostles Peter and Paul. Attila then moved his

vens Pannonias repetit, ubi non ita multo post, effundente se ubertim propter ebrietatem e naribus sanguine, moritur.

2   Leo vero ad Urbem rediens, totus ad confirmandam catholicam fidem convertitur, quae tum potissimum a multis haereticis impugnabatur, maxime autem a Nestorianis et Eutychianis. Nestorius enim Constantinopolitanus episcopus Virginem non Dei sed hominis tantummodo genitricem dixit, ut aliam carnis, aliam divinitatis[2] personam faceret et seiunctim alterum esse Dei filium, alterum hominis ostenderet. Eutyches autem Constantinopolitanus abbas, ne sentire cum Nestorio videretur, divinam cum humana natura in idem compositum recidisse affirmabat unumque factum, nec uno modo inter se distingui debere. Hanc haeresim, cum Flavianus Constantinopolitanus episcopus damnasset, Theodosio annuente synodus Ephesina indicitur, in qua, Dioscoro Alexandrino episcopo praesidente, Eutyches restituitur, Flavianus vero damnatur. At Leo, mortuo Theodosio in eiusque locum suffecto Marciano principe catholico, concilium Chalcidonense indicit, in quo sexcentorum et triginta episcoporum auctoritate decernitur credendum duas naturas in Christo fuisse, utque unus idemque Christus Deus et homo crederetur, ac statim Nestorius et Eutyches, nefandus Manichaeorum praesul, damnarentur. Combusti etiam publice sunt Manichaeorum libri; calcata et depressa est Dioscori superbia atque haeresis.

3   Interim vero, mortuo a suis Valentiniano, Maximus tyrannus imperium occupat Eudoxamque, quondam Valentiniani uxorem, sibi violentis nuptiis adiungit. Hanc ob rem Vandali, ex Africa acciti, Genserico duce Romam hostili manu ingressi, Maximum, in illo tumultu ab Urso milite Romano occisum, in Tiberim proiiciunt, urbem diripiunt atque incendunt, templa et sacraria spoliant, nec Leonem pontificem exaudiunt clamantem ut urbi et tem-

camp and returned to Hungary, where not much later he died from blood gushing out of his nostrils after a drunken rout.[2]

Leo returned to the city and devoted himself entirely to 2 strengthening the Catholic faith, which at that time especially was being attacked by many heretics, and by the Nestorians and the Eutychians in particular. Nestorius, the bishop of Constantinople, said that the Virgin was the mother, not of God but only of a man, so that he imagined one person of flesh and another divine, and he made known that they were separate, one the son of God and the other a son of man. Eutyches, an abbot of Constantinople, wished to differ from Nestorius and asserted that the divine with the human nature descended into the same compound, were made one, and should never be separated. After Flavianus, the bishop of Constantinople, condemned this heresy, with Theodosius' approval a synod was called in Ephesus, presided over by Dioscorus, the bishop of Alexandria, in which Eutyches was restored and Flavianus condemned. After Theodosius died and the Catholic emperor Marcian was appointed in his place, Leo summoned the council of Chalcedon, in which by the authority of 630 bishops it was decreed as an article of faith that there were two natures in Christ, and that one and the same Christ is believed to be God and man. Both Nestorius and Eutyches, the wicked bishop of the Manichees, were also condemned. The books of the Manichees were publicly burned, and the arrogance and heresy of Dioscorus was stamped out and suppressed.[3]

Meanwhile, after Valentinian was killed by his soldiers, the 3 usurper Maximus seized power and forced Valentinian's widow Eudoxa to marry him. Because of this, the Vandals were summoned out of Africa and forcibly entered Rome under Genseric their leader. Maximus was killed in the fray by a Roman soldier named Ursus, and the Vandals threw him into the Tiber. They sacked and burned the city, stripped the churches and chapels, and did not heed Pope Leo, who cried out to them to take spoils wher-

plis parcentes praedam quo vellent abigerent. Abeuntes decimo quarto die post urbem captam atque Eudoxam cum filia et ingenti captivorum numero secum trahentes, in Africam revertuntur.

4   At Leo, ad reparandam urbem et templa conversus, Demetriam ancillam Dei impulit ut basilicam beato Stephano via Latina tertio ab Urbe miliario in fundo suo conderet. Ipse vero in honorem beati Cornelii episcopi basilicam via Appia aedificavit. Templa diffracta restituit, sacrorum vasa comminuta aut ablata vel denuo renovavit vel ex integro, quoad fieri potuit, restituit. Cameras praeterea tres condidit in tribus basilicis, Ioannis,[3] Petri ac Pauli. Sepulcris quoque apostolorum custodes addidit ex clero Romano; hos cubicularios appellavit. Praeterea vero monasterium prope[4] sanctum Petrum condidit constituitque ut intra actionem mysterii diceretur 'Hoc sanctum sacrificium,' et cetera, neve ulla monacha velamen capitis benedictum acciperet, nisi approbatum fuisset eam quadraginta annis caste et integre vixisse.

5   Dum autem his curis vir sanctus intentus esset, subito exorta est Acephalorum haeresis. Qui ideo Acephali vocati sunt, quia sine cerebro et sine auctore habebantur. Ii autem Chalcidonense concilium improbant, proprietatem duarum substantiarum in Christo negant, unam tantum in eiusdem persona naturam praedicantes. Quam quidem haeresim epistolis suis eleganter et docte ad Christi fideles scriptis acerrime confutavit.

6   Sunt qui scribant Paulinum, Nolanae urbis episcopum, Prosperum Aquitanum, virum doctum, Mamercum Viennensem episcopum in pretio tum fuisse. Primus enim Mamercus, ut aiunt, supplicationes, quas Graeci *litanias* vocant, instituit ob frequentes terraemotus qui tum maxime Gallias vexabant.

ever they wanted, but to spare the city and its churches. Fourteen days after capturing the city they left and returned to Africa, taking with them Eudoxa, her daughter, and a large number of captives.[4]

Turning now to the restoration of the city and the churches, 4 Leo urged the handmaid of God Demetria to build a basilica to Saint Stephen on her estate on the Via Latina three miles from the city. He himself constructed a basilica in honor of the bishop, St. Cornelius, on the Via Appia. He restored shattered churches and repaired broken sacred vessels, replacing stolen ones or restoring them anew insofar as he could. He also built three vaults in the three basilicas of John, Peter, and Paul. He appointed some Roman clerics as custodians of the tombs of the Apostles, calling them *cubicularii*. He constructed a monastery near Saint Peter's, and decreed that while celebrating Mass the priest should say: "This holy sacrifice," etc. He also decreed that no nun should receive the consecrated veil unless it were proven that she had lived chaste and inviolate for forty years.[5]

While this holy man was intent on these concerns, the her- 5 esy of the Acephali suddenly arose. They were called Acephali since they were held to be without brains and without a leading figure. They did not accept the council of Chalcedon and denied the property of two substances in Christ, preaching that there was only one nature in Christ's person. Leo refuted this heresy with great incisiveness in his elegant and learned epistles to the faithful.[6]

Some write that Paulinus, the bishop of Nola; Prosper, a 6 learned man of Aquitaine; and Mamercus, bishop of Vienne, were held in esteem at this time. They say that Mamercus was the first to appoint public days of prayer, which the Greek call "litanies," on account of the frequent earthquakes which were greatly troubling Gaul at that time.[7]

7   Leo postremo creatis ex institutione sacrorum octoginta et uno presbyteris, diaconis triginta et uno, episcopis sex et octoginta, moritur ac sepelitur apud Sanctum Petrum in Vaticano IV Idus aprilis. Sedit annis uno et viginti, mense uno, diebus tredecim. Vacat tum sedes dies septem.

Finally, after ordaining eighty-one priests, thirty-one deacons, 7
and eighty-six bishops, Leo died and was buried next to Saint Peter in the Vatican on April 10. He was pope for twenty-one years,
one month, and thirteen days. The see was then vacant for seven
days.[8]

Note on the Text and Translation

ক৾৲৵

The Latin text in this volume is based principally on Giacinto Gaida's 1913 Latin edition, prepared for the distinguished series "Rerum italicarum scriptores." Gaida based his text on two manuscripts, Vatican City, Biblioteca Apostolica Vaticana, Vat. lat. 2044 (the dedication copy with autograph notes and corrections), and Rome, Biblioteca Angelica MS. 222 (another manuscript whose production was supervised by Platina and which contains marginal corrections in his hand), as well as on the first printed edition (Venice 1479), which Platina himself saw through the press. He also recorded readings found in two later printed editions: the edition of Eucario Cervicorno (Cologne, 1540) and Onofrio Panvinio's revised edition (Venice, 1562).[1] The present edition does not include the variant readings in these manuscripts and early editions since this information is readily available in Gaida's critical edition. I am grateful to Prof. Massimo Miglio and the Istituto Storico Italiano per il Medio Evo (Rome) for permission to make use of this text.

Gaida's numbering of the *Lives*, not found in the original Latin text, has been preserved to facilitate citation, but his punctuation and orthography (which sometimes but not consistently reflect that found in the manuscripts and early editions) have been modernized. The dates of each pope's reign have been supplied from *The Oxford Dictionary of the Popes*, ed. J. N. D. Kelly (Oxford, 1986). The notes are indebted to those in Gaida's edition, though they have been verified, updated and in some cases supplemented.

The most important discovery relevant to constituting the Latin text since Gaida's time was made by Piero Scapecchi, who identified in the Biblioteca Nazionale Centrale of Florence the manuscript (Conv. soppr. C 4 797) used as a printer's dummy for the first edition. This manuscript contains numerous marginal corrections in Platina's own hand.[2] This manuscript has been collated for the present edition and its variants (*F*) and Platina's revisions (*Fp*) have been recorded in the apparatus. In a

number of cases the text *ante correctionem* represents an earlier stage of the text than is attested in either the *editio princeps* or the two manuscripts used by Gaida, and affords insight into Platina's process of revision. The revisions disclose Platina's great concern for style, for correct names and titles, and for accurate historical information; they also reveal from time to time the theological and political pressures under which he worked. Platina made many adjustments to the rubricated *notabilia* and to the punctuation, which have not been recorded, and his minor adjustments to the spelling, transpositions of words and other banal corrections have generally been passed over in silence. Platina often gives proper names and adjectives in incorrect or inconsistent forms; these have generally been left unchanged in the Latin text but corrected in the translation.

The only translation in English of the *Lives* was published by Paul Rycaut in 1685, which was reprinted in the nineteenth century in a bowdlerized form.[3] The antiquated English in this translation is at best quaint, but often inaccurate and confusing, and significant details are frequently omitted, so much so as to suggest that the translator may have used an abridged text. The translation, for example, does not include Platina's preface, the entire lives of Christ and of Sixtus IV, and the lengthy detailed donation lists for each church. In the present translation, I have tried to remain as faithful to the Latin as is consistent with readable modern English. Platina tends to pile participle upon participle in extended periods which do not find their way easily into the ear of the modern reader; hence longer Latin sentences have often been broken up into two or more English sentences.

SIGLA

F	Florence, Biblioteca Nazionale Centrale, MS Conv. soppr. C 4 797
Fp	Platina's hand in *F*
Gaida	Gaida's RIS edition of 1913
[ ]	deleted
< >	added by editor

s.s.	superscript
in marg.	written in the margin
om.	omitted

NOTES

1. Gaida, XCVIII-XCIX.

2. Scapecchi, "Un nuovo codice."

3. The 1685 edition is available on Early English Books Online (EEBO). The second edition of this translation was published as *The Lives of the Popes from the Time of Our Saviour Jesus Christ to the Death of Paul II*, edited by William Benham (see Bibliography). Benham, xii, without further specification writes in the preface: "One passage only has been omitted, as containing matter coarser than meets our present ideas of good taste. It does not bear on the history at all."

Notes to the Text

1. *om.* F

2. *om.* F

3. ac aliis *om.* F

4. humanitatem *before correction in* F

5. arbitrantur *F*

LIFE OF CHRIST

1. Platynae historici liber de vita christi ac pontificum omnium qui hactenus ducenti et XXII fuere *Fp, correcting a previous title, also in Platina's hand, subsequently cancelled:* Platynae [historici *s.s.*] liber de vita christi ac pontificum omnium qui [hactenus *s.s.*] CCC et XXIIII fuere usque ad Sixtum IIII fuere [*sic*]

2. Et Iudeorum . . . notam *added in marg.* Fp

3. affinitatis *before correction by* Fp

4. Sebastias vel *added s.s.* Fp

5. relinquisse *before correction by* Fp

6. autem *before* puer *deleted* Fp

7. Cyrinum virum consularem] Quirinum *before correction by* Fp

8. Simeon vir iustus] vir iustus Symon *before correction by* Fp

9. unctus *added in marg.* Fp

10. primogeniorum F

11. viri optimi *added in marg.* Fp

12. Patitur *before correction by* Fp

13. trigesimo tertio F

14. etiam . . . distet *added in marg. Fp*

15. sceleris *added in marg. Fp*

I. PETER

1. e medio sublatus est] moritur *before correction by Fp*

2. homine] eo *before correction by Fp*

3. *See Suetonius, Caligula §9:* Caligulae cognomen castrensi ioco traxit *and Notes to the Translation ad loc.*

4. vero *after* Praeterea F

5. quod [fratrem *canc.*] Herodem accusaverat *added in marg. Fp*

6. ipsum autem ... relegat *added in marg. Fp*

7. Postremo autem *added in marg. Fp*

8. videlicet *after* senatorii *cancelled Fp*

9. non *corrected to* vix *s.s. Fp*

10. genus *added after* humanum *in marg. Fp*

11. alibi *before* Tu *cancelled Fp*

12. se *after* quidam *cancelled Fp*

13. *Fp corrected* immixto *to* illitis *in marg.*

14. *Fp corrected* decanis *to* diaconis *in marg.*

15. posse *added in marg. Fp*

16. ante *F*

17. autem *added in marg. Fp*

18. *Fp corrected* Eius *to* Cuius *in marg.*

19. *Fp cancelled* unus ex septuaginta apostolis *after* dicebatur

20. Plutarcho concaptivo comitante *added in marg. Fp*

21. *Fp corrected* ad septem ecclesias *to* ac quattuor *in marg.*

22. ad Colossenses una *added in marg. Fp*

23. habetur *before correction by Fp;* olim *added in marg. Fp*

24. *Fp corrected* Sunt *to* Erant etiam *in marg.*

25. lapidem *added in marg. Fp*

26. vero *om. F*

27. autem *added in marg. Fp*

28. Callicula *Gaida*

2. LINUS I

1. anno *added in marg. Fp*

2. *Fp cancelled* videlicet *after* pervenit

3. erat *after* Hiberia *cancelled by Fp*

4. *added s.s. Fp*

5. *added s.s. Fp*

6. videlicet *cancelled after* fuisset *Fp*

7. Petri *add in marg. Fp*

8. *Fp corrected* arguit *to* reprehendit *in marg.*

9. *Fp corrected* primus *to* secundus *in marg.*

10. tertius *after correction by Fp*

11. pontificatus munus *F:* munus *afterwards deleted F*

12. Matathiae *Gaida:* Matthiae *after correction by Fp*

13. annum *after* decimum *before correction by Fp*

14. *added s.s. Fp*

3. CLETUS I

1. phase *sic F*

2. Hac etiam in victos humanitate usus, ut omnes qui ex familia David superfuissent, velut ex regia stirpe conquisitos in pretio habuerit. Idem quoque] Vespasianus autem *before correction by Fp*

3. *added in marg. Fp*

4. *Fp corrects* theatrum *to* amphitheatrum *in marg.*

5. adhuc *after* partem *before correction by Fp*

6. denegaret *before correction by Fp*

7. imitator] sectator *before correction by Fp*

8. *added in marg. Fp*

9. Nec mirum: a se enim fere omnia acceperit quippe qui Christum in carne non norat *cancelled after* laudatur *by Fp*

10. Hierosolymitana urbe *before correction by Fp*

4. CLEMENT I

1. autem *added in marg. Fp*

2. quem herodes capitem multavit *cancelled by Fp*

3. vero *added in marg. Fp*

4. Christi anno in Domino quievit] domini anno mortuus ac sepultus est *before correction by Fp*

5. ANACLETUS I

1. qua . . . vastaret *after correction by Fp*

2. Anacletus autem *after correction by Fp*

3. *Fp corrects* Unde *to* Quare *in marg.*

4. *added s.s. Fp*

5. ossium *added in marg. Fp*

6. gubernat *before correction by Fp*

6. EVARISTUS I

1. acclamatum sit *before correction by Fp*

2. ac *before correction by Fp*

3. marmorea *before correction by Fp*

4. historiae *F*

7. ALEXANDER I

1. Qui pridie . . . clausulam *added in marg. Fp*

2. *Fp cancels* cum reliquo canone *after* meum

3. aetatem *before correction by Fp*

8. SIXTUS I

1. *corrected from* furiosum *by Fp*

2. ubi consecraverat] consecraturus *before correction by Fp*

3. Thesyphorus F, *cancelled as though for correction but not corrected by Fp*

4. *added in marg. Fp*

9. TELESPHORUS I

1. instauranda *before correction by Fp*

2. operis F

3. *Fp cancels* videlicet *before* hora

4. sectatorem *before correction by Fp*

5. Platonis *before correction by Fp*

6. *added in marg. Fp*

10. HYGINUS I

1. Thelesphorum *before correction by Fp*

2. eiusdemque F: -que *om. Gaida*

3. tigna F

4. licet re vera . . . matrima dicetur *added in marg. Fp*

5. Negabat . . . mundum fecerat *added in marg. Fp*

6. regnante *before correction by Fp*

7. Antiochensis F

8. *Isidore:* qui materiam non natam introducens, deo non nato eam comparavit, matremque elementorum et deam asseruit.

11. PIUS I

1. e medio sublato] defuncto *before correction by Fp*

2. cum naturae *Gaida:* naturae cum F

3. subiecto *before correction by Fp*

4. repetitam *Gaida:* repetita F

5. *Fp cancels* scilicet *after* repetitam

6. ut *before correction by Fp*

7. Penitentiam … XL] Peniteant inquit LX *before correction by Fp*

8. Ubinque *sic Gaida*

9. instatus *sic Gaida*

10. *Fp cancels* ipsius *after* sui

11. *Jerome:* Encratitarum heresim

12. Omnem . . . proposuisset *added in marg. Fp*

12. ANICETUS I

1. vel, ut quidam volunt, metropolitani *added in marg. Fp*

2. idolatras F

3. ante vel post] ulterius vel alterius (?) *before correction by Fp*

4. meas *Gaida*

13. SOTER I

1. Pauli apostoli doctrina] ab apostolo Paulo *before correction by Fp*

2. doctrina *before correction by Fp*

3. Scripsit et Philippus cretensis episcopus contra Marcionem praeclarum volumen. Idem fecit et Lusanus contra fratres quosdam qui ab ecclesia ad Enoratianam (?) haeresim transierant *cancelled after* apparuisse *by Fp*

4. habitas] factas *before correction by Fp*

5. XXI *before correction by Fp*

14. ELEUTHERIUS I

1. ut Ptolemaeus ait *added in marg. Fp*

2. *added in marg. Fp*

3. *Fp cancels* videlicet *after* Deum

4. autem *before correction by Fp*

15. VICTOR I

1. *Fp cancels* decreto *after* consulto

2. luna *added in marg. Fp*

3. *add s.s. Fp*

4. characterem *before correction by Fp*

5. iudaeos imitari] iudaezari *before correction by Fp*

6. arguitur quod adventum *added in marg. Fp*

7. *added in marg. Fp*

16. ZEPHYRINUS I

1. *Liber pontificalis:* Habundio

2. addidit] meritus est *before correction by Fp*

3. et Adiabenos] acadiabenos *before correction by Fp*

4. *added in marg. Fp*

5. penositatem *before correction by Fp*

6. Turbriensi *before correction by Fp*

7. et poenitentiam *after* confessionem *cancelled Fp*

8. *added s.s. Fp*

17. CALIXTUS I

1. *Fp cancels* videlicet *after* Bassiano

2. Antoninianas *Gaida:* Antonianas *F (see 19.4)*

3. ob *added in marg. Fp*

4. refertque *Gaida:* referretque *F*

5. Valentini *before correction by Fp*

6. sectatorem *before correction by Fp*

7. nunc *om.* F

8. Calopodii F

9. pridie *added in marg. Fp*

18. URBAN I

1. *Fp cancels* cum *before* magna

2. *Fp cancels* et ut quidam volunt *after* praestantissimum

3. Valeriani] sanctissimae virginis *before correction by Fp*

4. con- *added in marg. Fp*

5. Appia *before correction by Fp*

19. PONTIAN I

1. *Fp cancels* videlicet *before* Macrinus

2. et *after* habuit F

3. *added in marg. Fp*

20. ANTHERUS I

1. autem *before correction by Fp*

2. et vitae *in marg. Fp*

3. qui *added in marg. Fp*

4. ne *added s.s. Fp*

5. *Fp cancels* quemcunque *after* episcopum

21. FABIAN I

1. militum copiis] copiam militum *before correction by Fp*

2. quod est *added in marg. Fp*

3. senior *before correction by Fp*

4. urbis Romae] Romanae urbis *before correction by Fp*

5. Novatii *F*

6. erronea *before correction by Fp*

7. ut creditum est *added in marg. Fp*

8. visa est *added s.s. Fp*

22. CORNELIUS I

1. trusus *before correction by Fp*

2. Novatum *F*

3. Novati *F*

4. ordinatus *before correction by Fp*

5. apud Telluris templum *before correction by Fp*

6. imperii] rei publicae *before correction by Fp*

7. Martii *before correction by Fp*

8. credo *added in marg. Fp*

23. LUCIUS I

1. invasae *before correction by Fp*

2. *Fp cancels* videlicet *after* Romanae

3. diaconos quattuor *om. Gaida*

4. vacat *corrected to* tum vacat *in marg. Fp*

24. STEPHEN I

1. recommunicandum *F*

2. Orientalis *Gaida*

3. extitisse *before correction by Fp*

4. re *before correction by Fp*

25. SIXTUS II

1. *added s.s. Fp*
2. apud *added in marg. Fp*
3. Spiritu *Gaida*
4. erroneae *before correction by Fp*
5. *Fp cancels* videlicet *before* abundantiam
6. significet *before correction by Fp*

26. DIONYSIUS I

1. terminis *before correction by Fp*
2. Inter eundum enim] In itinere *before correction by Fp*
3. optimi cuiusque] cuiusvis optimi *before correction by Fp*
4. tutus *Gaida*
5. instatus *Gaida (sic)*
6. Huic autem] Tanto *before correction by Fp*
7. vacat *after* sedes *before correction by Fp*

27. FELIX I

1. quod *Gaida*

28. EUTYCHIAN I

1. *added in marg. Fp*
2. *Fp cancels* videlicet *before* bonam
3. *Fp cancels* quinquies toto pontificatu *after* ordinibus
4. in pontificatu vixisse *added in marg. Fp*

29. GAIUS I

1. Sirmum *F*
2. et licentia *added in marg. Fp*

3. graecam linguam ac latinam] Latinam linguam ac graecam *before correction by Fp*

4. *added in marg. Fp*

5. *added in marg. Fp*

30. MARCELLINUS I

1. ipsemet] manu propria *before correction by Fp*

2. Maximianum *added in marg. Fp*

3. autem herculeus *added in marg. Fp*

4. At Constantius] Constantius vero *before correction by Fp*

5. tertio *before correction by Fp*

6. *Orosius:* Gallinicum

7. ac *before correction by Fp*

8. Is autem *added in marg. Fp*

9. ex decreto *before correction by Fp*

10. *added s.s. Fp*

11. habita est *before correction by Fp*

12. moereri *Gaida*

13. *Fp cancels* Priscillae *after* coemiterio

14. quod Priscillae deinceps nomen habuit *added in marg. Fp*

15. *Fp cancels* dementiae *after* eo

16. post aliquot annos] postea *before correction by Fp*

17. nullum *before correction by Fp*

31. MARCELLUS I

1. *Orosius:* Galerio (*as throughout 31.1*)

2. forte *Gaida*

3. *Orosius:* Maximinum; *Fp cancels* scilicet *after* Maximianum

4. episcopatu . . . deponeret] episcopatum et Christianum nomen renuntiaret *before correction by Fp*

5. administrabat *before correction by Fp*

6. a *Gaida*

7. *Fp cancels* passim *before* ubique

32. EUSEBIUS I

1. in gratiam Herculei repudiatae filius] concubinae filius ut scribunt historici *before correction by Fp (following Orosius 7.25.16)*

2. Paulum *F*

33. MILTIADES I

1. Galero *F*

2. *added in marg. Fp*

3. *om. F*

4. vitamque Thessalonicae . . . persequeretur *added in marg. Fp*

5. inconstans *before correction by Fp*

6. in Calisti in crypta] Calisti crypta *F*

34. SYLVESTER I

1. *added s.s. Fp*

2. optimo quoque] quovis optimo *before correction by Fp*

3. secundam Romam . . . indicabant *added in marg. Fp,* est *after* conatus *cancelled*

4. ac Christianorum *before correction by Fp*

5. ut dixi *added in marg. Fp*

6. *Fp cancels* eos *before* lacerans

7. vel ut quidam volunt secesserat *added in marg. Fp*

8. *added in marg. Fp*

9. quoque *added in marg. Fp*

10. *added in marg. Fp*

11. his verbis Erat aliquando quando non erat *added in marg. Fp*

12. adhibita etiam impensa munifice quidem *added in marg. Fp*

13. in quo *before correction by Fp*

14. ex ipsa patris divinitate] ex ipsa dei patris deitate *before correction by Fp*

15. veritate *added in marg. Fp*

16. *om. F*

17. *Fp cancels* videlicet *after* soldos

18. quod *Gaida*

19. animi *added in marg. Fp*

20. Hanc ob rem Constantinus . . . uteretur *added in marg. Fp*

21. *added s.s. Fp*

22. alio pro cono . . . procellas deiecit *added in marg. Fp*

23. sepulchro] sarcophago *before correction by Fp*

24. *Liber pontificalis:* insulam Meseno … insulam Mattidiae, quod est montem Argentarium.

25. Graccorum] Graecorum *before correction by Fp*

26. Ne autem … etiam addidit *added in marg. Fp*

27. Certum enim vectigal . . . scribunt *omitted in F*

28. monendos *Gaida*

29. eius cibus . . . contemplationi deditus *added in marg. Fp*

30. *added s.s. Fp*

35. MARK I

1. una cum Crispo filio *added in marg. Fp*

2. pulsis ab Urbe tyrannis *added in marg. Fp*

3. dictum *after* aliter *Gaida:* [*illeg.*] dictum loquuntur *erased and cancelled in F*

4. via *Gaida (cf. 38.3)*

5. atque illic . . . baptizatum fuisse *added in marg. Fp*

6. rem hanc] historiae fabulam *before correction by Fp*

7. sentient] tenent *before correction by Fp*

8. qui sacris . . . mysteriis oraverat *added in marg. Fp*

9. non auctorum conficta nomina et eorum maxime qui, cum Graeci sint, sibi etiam in re ficta credi volunt. Nec mihi obiiciant Ambrosii auctoritatem, qui Graecorum opinionem secutus, dicit Constantinum in ultimis conscitum Baptismate lotum fuisse *cancelled by Fp within the marginal addition of Fp (see next note)*

10. Me certe non latet . . . scripsere *added in marg. Fp*

36. JULIUS I

1. *added s.s. Fp*

2. levandi ventris causa] humanae necessitatis causa *before correction by Fp*

3. conatur *Gaida*

4. Non destitit . . . ceteris praeferendam *added in marg. Fp*

5. omissis his contentionibus *added in marg. Fp*

6. videlicet *cancelled after* unam *Fp*

37. LIBERIUS I

1. quodque . . . nolebat *added in marg. Fp*

2. ut quidam volunt *added in marg. Fp*

3. Sunt tamen . . . precibus impetrasse *added in marg. Fp*

4. Pontifex] Liberius *before correction by Fp*

5. *i.e.* Liviae (Libiae *in the Liber pontificalis*)

6. Praeterea vero *added in marg. Fp:* quoque *after* Donatus *cancelled*

7. regnante *before correction by Fp*

8. partis *before correction by Fp*

9. Romanis] Romanae ecclesiae *before correction by Fp*

10. *One should probably read* pacatiorem

11. ad hominem enim . . . semper restitit *added in marg. Fp*

12. autem *before correction by Fp*

38. FELIX II

1. quippe qui . . . natus erat *added in marg. by Fp*

2. etiam *om. Gaida*

3. creatur *before correction by Fp*

4. apoplexia *added in marg. by Fp*

5. quarto et viginti *added s.s. Fp*

6. Hoc autem . . . Iuliano inciderat *added in marg. Fp*

7. cives *added in marg. Fp*

8. more anserum *added in marg. Fp*

9. *added s.s. Fp*

10. ob eloquentiam et versutiam *added in marg. by Fp*

11. hic *before correction by Fp*

12. dotavitque *after* aedificavit *cancelled Fp*

39. DAMASUS I

1. Eubolo . . . praeceptoribus usus *added in marg. Fp*

2. blandimentis *before correction by Fp*

3. Miror ego . . . martyrum aedificasset *added in marg. Fp*

4. Idem imperator *added in marg. Fp*

5. multo *added in marg. Fp*

6. incomposito agmine *added in marg. Fp*

7. aut *F*

8. quanquam sunt . . . avectus est *added in marg. Fp*

9. -arent *Gaida*

10. *Fp cancels* et urbis Romae *before* Damasus

11. *Fp corrects from* Ursinus

12. non longe a theatro Pompeiano] apud theatrum *before correction by Fp*

13. *Fp cancels* videlicet *after* Patena

14. circa basilicam] in circuitu basilicae *before correction by Fp*

15. cum matre et sorore] apud matrem et sororem *before correction by Fp*

40. SIRICIUS I

1. autem *added in marg. Fp*

2. Ioviano *F*

3. Precopium *F*

4. quidem] autem *before correction by Fp*

5. sex et XL annis *added in marg. by Fp*

6. *Fp cancels* scilicet *before* Macharii

7. eum *after* litterae Gaida, *but cancelled in F*

8. licet Themistii . . . mitiorem reddiderint *added in marg. Fp*

9. *i.e.* Athanaricus

10. *Fp cancels* quae consuetudo iam abolevit *after* dandos; abolevit *corrected to* exolevit *in marg. by Fp, then cancelled*

11. ab episcopo tantum] nisi ab episcopo *before correction by Fp*

12. propelleretur *before correction by Fp*

13. librum *before correction by Fp*

41. ANASTASIUS I

1. *added in marg. Fp*

2. *i.e.* Polemonem *(as in Jerome)*

42. INNOCENT I

1. Claudiani] cuiusdam *before correction by Fp*

2. *added s.s. Fp*

3. vel, ut alii volunt, iudicem suum *added in marg. Fp*

4. omnes *added in marg. Fp*

5. Affirmant quidam] Ferunt *before correction by Fp*

6. *added in marg.* Fp

7. vel *before correction by* Fp

8. et socio *added in marg.* Fp

9. *i.e.* Livianum (Libianam *Liber Pontificalis*)

10. Apollinarius *Gaida*

11. *Fp cancels* etiam *before* animam

12. vero Hierosolymitanus] autem Hierosolymae *before correction by* Fp

13. vero *before correction by* Fp

14. etiam *before correction by* Fp

43. ZOSIMUS I

1. enim *before correction by* Fp

2. *Fp cancels* videlicet *after* Ruffinum

3. Qui deinceps] Ii tamen *before correction by* Fp

4. animi *added in marg.* Fp

5. *Fp cancels* potissimum *after* incautos

6. Propinare *before correction by* Fp

7. ecclesiae Romanae] sanctae Romanae ecclesiae *before correction by* Fp

8. Hunc ego . . . ad se traduxissent *added in marg.* Fp

9. *added s. s.* Fp

44. BONIFACE I

1. *added s.s.* Fp

2. creatus *before correction by* Fp

3. lectissimis F

4. pepigit *before correction by* Fp

5. revelante *before correction by* Fp

6. etiam qui] qui etiam *before correction by* Fp

7. ob iniuriam *before correction by* Fp

45. CELESTINE I

1. *Fp cancels* quidem *before* perturbatione
2. *Fp cancels* ne civitatis suae calamitatem cerneret *after* episcopus
3. ab Anglis auxilium] Anglos in auxilium *before correction by Fp*
4. *added s.s. Fp*
5. apud Constantinopolim *before correction by Fp*
6. *Fp cancels* videlicet *before* argenteam
7. XV *Gaida*
8. atque *Gaida*

46. SIXTUS III

1. spatiis *before correction by Fp*
2. *i.e.* Liviae; *cf.* 37.2
3. titulus ipse *added in marg. Fp*
4. graeca orthographia *added in marg. Fp*
5. *Fp cancels* graecanicam illam asperitatem fugiens et *after* aetas
6. quoque *added s.s. Fp*
7. canitur *after* ubi *before correction by Fp*
8. Quod ego factum Celestini . . . sperare futura *added in marg. Fp*
9. XII *F*
10. via Tyburtina *Gaida*

47. LEO I

1. *added s.s. Fp*
2. deitatis *before correction by Fp*
3. *Fp cancels* videlicet *after* Ioannis
4. apud *before correction by Fp*

Notes to the Translation

☙❦☙

ABBREVIATIONS

Biondo-Piccolomini	Aeneas Silvius Piccolomini, *Supra Decades ab inclinatione imperii usque ad tempora Joannis XXIII Pontificis Maximi epitome*, in Pius II, *Opera quae extant omnia* (Basel, 1571), 144–281.
Cassiodorus	Cassiodorus, *Historia ecclesiastica vocata Tripartita, ex tribus graecis auctoribus, Sozomeno, Socrate et Theodoreto, per Epiphanium Scholasticum excerpta et in compendium redacta.* In PL 69: 879–1214.
Eusebius	Eusebius, *The Ecclesiastical History*, tr. K. Lake, 2 vols. (Cambridge, Mass., 1980).
Eusebius-Jerome	Eusebius and Jerome, *Chronique: continuation de la Chronique d'Eusèbe, années 326–378*, ed. and tr. R. Helm, B. Jeanjean and B. Lançon (Rennes, 2004).
Eutropius	Eutropius, *Breviarium ab urbe condita*, ed. C. Santini (Leipzig, 1979).
Isidore	Isidore of Seville, *Etymologiarum sive Originum libri XX*, ed. W. M. Lindsay (Oxford, 1911).
Jerome	Jerome, *De viris illustribus.* In PL 23: 597–720.
Josephus	Flavius Josephus, *Jewish Antiquities*, ed. and tr. H. St. J. Thackeray, R. Marcus, A. Wikgren and L. H. Feldman, in his *Works*, vols. 4–9 (Cambridge, Mass., 1966–69).
LP	*Le Liber pontificalis: texte, introduction et commentaire*, ed. L. Duchesne (Paris, 1981).
ODP	*The Oxford Dictionary of the Popes*, ed. J. N. D. Kelly (Oxford. 1986).

Orosius	Paulus Orosius, *Historiarum adversum paganos libri septem*, ed. C. Zangemeister (Leipzig, 1889).
Palmieri	Matteo Palmieri, *Liber de temporibus (aa. 1–1448)*, ed. Gino Scaramella, Rerum Italicarum Scriptores, n.s., vol. 26 (Città di Castello, 1905–15).
Paulus Diaconus	Paulus Diaconus, *Historia Romana*, ed. H. Droysen, Monumenta Germaniae historica, Scriptores rerum Germanicarum 49 (Munich, 1978).
PL	*Patrologiae cursus completus, series latina*, ed. J.-P. Migne, 221 vols. (Paris, 1844–91).
Ptolemy	Ptolemy of Lucca, *Historia Ecclesiastica*, ed. L. A. Muratori, Rerum Italicarum Scriptores, vol. 11 (Milan, 1727), 754–1242.
Rufinus	Rufinus, *Historia Ecclesiastica*. In *PL* 21: 461–540.
SHA	*Scriptores Historiae Augustae*, ed. and tr. D. Magie, 3 vols. (Cambridge, Mass., 1967–78).
Shotwell and Loomis	James T. Shotwell and Louise Ropes Loomis, *The See of Peter* (New York, 1927).

PREFACE

1. Virgil, *Aenead*, 8.63.

2. For Platina's belief that the earlier parts of the *Liber pontificalis (LP)* had been composed by Pope Damasus I (366–383), see 39.7 below and the Introduction.

LIFE OF CHRIST

1. The full title as given in the rubrics to the various manuscripts and the 1479 edition is: *The Historian Platina's Lives of Christ and All the Popes who thus far number 220.*

2. Diogenes Laertius 3.88–89. Plato is said to have identified four sources of nobility: just and good ancestors; ancestors who held power; ancestors who were famous, and innate high-mindedness.

3. Eusebius 1.2 and Ptolemy 1.2 both discuss the excellence and nobility of Christ.

4. Genesis 49:10; Eusebius 1.8; Ptolemy 1.1.

5. Compare Leviticus 21:10.

6. Eusebius 1.6–8; Ptolemy 1.2.

7. Suetonius, *Augustus*, 51, 60, 66, 28.

8. Sebaste is the usual Greek translation for Augustus.

9. Ibid. 28.3.

10. Ptolemy 1.3. Compare Orosius 6.22.

11. Eusebius 1.5. Compare Luke 2:1–2.

12. Isaiah 9:5–7.

13. Augustine, *City of God*, 16.26; Ptolemy 1.3–4.

14. Isidore 7.2.

15. Ptolemy 1.5; Eusebius 1.8; Matthew 2.

16. Isaiah 19:1.

17. Matthew 2; Ptolemy 1.5. Compare Eusebius 1.8; Palmieri 8.

18. Ptolemy 1.6–7.

19. Josephus 18.63–64. Compare Eusebius 1.11; Ptolemy 1.8.

20. Josephus 18.116–119; Eusebius 1.11.

21. Ptolemy 1.9.

22. Matthew 18; Palmieri 10.

23. Orosius 7.4. Compare Eusebius 2.2; Palmieri 10.

24. Palmieri 11. Compare Eusebius 2.7.

I. PETER

1. Acts 2; Ptolemy 1.10. Compare Jerome 1.

2. *LP* 1.1. Compare Jerome 1.

3. Eutropius 7.11; Orosius 7.4. Compare Suetonius, *Tiberius*, 32, 37, 70; Palmieri 9.

4. Platina here calls Caligula 'Callicula,' misled probably by a corruption in his manuscript of Suetonius, *Caligula*, 9: Suetonius says that Caligula acquired his name, which means "little boot," *a castrensi ioco*, from a military joke, because he had been brought up among soldiers in the dress of a common soldier; Platina's source must have read *a castrensi loco* and possibly also offered the odd variant 'Callicula' for Caligula.

5. Suetonius, *Caligula*, passim; Orosius 7.5. Compare Eutropius 7.12; Palmieri 10–11.

6. King of Arcadia, turned into a wolf by Zeus for sacrificing a child on an altar.

7. Ptolemy 1.10; Matthew 16.

8. Eutropius 7.13; Orosius 7.6; Palmieri 12. Compare Suetonius, *Claudius*, 20, 25, 26, 44, 17.

9. For an exhaustive survey of the tradition and sources concerning Simon Magus, see Shotwell and Loomis, pp. 120–207.

10. Justin Martyr, *Apologia Prima*, in Shotwell and Loomis, 130–131.

11. Suetonius, *Nero*, 12, reported a magician's attempt to fly and fall to death.

12. This conflation orginates in Irenaeus, *Adversus Haereses*, in Shotwell and Loomis, 131.

13. Ptolemy 1.13; Eusebius 2.13; Acts 8; Jerome 1.1; Palmieri 12; *LP* 1.4.

14. Not in Jerome but from the so-called "Monarchian prologues" or arguments (third century?) handed down with the Vulgate text of the New Testament and often mistakenly attributed to Jerome by medieval scholars.

15. Jerome, 8.1–5. Compare Palmieri 13–14.

16. Gospel of Hebrews, quoted in Jerome 2.

17. Jerome 2 and 6; Ptolemy 1.14; Acts 4 and 15. Compare Palmieri 13. Gaida 7, n.5, says that Platina quotes Josephus by memory from a second-hand source.

18. Jerome 5; Acts 27. Compare Acts 7 and 9; Eusebius 2.22. Before revision in *F* Platina had written "is regarded as dubious, . . . there are some who . . ."

19. Jerome 1. Compare *LP* 1.2; Ptolemy 1.16.

20. *LP* 1.3. Compare Ptolemy, 1.16.

21. *LP* 1.5.

22. Jerome 1 and 5; Ptolemy 1.17. Compare *LP* 1.1 and 6.

23. I.e., a Montanist heretic.

24. Eusebius 2.25 (who cites Gaius).

25. Tacitus, *Annales*, 15.39–40.

26. Eutropius 6.14–15. Compare Suetonius, *Nero*, passim; Orosius 7.7; Ptolemy 1.15.

2. LINUS I

1. *LP* 2.1. Compare Ptolemy 2.1. *LP* states that his father was named Herculanus.

2. Eutropius 7.16–18; Orosius 7.8; Suetonius, *Galba*, 20, 11; *Otho*, 1, 9, 11; *Vitellius*, 13, 14, 17; Palmieri 15.

3. Ptolemy 2.1; Jerome 15.

4. *LP* 2.2. Compare Ptolemy 2.1–2.

5. Jerome 11. Compare Ptolemy 2.3–4.

6. *LP* 2.1–2; Ptolemy 2.2.

3. CLETUS I

1. *LP* 3.1; Ptolemy 2.5. His name is more correctly given as Anacletus; Cletus is a shortened form. *LP*, followed by Platina, distinguishes this Cletus from Anacletus I (§5, below) but modern authorities regard Cletus and Anacletus I as the same person; see *ODP*, 7.

2. Orosius 7.9; Palmieri 15; Suetonius, *Vespasian*, 5. Compare Eusebius 3.5.

3. I.e., the Colosseum. Orosius 7.9; Suetonius, *Domitian*, 2; *Vespasian*, 9, 14, 16–17; Eutropius 7.19–20. Compare Eusebius 3.12.

4. Suetonius, *Titus* 1.

5. Eutropius 7.20–22; Suetonius, *Titus*, 7–8.

6. Jerome 7. Compare Ptolemy 1.5.

7. Ptolemy 2.7. Compare Eusebius 3.31.

8. *LP* 3.1–2.

4. CLEMENT I

1. *LP* 4.1.

2. Eutropius 7.23; Orosius 7.10; Suetonius, *Domitian*, 3, 13, 17; Palmieri 17.

3. Jerome 15.

4. Ptolemy 2.9; see 2.5, above.

5. Jerome 15.

6. Jerome 9.

7. Ptolemy 2.11.

8. *LP* 4.1, 4.

5. ANACLETUS I

1. Ibid. 5.1. On his identity, see note 3.1, above.

2. Eutropius 8.1–3; Orosius 7.11–12; Palmieri 17–18.

3. Ptolemy 2.14.

4. This is a standard phrase used when taking extraordinary measures.

5. Ibid. 2.12.

6. Jerome 16; Palmieri 18.

7. Pliny the Younger, *Letters* 10.96–97; Eusebius 3.33; Palmieri 18.

8. Ptolemy 2.12; Palmieri 18.

9. *LP* 3, 5; Ptolemy 2.14.

10. *LP* 5.1–3.

6. EVARISTUS I

1. *LP* 6.6. Compare Ptolemy 2.17.

2. I.e., the column of Trajan, in the Forum of Trajan. Eutropius 8.4–5. Compare Orosius 7.12.

3. *LP* 6.2; Ptolemy 2.17.

4. Jerome 18–20. Compare Ptolemy 2.18; Palmieri 19.

5. Orosius 7.13. Compare Eusebius 4.8–9; Palmieri 19.

6. *LP* 6.1, 3; Ptolemy 2.17.

7. ALEXANDER I

1. *LP* 7.1; Ptolemy 2.19.

2. Orosius 7.13; Eusebius-Jerome 165, 167; Eutropius 8.7; Palmieri 19.

3. *SHA, Hadrianus*, 11, 14, 19, 26. The last sentence is defective in Platina's Latin (see Gaida 21), probably the result of censorship by Platina himself so as not to detract from Hadrian's (or perhaps Suetonius') reputation; the text in brackets has been supplied from Platina's source, *SHA, Hadrianus*, 11. 3.

4. This means that he introduced the Last Supper narrative into the Mass.

5. *LP* 7.2; Ptolemy 2.20.

6. Jerome 21. Compare Ptolemy 2.20.

7. Orosius 7.13. Compare Eusebius 4.6; Ptolemy 2.20.

8. Ptolemy 2.20. Compare Eusebius 4.6.

9. *LP* 7.1, 3; Ptolemy 2.19.

8. SIXTUS I

1. *LP* 8.1; Ptolemy 2.21.

2. *SHA, Hadrianus*, 18–19, 25.

3. *LP* 8.2. Ptolemy 2.21.

4. Ptolemy 2.21–22.

5. Compare Ptolemy 2.23; Eusebius 2.18.

6. *LP* 8.1, 3.

9. TELESPHORUS I

1. Ibid. 9.1. Compare Ptolemy 2.24.

2. I.e., the Aurelian Column (or Column of Marcus Aurelius) in the Piazza Colonna, from which the region (and family) of Colonna took its name. Orosius 7.14; *SHA, Antoninus Pius*, 1, 2, 6, 8, 9.

3. Ptolemy 2.24, 782; Mark 15; *LP* 9.2.

4. Jerome 23; Eusebius 4.16.

5. Isidore 8.5; Ptolemy 2.24.

6. *LP* 9.1–3; Ptolemy 2.24.

10. HYGINUS I

1. Ptolemy 2.27; *LP* 10.1.

2. Eutropius 8.8; *SHA, Antoninus Pius*, 9, 13; Palmieri 21.

3. Festus 14; *LP* 10.2; Ptolemy 2.27.

4. Jerome 17; Ptolemy 2.28; Palmieri 21.

5. Jerome 24; Ptolemy 2.29; Palmieri 21.

6. Jerome 25; Isidore of Seville, 8.5. Compare Ptolemy 2.29. Platina is here following a corrupt text of Isidore, his source; the original makes a good deal more sense (see Notes to the Text *ad loc.*): "who posited eternal matter and compared it to an eternal god, and asserted it was the mother of the elements and a goddess."

7. *LP* 10.1–2.

11. PIUS I

1. Ibid. 11.1.

2. Platina means Marcus Cornelius Fronto, the orator, appointed tutor to the emperor Marcus Aurelius by Antoninus Pius.

3. Plato, *Rep.* 5.473d.

4. Orosius, VII.15; *SHA, Antoninus Pius,* 10–11. Compare Eutropius 8.11–12.

5. *LP* 11.2–4.

6. Ptolemy 3.2.

7. I.e., Marcus Antoninus Verus; in fact the book was presented to the later emperor Marcus Aurelius *c.* 172.

8. Jerome 26; Isidore 8.5; Palmieri 22.

9. Jerome 29; Isidore 8.5.

10. Jerome 30–31; Eusebius 4.28–29.

11. *LP* 11.1, 5.

12. ANICETUS I

1. Ibid. 12.1.

2. Eutropius 8.13; *SHA, Antoninus Pius,* 7, 8, 12; Orosius 7.15; Palmieri 22.

3. *LP* 12.2; Ptolemy 3.6.

4. Jerome 22. Compare Ptolemy 3.6; Palmieri 21.

5. Ptolemy 3.6.

6. *LP* 12.1–2.

13. SOTER I

1. *LP* 13.1; Ptolemy 3.7.

2. Orosius 7.15–16; Eutropius 8.15. Compare Palmieri 23.

3. Ptolemy 3.7. Compare *LP* 13.2.

4. Jerome 37; Isidore 8.5. Compare Ptolemy 3.8; Palmieri 22.

5. Jerome 38, 28. Compare Palmieri 23.

6. *LP* 13.1, 3; Ptolemy 3.7.

14. ELEUTHERIUS I

1. *LP* 14.1.

2. Orosius 7.16; Eutropius 8.15; *SHA, Commodus,* 17. Compare Palmieri 23.

3. Ptolemy 3.9. Compare *LP* 14.2.

4. Ptolemy 3.11. Compare *LP* 14.2.

5. Ptolemy 3.12. Compare Palmieri 23.

6. Eusebius 5.13.

7. Isidore 8.5; Eusebius 5.15. See Genesis 1:31.

8. Isidore 8.5. See Isaiah 45:7.

9. Compare Palmieri 20.

10. Jerome 32–33. Compare Palmieri 22.

11. *LP* 14.1, 3.

15. VICTOR I

1. Ibid. 15.1.

2. Eutropius 8.16–17; Orosius 7.16; *SHA, Pertinax*, 6, 12.

3. *LP* 15.2–3. Compare Ptolemy 3.13.

4. Jerome 45.

5. *LP* 15.2.

6. Ptolemy 3.14–15. Compare Palmieri 24.

7. Jerome 49–52; Eusebius 5.28.

8. *LP* 15.1, 4.

16. ZEPHYRINUS I

1. Ibid. 16.1.

2. Eutropius 8.18–19; *SHA, Septimius Severus*, 19. Compare Orosius 7.16; Palmieri 24. This is Platina's first jibe against Paul II.

3. Ptolemy 3.16–18. Compare *LP* 16.2.

4. Matthew 19:12.

5. Jerome 54; Eusebius 6.2–5; Palmieri 24; Ptolemy 3.22–3.

6. *LP* 16.1, 3.

17. CALIXTUS I

1. Ibid. 17.1.

2. Orosius 7.17–18; Eutropius 8.18–20; *SHA, Severus,* 21; *Caracalla,* 5, 7, 9–10. Compare Palmieri 24–25.

3. *LP* 17.2; Ptolemy 3.20–21.

4. *LP* 17.3–4; Ptolemy 3.20–21.

5. Jerome 53. Compare Ptolemy 3.23.

6. I.e., six thousand papyrus rolls containing his books, not six thousand books, since many rolls might be required for a single book.

7. Eusebius 6.14–15; Jerome 56; Ptolemy 3.22–26.

8. *LP* 17.1, 4.

18. URBAN I

1. Ibid. 18.1. Compare Ptolemy 3.24.

2. Eutropius 7.22; Orosius 7.18.

3. *SHA, Elagabalus,* 6, 16, 25–27, 31–33; Jerome 63; Palmieri 25.

4. *LP* 18.3; Ptolemy 3.25. See 17.2.

5. Jerome 57, 58; Ptolemy 3.29; Eusebius 6.16.

6. *LP* 18.1, 4.

19. PONTIAN I

1. Actually 235 AD. Ibid. 19.1. Compare Ptolemy 3.27.

2. Eutropius 8.21; *SHA, Clodius Albinus,* 11. Compare Orosius 8.18.

3. I.e., Julia Mamaea.

4. Eutropius 8.23; *SHA, Severus Alexander,* passim; Orosius 7.18.

5. Ptolemy 3.27. Compare *LP* 19.2.

6. Jerome 60; Eusebius 6.17. Compare Ptolemy 3.26, 23; Palmieri 25.

7. Eusebius, 6.16. Compare Jerome 54; Ptolemy 3.29; Palmieri 26.

8. *LP* 19.1, 3.

20. ANTHERUS I

1. Ibid. 20.1; Ptolemy 3.30.
2. Orosius 7.19; *SHA, Maximini Duo*, passim. Compare Palmieri 26.
3. *LP* 20.2; Ptolemy 3.30.
4. Eusebius 6.23; Jerome 63, 54. Compare Ptolemy 3.32; Palmieri 25.
5. *LP* 20.1, 3.

21. FABIAN I

1. Ibid. 21.1. Compare Ptolemy 4.1.
2. Orosius 7.20; Eutropius 9.3; *SHA, Gordiani Tres*, 18, 23; Palmieri 26. Compare Eusebius 6.25; Jerome 54.
3. *LP* 21.2; Ptolemy 4.1.
4. Ptolemy 4.2; Eusebius 6.33; Jerome 70.
5. Ptolemy 4.3–4; Eusebius 6.19–20.
6. Eusebius 6.8–9.
7. Ibid. 6.29.
8. *LP* 21.1, 5.

22. CORNELIUS I

1. Ibid. 22.1. Compare Ptolemy 4.6.
2. Orosius 7.21; Eutropius 9.4.
3. *LP* 22.2–3. Compare Ptolemy 4.6.
4. Eusebius 6.33; Ptolemy 4.6.
5. Eusebius 6.35; Jerome 69. Compare Ptolemy 4.7–8.
6. *LP* 22.4–6. Compare Ptolemy 4.7–8.
7. *LP* 22.5; Jerome 67.
8. *LP* 22.1, 7.

23. LUCIUS I

1. Ibid. 23.1.

2. Orosius 7.21–22; Eutropius 9.5–8.

3. *LP* 23.3; Ptolemy 4.10; 4.12; Jerome 67–68.

4. *LP* 23.1, 4–5.

24. STEPHEN I

1. Ibid. 24.1.

2. Orosius 7.22; Eutropius 9.9. Compare Palmieri 28.

3. *LP* 24.3; Ptolemy 4.13–14.

4. Jerome 71; Ptolemy 4.13–14, 20; Isidore 8.5. Compare Eusebius 7.25.

5. *LP* 24.1–2, 4.

25. SIXTUS II

1. Ibid. 25.1; Ptolemy 4.15.

2. Eutropius, 9.22. Compare Orosius, 7.22.

3. Eusebius, 7.5, 23, 22, 25; Isidore 8.5; Ptolemy 4.18.

4. Ptolemy 4.17; *LP* 25.2–3.

5. *LP* 25.1, 4.

26. DIONYSIUS I

1. Ibid. 26.1–2; Ptolemy 4.19.

2. Orosius 7.23. Compare Eutropius 9.11–12; Palmieri 28.

3. Eusebius 7.27–30; Jerome 71; Isidore 8.5. Compare Ptolemy 4.20.

4. *LP* 26.1, 3.

27. FELIX I

1. Ibid. 27.1. Compare Ptolemy 4.22.

2. Eutropius 9.13–16; Orosius 7.23. Compare Palmieri 28.

3. Ptolemy 4.22–23; *LP* 27.2. Compare Palmieri 29.

4. *LP* 27.1–3.

28. EUTYCHIAN I

1. Ibid. 28.1. Compare Ptolemy 4.24.

2. Eutropius 9.16; Orosius 7.24.

3. *LP* 28.2; Ptolemy 4.24–25; Eusebius 7.30, 32; Isidore 8.5.

4. *LP* 28.1, 3. Compare Ptolemy 4.24.

29. GAIUS I

1. *LP* 29.1. Compare Ptolemy 4.26.

2. I.e., Transalpine and Cisalpine Gaul.

3. Orosius 7.24–25; Eutropius 9.17–18. Compare Palmieri 29–30.

4. *LP* 29.2–3; Ptolemy 4.26–28; Jerome 74–75.

5. Ptolemy 4.27; *LP* 29.1, 3–4.

30. MARCELLINUS I

1. *LP* 30.1. Compare Ptolemy 4.29.

2. Orosius 7.25. Compare Eutropius 9.20–24; Palmieri 30.

3. Eusebius 8.2, 4–7, 9, 11, 13, 14.

4. *LP* 30.2; Eusebius 8.13. Compare Ptolemy 4.29.

5. *LP* 30.2–4; Ptolemy 4.29–30.

6. Eusebius 8.16–17; 8.1.

7. *LP* 30.1, 5. Compare Ptolemy 4.33.

31. MARCELLUS I

1. *LP* 31.1. Compare Ptolemy 4.33.

2. Orosius 7.25; Eutropius, X.1–2; Palmieri 31.

3. Ptolemy 4.33; *LP* 31.2–5;

4. *LP* 31.1, 6.

32. EUSEBIUS I

1. *LP* 32.1. Compare Ptolemy 4.35.

2. The earlier redaction in *F* read "his son Constantine by his concubine Helen, as historians write." See Orosius 7.15.16.

3. Eutropius 10.2–3. Compare Orosius 7.28.

4. Ptolemy 4.35; 5.3. Compare *LP* 32.2; Palmieri 33.

5. Jerome 80, 81. Compare Ptolemy 4.34, 36.

6. *LP* 32.1, 3.

33. MILTIADES I

1. Ibid. 33.1; Ptolemy 4.37.

2. Eutropius 10.4; Eusebius 8.16–17; 9.9.

3. Eutropius 10.4–6; Eusebius 9.9–10; Orosius 7.28.

4. Eusebius 9.9–10; Orosius 7.28.

5. Eusebius 8.14.

6. *LP* 33.1–3; Ptolemy 4.37; Eusebius 7.32.

34. SYLVESTER I

1. *LP* 34.1; Ptolemy, 5.1. Onofrio Panvinio's edition of 1562 corrected this erroneous date to 314.

2. Eutropius 10.7–8. Compare Palmieri 32.

3. Cassiodorus 1.4–5; Eusebius 9.9–10.

4. *LP* 34.2–3; Ptolemy 5.1. Compare Palmieri 32.

5. Rufinus, 1.1–5; Isidore 8.5. Compare Ptolemy 5.6; Palmieri 33.

6. In fact they were condemned at the Council of Constantinople in 381.

7. *LP* 34.4; Isidore 8.5; Rufinus 1.2, 6.

8. *LP* 34.6–8. Ptolemy 5.8.

9. *LP* 34.9–14.

10. Ibid. 34.16–21.

11. Ambrose, *De obitu Theodosii oratio*, 41–49.

12. *LP* 34.22; Rufinus 1.7–8.

13. *LP* 34.23–27.

14. Ibid. 34.28–33.

15. Rufinus 1.9, 10, 8; Jerome 887, 88. Compare Ptolemy 5.11.

16. *LP* 34.1, 34.

35. MARK I

1. Ibid. 35.1. Compare Ptolemy 5.12.

2. Rufinus 1.11. See also 38.3, below.

3. On the controversy over Constantine's baptism in the Renaissance, see Charles L. Stinger, *The Renaissance in Rome* (Bloomington, Indiana, 1985) 253.

4. Cassiodorus 1.5–6.

5. For the context of this passage, see the Introduction. By his silence in the life of Sylvester and by his rejection here of the story of how Constantine was cured of leprosy, Platina is implicitly rejecting the authority of the Donation of Constantine, wherein Constantine supposedly gives temporal power over the Roman Empire to Pope Sylvester in gratitude for being cured of leprosy; compare Platina's account here to the forged "Donation of Constantine," published in this I Tatti series: see Lorenzo Valla, *On the Donation of Constantine*, ed. and tr. G. W. Bowersock (Cambridge, Mass., 2007), Donation, §§6–8. Platina also repeats Valla's argument (*Oration* §32) about the lack of contemporary witnesses to the Donation. It may be significant that this controversial passage in Platina's text was contained in a marginal addition to the printer's dummy (see *Notes to the Text*).

6. Ptolemy 5.1; Eutropius 10.8.

7. *LP* 35.1–5; Ptolemy 5.12, 14; Jerome 84; Palmieri 34.

36. JULIUS I

1. *LP* 36.1. Compare Ptolemy 5.16.

2. Eutropius 10.9; Ptolemy 5.16. Compare Orosius 7.29; Palmieri 35.

3. Rufinus 1.16–19, 13. Compare Ptolemy 5.22.

4. *LP* 36.1–3; Eutropius 10.9.

5. Jerome 86, 89, 110; *LP* 36.1, 4.

37. LIBERIUS I

1. *LP* 37.1. Compare Ptolemy 5.20.

2. Orosius 7.29; Eutropius 10.9; Rufinus 1.20–21.

3. *LP* 37.2–5. Compare Ptolemy 5.20.

4. *LP* 37.7.

5. Jerome 91–95, 97; Isidore 8.5. Compare Palmieri 36.

6. Jerome, 99; Cassiodorus 5.26. Compare Palmieri 37.

7. *LP* 37.1, 8; Ptolemy 5.20.

38. FELIX II

1. *LP* 38.1

2. Eutropius 10.14–15; Rufinus 1.26. Compare Orosius 7.29; Palmieri 38.

3. Plutarch, *Life of Pyrrhus*, 19.

4. Ammianus Marcellinus 16.10, 4–17.

5. Jerome 98; *LP* 38.1; Rufinus 1.25.

6. Ptolemy 5.25, 26, 27; Jerome 98; *LP* 38.1–3.

39. DAMASUS I

1. *LP* 39.1. Compare Ptolemy 6.1.

2. Rufinus 1.32; Ammianus Marcellinus 22–25.

3. Psalm 97:7.

4. Rufinus 1.33, 35.

5. Luke 19:44.

6. Compare Rufinus 1.37.

7. Orosius 7.30.

8. Orosius 7.31. Compare Palmieri 39.

9. Now Santa Maria Maggiore in Rome.

10. Platina believed that Damasus was the author of the *Liber Pontificalis* on the basis of a misreading of the exchange of letters between Damasus and Jerome that stands in most manuscripts at the head of the work.

11. *LP* 39.1–5; Ptolemy 6.1, 2; Rufinus 2.10. Compare Palmieri 39.

12. *LP* 39.1, 6.

40. SIRICIUS I

1. Ibid. 40.1. Compare Ptolemy 6.9.

2. Orosius 7.32; Rufinus 2.3. Compare Palmieri 38–39.

3. Rufinus 2.8, 4, 6.

4. Orosius 7.32; Rufinus 2.13. Compare Palmieri 39–41. The Goths' victory at Adrianople in 378 marked the end of the Roman empire for Ammianus; see 31.12–13.

5. Ptolemy 6.9, 10; *LP* 40.2–3.

6. Jerome 100, 101, 105, 107, 109–111; Isidore 8.5. Compare Ptolemy 5.24, 27.

7. *LP* 40.1, 4.

41. ANASTASIUS I

1. *LP* 41.1. Compare Ptolemy 6.15.

2. Rufinus 2.13, 14; Orosius 7.34; Palmieri, pp. 41–42.

3. Rufinus 2.15; Ptolemy 6.7.

4. Ptolemy 6.15; *LP* 41.1–3.

5. Ptolemy 6.16, 6.4, 6.8; Rufinus 2.2, 9; Jerome 106, 107, 104, 105.

6. *LP* 41.1, 3.

42. INNOCENT I

1. Ibid. 42.1. Compare Ptolemy 6.19.

2. Orosius 7.35; Paulus Diaconus 12.2. Compare Palmieri 42. The lines are from Claudian's *De tertio consulatu Honorii Augusti*, 96–97.

3. Paulus Diaconus 12.2, 8; Rufinus 2.18–19. Compare Orosius 7.35.

4. Ptolemy 6.19–20. Compare *LP* 42.1–2.

5. *LP* 42.3–8. Compare Ptolemy 6.21.

6. Rufinus 2.20; Jerome 104, 106, 112–113. In Jerome Martian is called Pacian, and Esicius is more correctly written as Euzoius.

7. Ptolemy, 6.11; Isidore 8.5. Compare Palmieri 42.

8. *LP* 42.1, 8.

43. ZOSIMUS I

1. Ibid. 43.1. Compare Ptolemy, 6.25.

2. Orosius 7.37.

3. Orosius 7.36–37, 39, 43. Compare Palmieri 44.

4. *LP* 43.1; Ptolemy 6.25.

5. Jerome 118, 119, 123, 125, 126.

6. Palmieri 43–44.

7. Palmieri 45; Ptolemy 6.27–28, 12.

8. *LP* 43.1–2.

44. BONIFACE I

1. The basilicas of Santa Maria in Trastevere and San Pietro, respectively.

2. Ibid. 44.1–4. Compare Ptolemy 6.29.

3. Paulus Diaconus 13.2–3. Compare Orosius 7.43; Palmieri 45–46.

4. *LP* 44.5–6. Compare Ptolemy 6.30.

5. Jerome 135, 130, 132–34. Jerome writes, more correctly, Euzoius for Eunomius, Pacian for Patian, Amphilochius for Amphilotius.

6. Ptolemy 6.31.

7. *LP* 44.1, 4, 7.

45. CELESTINE I

1. Ibid. 45.1.

2. Paulus Diaconus 13.9–10. Compare Biondo-Piccolomini 1.2; Palmieri 46–47.

3. Paulus Diaconus 13.13, 17–18, 16. Compare Palmieri 47.

4. *LP* 45.1–2; Ptolemy 7.1.

5. Ptolemy 7.2. Compare Palmieri 46–47.

6. *LP* 45.1, 3.

46. SIXTUS III

1. *LP* 46.1. Compare Ptolemy 7.6.

2. Paulus Diaconus 14.1, 13.12. Compare Palmieri 47.

3. Paulus Diaconus 14.2–7. Compare Palmieri 48.

4. *LP* 46.1–4. Compare Ptolemy 7.6–7.

5. *LP* 46.8.

6. Ptolemy 7.9–10.

7. *LP* 46.1, 9; Ptolemy 7.7.

47. LEO I

1. *LP* 47.1. Compare Ptolemy 8.1.

2. Paulus Diaconus 14.8–13. Compare Palmieri 49; *LP* 47.7. On humanist praise for Attila, see Anthony F. D'Elia, "Genealogy and the Limits of Panegyric: Turks and Huns in Fifteenth-Century Epithalamia," *The Sixteenth Century Journal* 34.4 (Winter 2003): 973–991.

3. Ptolemy 8.1–2; Isidore 8.64. Compare *LP* 47.2–5; Palmieri 48–49.

4. Biondo-Piccolomini 1.2.

5. *LP* 47.1, 6–8.

6. Isidore 8.5. Compare Ptolemy 8.12; Palmieri 50.

7. Ptolemy 8.5.

8. *LP* 47.1, 9.

Bibliography

❧❦❧

EDITIONS OF THE LATIN TEXT

Vitae pontificum. Venice: Johannes de Colonia and Johannes Manthen, 1479.

In vitas summorum pontificum ad Sixtum IV. Nuremberg: Anton Koberger, 1481.

Vitae pontificum ad Sixtum IV. Treviso: Johannes Rubeus Vercellensis, 1485.

Hystoria de vitis pontificum periocunda. Venice: Filippo Pincio, 1504.

Hystoria de vitis pontificum periocunda. Paris: François Regnault, 1505.

Hystoria de vitis maximorum pontificum historia periocunda. Venice: Filippo Pincio, 1511.

Hystoria de vitis pontificum. Lyon: de Villiers, 1512

De vitis maximorum pontificum historia periocunda. Venice: Gulielmus de Fontaneto de Monteferrato, 1518.

De vita et moribus summorum pontificum historia. Cologne: Eucharius Cervicornus, 1529.

De vita et moribus summorum pontificum historia. Paris: Jean Petit, 1530.

De vitis ac gestis summorum pontificum. Cologne: Eucharius Cervicornus, 1540.

De vitis ac gestis summorum pontificum. Cologne: Jaspar Gennepaeus, 1551.

Opus de vitis ac gestis summorum pontificum ad sua usque tempora deducta. Edited by Onofrio Panvinio. Cologne: Maternus Cholinus, 1562.

Historia de vitis pontificum romanorum. Edited by Onofrio Panvinio. Venice: Michael Tramezinus, 1562.

Historia de vitis pontificum romanorum. Edited by Onofrio Panvinio. Cologne: Maternus Cholinus, 1568.

Historia de vitis pontificum romanorum. Louvain: Ioannes Bogardus, 1572.

Historia de vitis pontificum romanorum. Edited by Onofrio Panvinio. Cologne: Maternus Cholinus, 1574.

De vitis pontificum romanorum. Edited by Onofrio Panvinio. Cologne: Maternus Cholinus, 1593.

Vitae romanorum pontificum ... ex Platinae historia in Epitomen redactae. Lüttich, 1597.

De vitis pontificum romanorum. Edited by Onofrio Panvinio. Cologne: Bernardus Gualtherius, 1600.

Historia de vitis pontificum romanorum. Edited by Onofrio Panvinio. Cologne: Gosuinus Cholinus, 1610.

The same. Cologne: Gosuinus Cholinus, 1611.

The same. Cologne: ex officina Choliniana, 1626

Opus de vitis ac gestis summorum pontificum. Leiden: Elsevier?, 1645.

Opus de vitis ac gestis summorum pontificum. [n. pl.], 1664.

Liber de vita Christi ac omnium pontificum. Ed. Giacinto Gaida. Rerum Italicarum Scriptores, ser. 2, vol. 3.1. Città di Castello: Lapi and Zanichelli, 1913–1932.

ENGLISH TRANSLATION

The Lives of the Popes from the time of Our Saviour Jesus Christ, to the Reign of Sixtus IV, Written originally in Latine by Baptista Platina . . . and translated into English, and the same history continued from the year 1471 to this present time, wherein the most remarkable passages of Christendom, both in church and state are treated of and described by Sir Paul Rycaut. London: Christopher Wilkinson, 1685. "Rendred into English by an unknown hand."

Second edition, corrected. 1688.

The Lives of the Popes written originally in Latin by B. Platina, and translated into English. Edited by William Benham. 2 vols. London: Griffith, Farran, Okeden and Welsh, 1888. A reprint of the 1688 edition.

SELECTED MODERN STUDIES

Bauer, Stefan. "Platina, Bartolomeo." In *Biographisch-Bibliographisches Kirchenlexikon*, vol. 22, cols. 1098–1103. Herzberg: T. Bautz, 2003.

Idem. "'Platina non vitas, sed vitia scripsit': le censure sulle *vite dei papi*." In *Nunc alia tempora, alii mores: Storici e storia in età postridentina*, ed. Massimo Firpo, 279–89. Florence: Olschki, 2005.

Idem. *The Censorship and Fortuna of Platina's Lives of the Popes in the Sixteenth Century*. (Late Medieval and Early Modern Studies, 9). Turnhout, Belgium: Brepols, 2006.

D'Amico, John F. *Renaissance Humanism in Papal Rome: Humanists and Churchmen on the Eve of the Reformation*. Baltimore: The Johns Hopkins University Press, 1983.

Fubini, Riccardo. "Papato e storiografia nel Quattrocento: storia, biografia e propaganda in un recente studio." *Studi medievali*, ser. 3, 18 (1977): 321–351. Review of Miglio, *Storiografia pontificia*, as below.

Miglio, Massimo. *Storiografia pontificia del Quattrocento*. Bologna: Patròn, 1975.

Miglio, Massimo. "Tradizione storiografica e cultura umanistica nel *Liber de vita Christi ac omnium pontificum*." In *Bartolomeo Sacchi, il Platina (Piadena 1421-Roma 1481): Atti del Convegno internazionale di studi per il V centenario (Cremona, 14–15 novembre 1981)*, ed. Augusto Campana and Paola Medioli Masotti, 63–89. Padua: Antenore, 1986.

Peter Partner. *The Pope's Men: The Papal Civil Service in the Renaissance*. Oxford: The Clarendon Press, 1990.

Scapecchi, Piero. "Un nuovo codice del *Liber de vita Christi ac omnium pontificum*." *Roma nel Rinascimento* (1999): 247–52.

Stinger, Charles L. *The Renaissance in Rome*. Bloomington: Indiana University Press, 1985, 1998.

Index

 རེ་ལིཏ

Lowercase roman numerals refer to pages in the Introduction. Two-part arabic numbers (19.3, 47.5) refer to chapter number and paragraph in the *Lives of the Popes*. Arabic numbers with "n" (303n4) refer to page and note numbers in the Notes to the Translation. References to Platina's *Life of Christ* and Preface are given as *LC* plus paragraph number and Pref. plus paragraph number, respectively. Italicized numbers refer to location (book or chapter) in cited primary sources.

Publication of this volume has been made possible by

The Myron and Sheila Gilmore Publication Fund at I Tatti
The Robert Lehman Endowment Fund
The Jean-François Malle Scholarly Programs and Publications Fund
The Andrew W. Mellon Scholarly Publications Fund
The Craig and Barbara Smyth Fund
for Scholarly Programs and Publications
The Lila Wallace–Reader's Digest Endowment Fund
The Malcolm Wiener Fund for Scholarly Programs and Publications